NICKI MINAJ
HIP POP MOMENTS 4 LIFE

ISOUL HARRIS

OMNIBUS PRESS

London / New York / Paris / Sydney / Copenhagen / Berlin / Madrid / Tokyo

Exclusive Distributors
Music Sales Limited,
14/15 Berners Street,
London, W1T 3LJ.

Music Sales Corporation,
257 Park Avenue South,
New York, NY 10010, USA.

Macmillan Distribution Services,
56 Parkwest Drive
Derrimut, Vic 3030,
Australia.

Every effort has been made to trace the copyright holders of the photographs in this book but one or
two were unreachable. We would be grateful if the photographers concerned would contact us.

Typeset by Phoenix Photosetting, Chatham, Kent
Printed in the EU

A catalogue record for this book is available from the British Library.

Visit Omnibus Press on the web at www.omnibuspress.com

Contents

Acknowledgements

There are several people in my life who have contributed to the creation of this book. Thank you Mary (you are my best friend and I love you for it); John (I am you and I love you for that); my hard working literary agent Dawn Hardy (who says Twitter is worthless?); Chezon Jackson (the world renowned Sequoia leaf expert); Keisha Hines (thank you for the light bulb); Ursula Doyle (thank you for the skill); Derek Eubanks (your push at Morehouse landed me here); David Augusta (thanks for growing up with me); Sean Moore (we will always have *Scream*); Bryan Young (thanks for helping me believe); Cliff Boyce (thanks for helping me help myself); Derrick Hemphill (most people depart, thankfully you returned); Munson Steed (thanks for the genesis); Angela Bronner Helm (Paris is more magical because of you); Ronda Racha Penrice (thanks for talking me off the ledge at 1am); Kym Backer (my South American ride-or-die bitch); Marlon Jones (the strongest and most courageous man I know); Larry Johnson (our walks through New York are now legendary); Reginald Weekes & Anthony Preston (we were kids, now... we are kids!); Kelly Harrington (the little sister I never had despite my resistance ☺).

Introduction

Cookie Was The First

Nicki Minaj must be a cartoon character.

It's not just that she dresses in candy-coated outrageousness: sporting severely dyed wigs and rocking colour-clashing and second skin get-ups that have pushed the boundaries of hip-hop and fashion. It's also not that during the few short years of her time on the rap scene, she has unleashed some of the most ridiculous lyrics ever heard, such as: "First thing's first, I'll eat your brains/Then I'mma start rocking gold teeth and fangs," which she memorably quipped on the Kanye West-produced 2010 hit song 'Monster'. Minaj gave a lyrical lashing to her (non-existent) competitors, an about-face to the song's co-stars (including a couple of guys named Jay-Z and Rick Ross) and an overall unapologetic middle finger to all those who, at the time, still doubted that she could even rap.

No, it's more than that.

To call the self-described Harajuku Barbie unreal (Harajuku being the over-the-top street style of Japanese girls hanging out at Harajuku Station in Tokyo, introduced to the pop music world back in 2004 by Gwen Stefani in her track 'Harajuku Girls') may be the only way to make sense of her nearly impossible, beyond meteoric rise to superstardom. How else could this Caribbean-born, Queens-bred wannabe rapper leap from the realms of the unknown rap amateur in urban street hip-hop DVDs to performing and dropping it low alongside the most legendary pop star to walk the planet during the Super Bowl halftime show – the most watched entertainment performance every year around the world?

Nicki Minaj's ascendancy to the upper echelons of the music industry is a testament to the drastically different times we now live in, where fame is certainly more attainable than ever before, but it is also an example of someone identifying a void and quickly filling it. When Nicki emerged nationally, the lane for female rappers was essentially closed. At the time, there weren't any female rappers still relevant on a large scale, and Nicki saw her chance.

The few preceding years before Nicki Minaj emerged as a force to be reckoned with in 2010 had seen many give up on the idea of another female rap superstar. We were entering another decade and, while the future of hip-hop was undoubtedly exciting, the landscape for female MCs was not. Miss Hill walks, talks and performs among the living, but Lauryn Hill – the mega-watt MC and former Fugees singer who won over the world – died off long ago. Missy "Misdemeanor" Elliott's last major hit was in the middle of the last decade. Lil' Kim, well, Kim was off being Lil' Kim and, unfortunately, because of bad decisions and curious cosmetic surgery, the Queen Bee had become a self-constructed caricature of the feminine hip-hop force that had seen her worshipped. She was the first and last iconic female rapper.

Until now.

Nicki Minaj, with her otherworldly, free-spirited, make-the-rules-as-I-go persona(s) is the new embodiment of the female rapper: a gorgeous blend of eighties femme bravado and nineties femme fatale, sexy pin-up and the same decade's funky fembot style. She represents the new breed: the femcee without constraints, able to leap tall *Billboard* charts at a single bound; a raptress succeeding as the most revered figure in music: the pop star.

A lot has been said about hip-hop's newest female superstar: the accolades are as numerous as the criticisms. But since 2010 she has been breaking records non-stop, which means that Miss Minaj will have history on her side, even if the naysayers are not.

While some of the critique may be valid, much is simply born out of misunderstanding or from a refusal to even try to understand. In this millennial age, everyday life has become more digital and fluid and the entertainment industry is not immune to that. While Nicki's rise is certainly due to her irresistible mix of potent skill, borderline batty charisma and frequently fantastic flows, her success is also just a sign of the times. All around the world, from Toledo to Tokyo, the question still lingers: "Who is Nicki Minaj?" What we know for sure: she is really, really, really famous. She is known from the bodegas of the Bronx to the boardrooms in Silicon Valley. She is beloved by both suburban soccer moms as well as single ladies in the city. She is loved by pop radio and lyrically revered by hardcore male rappers.

There was a time in Nicki's career when she was solely a straight-spittin' raptress with an unforgiving flow and an even more merciless attitude – "Gutter Nicki" as some of her longtime fans refer to that early part of Nicki's fast-paced career. Safaree Samuels, Nicki's longtime friend and business partner, said she was not allowing herself to venture beyond. "Before, she was playing it so safe and then when se started to play around with the music a little more, she became free with it," he said in the E! special documentary on Nicki's road to stardom.

So who is the true Nicki Minaj? Is she schizophrenic?

Much has been said about Nicki's alter egos. When she debuted the different voices and characters some people thought she was a momentary gimmick, others saw her as a genius. "The voices show her character," Swizz Beatz also told E!. "It shows that she is not so serious. A lot of artists in her position don't have fun. They are stressed out and take everything so seriously. If you are not having fun at what you're doing, you are wasting your time."

She introduced the characters to not only enliven her work and set herself apart as a rapper, but to keep herself balanced, despite the pressures of being Nicki Minaj. "They keep each other from being suicidal at times," Nicki told *The Guardian*. "And I hate to use that word loosely, but... you can tell people, 'Don't kill yourself, don't be weak,' but until you walk a day in someone's shoes you don't know what the real pressure is. We're human. I create personalities so I can get through the day. It's like a defence mechanism for me so I don't have to deal with everything."

Initially she used the voices to sustain her own well-being, but when everyone began to talk about them, then she decided to name them. "I have a few personalities," she said to Yahoo! Music. "When people started making a big deal out of it, I started making names for these people. I can't control it and it's kinda scary, but it's fun." Some of those personalities include the crazy Roman Zolanski and his equally unbalanced British mother, Martha. "Roman's a little gay boy who lives in me," she told *The Guardian*. "And every time I talk he sort of just appears and I tell him, 'Roman, you know, stop it, you've gone mad, I tell you, mad.' He's an outlet to say what I need to say but sometimes don't want to." Nicki describes Roman, who first debuted his lethal tongue twisters on Trey Songz's 2010 track 'Bottoms Up', as "an outlandish lunatic who does not care about anyone's feelings and pulls your card if you get slick. He is very mischievous, he is very crazy and he likes to stir up the pot."

Nicki has said her penchant for creating personas grew from her being terrified of her father and the verbal and physical abuse she and her mom would endure at his hands. Sitting in her bedroom, she would cancel out the chaos going on in the other rooms by coming up with characters. "To get away from all their fighting, I would imagine being a new person," Nicki told *New York* magazine. "'Cookie' was my first identity – that stayed with me for a while. Then, I went on to Harajuku Barbie, then Nicki Minaj. Fantasy was my reality. I must have been such a fucking annoying little girl. Everywhere we went I was up singing or acting, like, 'Hey look at me!'"

And those characters have helped Nicki to circumvent the usual trajectory of the hip-hop female. Before her – when Lil' Kim and Foxy Brown rewrote the rules for women and rap in the mid-nineties – female rappers more or less relied on the requisite co-sign (endorsement) from a more successful male rapper, which had typically then served as shackles. A female rapper had limited conversation, her dialogue consisting mainly of boasts about her bedroom skills over anything else. But Nicki Minaj has changed the rules: a woman rapper can now believe she is the love child of David Bowie and Grace Jones and not have every door immediately slammed in her face. Because of Nicki's brash and bold-faced attack on the industry, there is a future for the girls that are writing their rhymes right now at the cafeteria table during their lunch period, waiting for the day that they can battle (the form of rap when an MC takes a stance against another rapper with rhymes full of boasts, put-downs and often funny criticisms) – and beat – the boys at the sport that remains overwhelmingly male-dominated.

Nicki is a trailblazer.

She was once just an ambitious young lady navigating life in New York, walking the tightrope between her passions for the future and surviving in the present. She worked thankless jobs and sold mix-tapes from the trunk of her car with only a dream and a belief that she was talented and unique enough to not only get a record deal, but become world famous one day. She watched female rappers and singers blow up in front of her eyes and she imagined the day that she would experience a taste of success. This drive enabled her to dodge the obstacles and jump the walls that stood in the way of what we now know was inevitable. A global superstar, Nicki is on the fast track to achieving all that her idols have done, and more.

She is now Nicki Minaj.

And this is her story.

Chapter 1

Coming To America

On October 30, 2010, Nicki Minaj returned to her native Trinidad for the first time since she was five years old. She performed the parade of hit songs she had amassed in two short years of releasing popular mix-tapes and making show-stealing guest appearances on the songs of artists far more famous and storied than her – from Lil Wayne to Mariah Carey. On that balmy night in the country that had birthed hip-hop's latest sensation, the 3,000-plus crowd didn't care that their native daughter didn't yet have an actual album under her designer belt. They were there to witness an impossible dream realised.

The self-named Harajuku Barbie's quick-witted and quirky rhymes captivated the throng of dancing Barbz and Ken Barbz – her gang of fanatics who follow and often imitate her chameleonic looks, circus-like gestures and street attitude. "Go to school and stay in school. Ladies, don't depend on a man for anything. Get your own!" the rapper shouted to the crowd. If the young women in the audience were to take advice from anyone, why not from Nicki Minaj?

Here was a woman, not far in age from them, quickly becoming world famous and commanding $50,000 to rap a minute-long verse, as she boasted on the Kanye West song 'Monster', which she also performed that night. Nicki was home and she was revelling in the sincere love from a people she did not know, but who felt they knew her. What's more, some of the Caribbean Barbz felt an unexplainable bond with their fellow Trini, who now resided in an unreachable stratosphere of fame.

Before leaving the stage (after performing well over her allotted time), she let down her superstar guard and stepped out from behind the persona. "This is the most emotional show I've ever had to do. I don't even know how I'm holding up," Nicki told the crowd. "It's been a long time coming back here and you guys have treated me so beautifully, I really couldn't ask for anything more."

But, of course, she *has* asked for more throughout her life, which is what brought her to the stage that night. Her success was born from a desire for a better life for her and her family, and it all started in Trinidad.

Onika Tanya Maraj was born on December 8, 1982, in St James, Trinidad and Tobago, a country in the South Caribbean, near Venezuela and Grenada. World-renowned kick boxer/martial artist Gary Goodridge is also a native, but Minaj is now the country's claim to fame and source of pride. Her parents, Omar and Carol Maraj, like most parents, wanted the best for their children and decided that the United States, in particular New York, was the place to raise their family.

In order to make the transition, the Marajs made the difficult decision to move to New York to get jobs and a home, with the intention of moving the children there once they had settled, and they left Onika and her siblings with their Trinidadian family. "I lived with my grandmother, and there were a lot of people that lived there. [I remember] 10-15 aunts, cousins and uncles," she told MTV. Her life on the island was far from plush. "In Trinidad we didn't have much," she told the *Trinidad Guardian*. Despite living in one of the most beautiful and idyllic places in the world, Onika's early childhood memories are not chock-full of carefree days bumming at the beach or exploring the island on her bicycle. Rather, living with a large group of family members in an extremely small home, she was far from comfortable and, although only a toddler at the time, Nicki remembers this as being a tough period in her life. "A lot of times, when you're from the islands, your parents

14

leave and then send for you," she told *MTV News*. "Because it's easier when they have established themselves; when they have a place to stay, when they have a job." The little Onika understood why her parents were going away, but she had no concept of the time it would take for them to finally reunite. "I thought it was gonna be for a few days, it turned into two years without my mother."

Carol was focused on making a life for her children in the States, but she would come home every so often to check up on Nicki (as her family began to call her) and her older brother Jelani. On the last day of each of her mother's pop-up visits, Onika would quietly pack all of her clothes, get dressed and sit patiently, hoping that this would be the day she would finally join her mother. "I would sit there and wait for her to leave, knowing that if she sees that I'm dressed, she'll take me with her," Nicki told *Vibe* magazine.

Eventually that day finally arrived. No one was more excited than Nicki, who had dreamed of moving to America. Ironically, despite the fact that she was actually leaving one, she thought of New York as an oasis.

In 1983, just four years before Nicki would depart Trinidad, the legendary hip-hop group Grandmaster Flash and the Furious Five released their classic single 'New York, New York'. The chorus is cautionary: "New York, New York, big city of dreams/And everything in New York ain't always what it seems/You might get fooled if you come from out of town."

Sadly, those words would prove prophetic for Onika.

During the flight from Trinidad and Tobago, Onika replayed the visions of the fantastical life she had dreamed of in the Big Apple. As fate would have it, after landing and collecting their bags, the freshly departed island child stepped into a chilly and wintry New York day. "I got off the plane and it was cold. I remember the smell. I could always remember the smell when I got out of the airport, and the snow," she said to MTV. Her arrival in Queens was remarkably similar to the scene in the 1988 Eddie Murphy film, *Coming To America*, when Murphy's character, Prince Akeem Joffer from the fictional African country of "Zamunda", leaves the tropical climate and luxury of his kingdom, on a quest to find a wife, and arrives in Queens to find frosty urban decay. The elements of the northeastern US were foreign to her. She was a stranger in an even stranger land. "I had never seen snow," she continued.

Her parents secured a modest house in Jamaica, Queens, one of the boroughs of New York City. Originally a haven for Irish immigrants settling in the city, the area was beginning to experience a change in racial make-up as many of the Irish and other groups of European descent began to move to other regions, a phenomenon that became known as "the white flight". As a result of their exit, African-Americans and immigrants of West Indian descent moved into the vacant homes.

Having lived with a motley crew of family in one small house, the five-year-old was hoping for a new home in New York worthy of a Disney film. But the home and its surroundings were particularly disappointing to the wide-eyed Onika. Where was the white picket fence? She told MTV: "I remember the house… I thought it was gonna be like a castle… like a fairy tale. I remember [going inside and] the furniture wasn't put down. It was, like, piled up on each other, and I didn't understand why." And unfortunately the truth only deepened her disappointment. Her father had fallen prey to a plague sweeping through most of the urban centres around the country, a seemingly unstoppable widespread affliction destroying families and ending lives: crack cocaine.

The flight of the Irish population had resulted in debilitating consequences for the neighbourhood and had a drastic effect on its economy. By the beginning of the seventies all of the big-name brand businesses, such as American department store juggernaut Macy's, had shuttered their stores in the area, which were either abandoned or replaced by less desirable discount stores. These conditions, along with rampant unemployment, created the perfect conditions for the crack wave to bed in.

Originating as early as 1981 in Los Angeles, by mid-decade the cheap and deadly drug was so ubiquitous in New York it was common to walk down sidewalks in certain neighbourhoods that were littered with empty crack vials. The city was hardly prepared for this unnatural disaster. "Twenty years ago, crack was headed east across the United States like a Mack truck out of control," said then New York State Senator Charles Schumer in 2004, "and it slammed New York hard because we just didn't see the warning signs."

Onika Maraj, barely in her adolescence at the time, did not see the warning signs either. Unknown to her, her father, Omar, had succumbed to the lecherous hook of the drug a short time before she arrived in the States. And upon her arrival in New York, she soon noticed that things weren't quite right. The cold and hard reality shook her to the core: Onika's father was taking the family furniture and selling it for drugs: "You come home from school and find your couch is gone, [and] you're like 'What happened?'" Nicki told *Vibe* magazine. Speaking to MTV, she said "When you are on crack, you can't keep a job. And when you can't keep a job, you don't have money. And when you don't have money, you steal and you steal from your family."

Like most children, she had dreamed of a life book-ended by two loving parents and filled in between with a nice home, nice things and just good ole' plain happiness. However, the Marajs were not the Huxtables (although, at one point, *The Cosby Show* was actually filmed a few miles away from the Maraj home in Astoria, Queens). "I thought we would be happy," she told *Vibe*. "But with a drug-addict parent there is no such thing as being happy."

Her father's addiction was also causing his marriage to deteriorate. Scared for her mother, Onika would listen closely to the fallout. "I started hearing a lot of arguing, and I didn't know why. I was always very nervous, very afraid. So, I knew it was not normal," she told MTV. "[He] would yell and curse a lot." Nicki has claimed that her father was verbally and physically abusive and would allegedly beat her mother. Onika witnessed him pull her mother out of a car and drag her two blocks down the street. "After that I had a phobia about unlocked doors," she told *Cosmopolitan*. "Anywhere my mother and I were, I made sure the door was locked, because that was my only way to protect her." Soon her father's behaviour began to worsen. "He would beg, cry [and] stalk us," she continued.

One night, Onika and her brother were staying at a neighbour's house and they were awakened in the middle of the night by the neighbour, who had received a call to say that the Maraj house was aflame. "We ran three to five blocks to our house and all we saw was smoke," Nicki told Wendy Williams during a visit to *The Wendy Williams Show*. "My dad burned the house down, with my mother still in it. She had to run out at the last minute, but she had a dream the night before that the house was going to be burned down."

Luckily, no one in the family was physically hurt, but it undoubtedly left scars on a still impressionable and young Onika, who lost a lot in the fire after all. "All my dolls, all my stuffed animals, all my pictures [were] burnt," she told *Vibe*. "I was one of those kids that kept all that stuff. I cared a lot. I swear you'd have to hypnotise me to get me to remember some things that happen. I think psychologically I blocked them away."

Onika's defence mechanisms helped her deal with the trauma surrounding her life. As another way of coping, she began to create characters in her head that she would play out, eventually forming her own world.

Yet, every day she would pray that her mother would gather the courage to leave her father, but she has since admitted that it was difficult for Carol to break away and has hinted that she may have suffered from battered women's syndrome. "My father was very abusive, and it was hard for my mother at first to leave because we had depended on him for so long," she told *The Guardian*. "Sometimes you kind of get adjusted to getting that beating."

After various encounters with her father, living in perpetual fear, she declined invitations from friends to stay overnight at their homes. She was constantly worried that her father would injure her mother. "I wanted to kill him," Nicki told Nightline. "I wished he were dead."

Every night, Onika would flood her prayers with wishes for wealth, but not to benefit herself. "I would go in my room and kneel down at the foot of my bed and pray that God would make me rich so I could take care of my mother," Nicki told *Rolling Stone*. "Because I always felt like if I took care of my mother, my mother wouldn't have to stay with my father, and he was the one, at that time, that was bringing us pain."

Despite her mother having left Onika in Trinidad for three years, the two had developed an unshakable bond that is still intact today. In 2010, Nicki told MTV personality Sway about her relationship with her mother: "When I was growing up, I was really close to my mother. I talk with her about everything that's going on in life, and it's still like that now."

Mommy Maraj is quite the joker, according to Nicki. And despite all that went on with her father and his struggles with substance abuse, the Maraj house eventually became one of warmth, filled with laughter. She told Sway: "My mother is hilarious, she's a Capricorn. She was always making me laugh so I get my sense of humor directly from [her]. To this day me and my mother cannot be on the phone without busting out laughing at something."

A precocious child, Onika had showed signs of an aptitude for music aged three, according to her relatives. As she got older, she began to develop an outgoing personality and her search for attention began at home. Jelani (she also has a younger brother, TK, and sister, Maya) was often the target of her insatiable energy. "He was quiet and could sit in front of a TV and watch cartoons or play video games for hours," she told MTV. "I could never sit for hours. I wanted attention so bad from [him] that I would rather him hit me or us fight than us not communicating. So, I would do crazy things and I [knew] sooner or later [that] he was going to punch me. Then I'm going to fight him and then when I start crying, I'll go to my mother. It was chaotic but it was all love," she remembered.

By the time Onika entered junior high, she no longer had to seek attention; she attracted it. She attended Elizabeth Blackwell Middle School 210 – named after the first woman to obtain a medical degree in the United States – in the Ozone Park area of Queens. The neighbourhood is famous for being the setting for the 1990 Academy Award-winning, Martin Scorsese-directed film *Goodfellas*. It was also an area dominated by convicted crime boss John Gotti. And, similar to those belligerent wise guys, Nicki got into her fair share of fights. She would even act as a protector of sorts for her friends, eagerly stepping in between them and their potential opponents.

During one such incident, she asked, "What's the problem?" and things turned ugly very quickly. According to an interview she gave to *Vibe*, she tore into the other girl's neck and chest with her fingernails, ripping the girl's shirt in the process and exposing her breasts. "She was Puerto Rican [and] you could see every scratch," she recalled.

Despite her penchant for outbursts, Nicki surprisingly took up the peaceful practice of playing the clarinet in junior high. When it was time to choose a high school (in New York, students can apply to various magnet high schools with areas of special concentration) it was a no-brainer for the outgoing girl, who was already a musician and who also loved to sing, to select LaGuardia High School of Music & Art and Performing Arts.

But, she was not a shoo-in.

LaGuardia High School was made famous by the 1980 film *Fame*, which placed a fictional spotlight on the talented students at the revered institution. The movie spawned a long-running television spin-off in 1982 (a pre-superstar Janet Jackson starred in the fourth season) and a film remake in 2009. Debbie Allen is the only actress to have starred in all three incarnations of the brand and her advice to the incoming students is world famous and wildly parodied: "You've got big dreams? You want fame? Well, fame costs. And right here is where you start paying... in sweat." When Nicki Maraj stepped into the halls of the celebrated school, she was ready to begin her quest for fame.

Well, at least she thought so.

The auditions for the school are notoriously difficult. Running at an average of three hours, the process is stressful and many applicants crumble, leave and return home, defeated and disappointed. Nicki was almost one of those people. During her singing audition, her voice failed her. She was hoarse. More often accustomed to getting what she wanted, she fled the room, very much defeated and disappointed.

"I was crying and embarrassed and I didn't want anyone in the school to see me. I just wanted to go home," she recalled to *Vibe*. "That was the first time in my adolescent life where my mother put her foot down. Normally, I made the rules."

Carol Maraj is a woman heavily steeped in religious faith. During an interview with MTV, Nicki revealed that it was her mother who gave her the support she needed to keep going when, at one stage, it all seemed pointless. "She was the one when I was on the verge of giving up that was there, praying for me every day. Her faith is unmatched. I get that 'where there is a will, there is a way' from my mother. She never looks at anything like 'no'."

Immediately following her failed audition, Momma Maraj grabbed her notoriously headstrong daughter, looked directly into her mahogany-tinted eyes and told her, "No. You are not finished. Go and try the drama major audition."

Following orders, albeit reluctantly, Nicki headed downstairs to the auditorium and went for it. She was shocked at what happened next. It was easy. She felt at home. More importantly, she felt like she was born to act. She continued to *Vibe*: "You know when you're doing something you were out here to do... and you're like, 'Wait, not everyone can do this?'" She was accepted.

Nicki, who was known for her loud and rambunctious behaviour, did well in the programme and, according to a former classmate, she also excelled in drama outside of the classroom. "Her friends were kind of like the mean girls. You got the sense when you walked past her that she was talking about you or had some kind of joke going on," the source told *Vibe*. "But, I wouldn't say that she was mean... you could tell at LaGuardia what someone's major was based on their behaviour and Nicki was definitely a drama major."

In equally dramatic fashion, she announced her new choice of career to her schoolmates. "I wanted to do what the boys were doing. I always wanted to compete with [them] and I walked into the booth one day and said, 'I'm a rapper,'" she told *King* magazine. "Everyone was looking at me like I had five heads."

Nicki graduated from LaGuardia in 2000. Tired of living with so many people under one roof, she wanted her own apartment and a car as quickly as possible. She also wanted something a little loftier: a career as a rapper, which meant she also needed money to book studio time to record. So, first of all, she needed a job. Armed with a high school diploma and acting skills learned from some of the best instructors in New York, she landed the inescapable prize for most actors: a job waiting tables. In fact, because she was constantly getting fired from various positions, she had multiple customer service and waitressing jobs.

"I probably got fired 10 times. That whole time was so horrible," she told *Blackbook* magazine. Her stint as a waitress included slinging entrées at Red Lobster. She remembers working at the Bronx outpost of the seafood chain as being equally frustrating and amusing. Whether it was her nails popping off onto customer's plates or patrons refusing to tip, she made sure she was always remembered, which led to her eventual firing. A former co-worker told *Vibe* that Nicki followed a customer out to his car, tapped on his window and gave him the middle finger. "He stole my pen! I gave him the pen to sign the credit card slip, and I was going to show him: I will lose my job for a pen," she said. For someone who actually needed the job, her behaviour was a little cavalier.

Prior to that she had worked as an office manager in a customer service centre, a job that put an end to her nine to five life. "[We were] in a little tiny room where I literally wanted to strangle this guy because he was so loud and obnoxious," Nicki told *Billboard*. "I would go home with stress pains in my neck and my back." She was ready to get on with the business of becoming famous. "At the end of the day of whatever job I hated, I would get all dressed up and go out with the hope of getting a record deal. At night, I was an artist; during the day I was a slave," she told *Blackbook*.

By the time she had lost her final nine to five, she'd exhausted all of her options. She had no money and she couldn't even consider calling her mother to tell her that she would be coming back home. In fact, even with an empty refrigerator and no income, she talked to her mom every day, never revealing her struggles. "My mother would call. I would be like 'Everything is great!' I refused to ask for anything."

Her pride and insistence on making it on her own were admirable, but almost equally detrimental. Being alone, broke, hungry and desperate for a break in a seemingly impenetrable industry propelled her into a deep depression. During this period, she contemplated making a move she could never come back from. "I kept having doors slammed in my face. I felt like nothing was working," she told *Cosmopolitan*. "I had moved out on my own, and here I was thinking I'd have to go home. It was just one dead end after another. At one point, I was, like, 'What would happen if I just didn't wake up?' That's how I felt. Like maybe I should just take my life."

Fortunately, she persevered and she credits her faith in God and her love for her family for keeping her alive. "The only thing that got me through that time was the fear of what would happen to my family if I didn't make it," she said to *Blackbook*. "I remember thinking, I don't know if this is ever going to work, but I'm going to give it one final try."

All of her male friends in Queens were rappers and aspiring artists and she fed off their energy and wanted to see where collaborations with them could possibly take her, but because she was a girl – and a pretty one – they only wanted her to sing the hooks and choruses to their songs. "I hated doing anything that made me seem like a girl at that time," she told *Vibe*. Determined to show them that she belonged, she used her small pot of savings that she miraculously was able to amass after deciding to refocus on her dream to book studio time and record the songs that she had been writing. "I wanted to be as strong as the boys and as talented as them and I wanted to show them I could do what they did."

Her plan worked. Wherever she would go around the city, she played her music. People began to notice her distinctive hard-edged but sexy voice, which showed real promise.

At the behest of a friend, Nicki placed her music on MySpace. Then a guy from Brooklyn, calling himself Fendi, liked what he heard.

Nicki was on her way.

Chapter 2

Alleys To Arenas

In 2006, MySpace was the premiere social networking site on the web. Along with the usual exchanges between users, established artists were able to preview new music and aspiring ones could upload their music to the site and some even secured major label deals as a result, such as British singer Lily Allen and American pop star Sean Kingston. It made sense that, after finally laying down tracks that she was proud of, Nicki decided to post her music on the site. The CEO of Brooklyn-based label Dirty Money Records, Fendi, listened to the upstart femcee and reached out to her.

"I was coaxed into starting a MySpace page and [I sent] out friend requests [to] some insiders in the [industry]. Fendi happened to be a person I sent a request to," Nicki told rapindustry.com. "He hit me up and began relentlessly pursuing me."

Fendi, who had admitted to having been a former drug dealer, started Dirty Money in the late nineties after serving a stint in prison. He learned the business by travelling on tours with artists such as hip-hop legends Big Daddy Kane and Busta Rhymes. While touring, he forged relationships with noted rappers such as Tupac and Jay-Z. A charismatic guy, Fendi says he first noticed Nicki because of her profile picture on MySpace and was intrigued because she looked Asian.

"I saw a picture of her with a Chinese look. Back then, when you landed on someone's page the music would start playing. I'm on her page and the music starts playing and I'm like 'Who is this? This can't be her. This shit sounds hard," Fendi told NCHipHopConnect.com. "When I met her on MySpace her name was actually Nicki Miraj. We had a mutual friend and I reached out to him and asked about her."

A proverbial game of cat and mouse ensued. Nicki was not sure of Fendi's intention so she initially ignored his repeated requests. "Fendi hit me up and I was afraid of him," Nicki told talk show host Wendy Williams. "But he went through someone else and they said he was good people, so I contacted him."

Once they hooked up and Nicki decided to give him a trial run as her manager, Fendi suggested something that sent her into an orbit of anger. He continued to NCHipHopConnect.com: "I saw the potential but I needed something with shock value. So I told her that I wanted to change her name to Nicki Minaj. Of course, me and Nicki weren't seeing eye to eye. She wasn't trying to hear it. She wasn't feeling the name Nicki Minaj. I told her in this game you need shock value but she was like, 'Fuck that!' She felt that it was degrading her." Nicki initially took offense to the suggestion that she use Minaj as her stage surname because of its similarity to the word *ménage* (from the term *ménage à trois*). In hip-hop, the idea of a threesome between a man and two women is often celebrated and even encouraged in lyrics. Nicki felt the name would demean her. But, with a little convincing, Fendi persuaded her that "Minaj" would garner the type of attention she needed to launch her career in the competitive rap world. "So I fought with her, and as you can see I won the argument," Fendi said to the site.

And with that the two commenced their working relationship and Nicki began making the rounds of New York City's underground hip-hop scene. She was pretty but she played down her looks because she wanted people, especially the guys, to take her seriously as a female rapper, not to see her as a sexpot. Her early rhymes and image were quite different to the Nicki Minaj that would emerge years later. It was not surprising to find the former Nicki in dark baggy clothes with a fitted baseball cap, rhyming on street corners. However, in an effort to find the middle ground between showcasing both her skills and her beauty, she began to evolve.

Fendi created a DVD series called *The Come Up*, which featured various rising artists on the rap scene from around the country, alongside established veterans. He was planning the 11th installment, *The Carter Edition*, named after Lil Wayne, who would make an appearance on the DVD (Dwayne Carter is the rapper's given name) and invited Nicki to appear on it as well. "*The Come Up* was my introduction to the world as Nicki Minaj and the stars were aligned," Nicki told *Rock Me TV*. "The appearance almost did not happen because Fendi called at the last minute, while he was coming back from North Carolina, and he said that I was filming a video that day and I told him, 'No, I am not ready.' He said, 'You are doing the video.' So I went and got dressed real quickly. I think I did my make-up at the MAC counter! It was so last minute and I was so mad, I really did not want to do it, but he really wanted me to be on the DVD."

Fendi's insistence on Nicki's participation in the project was a part of his grand plan for her career. Although, according to him, she was signed to Dirty Money Entertainment and he was working to get Nicki a distribution deal. Plus, he knew how much she admired Lil Wayne, the artist having gone from popular New Orleans rapper to worldwide superstar, whose album at the time, *Tha Carter 3*, had sold one million copies in its first week of release. "When I met Nicki, one of her biggest dreams was to meet Lil Wayne. Me and Lil Wayne had a great relationship. I used *The Carter Edition* as a marketing tool to get Wayne's attention [on] Nicki. I put Nicki's footage right after the Wayne interview. I knew he was going to watch it. I knew as soon as he watched her he was gonna give me a call."

Fendi's calculations were perfect. At the time, Wayne was receiving bombastic accolades from the record industry, critics and fans alike, including being called "the greatest rapper alive" on numerous occasions, and with an expanded fanbase (skater kids, hipsters and Wall Street yuppies all took a liking to Wayne's clever but irreverent post-millennial flow), he decided it was time to expand his own empire. After Wayne witnessed Nicki perform a rendition of Biggie's classic street anthem 'Warning' (replete with her own personalised story), he began to think of the future. Nicki's choice of song – a track from one of the most revered rappers ever – was a controversial one and caused a tsunami of buzz on the street. Wayne took notice of the stir she was causing.

Although one of the original signees at Cash Money Records (he joined the label as a child in 1995), Wayne launched Young Money Records (as an imprint of Cash Money/Universal Records) and thought that Nicki might be a great addition to the roster of fiery rappers he was assembling. "Wayne hit me and was like 'I wanna sign this chick Nicki.' I was doing a party with him in Greensboro, North Carolina. So I flew Nicki out to meet him and the rest is history," said Fendi. Nicki was ecstatic. "Never in a million years did I think that he would not only just like me, but want to sign me," she told *Rock Me TV*.

From there, Nicki released a series of mix-tapes that garnered sales success and critical acclaim. The first of the tapes, 2007's *Playtime Is Over*, featured Nicki as a Barbie in a box on the cover in an obvious homage to iconic female rapper Lil' Kim, who had appeared as the doll in a box almost a decade before. It included a song called 'Dreams '07', a cover of the Biggie song of the same name. In the original, the deceased Brooklyn rapper rhymes about "dreaming of fucking an R&B bitch" and proceeds to comically drop names and ways in which he would bed them: "As I sit back relax... sip a Becks/Think about the sexy singers that I wanna sex/I'd probably go to jail/For fuckin' Patti LaBelle... Got Whitney Houston boostin' from Bobby/Jasmine Guy was fly/Mariah Carey's kinda scary/Wait a minute, what about my honey Mary?"

Nicki's version is similar at first, but she flips the theme. Instead of wanting to have sex with famous R&B male singers, she is dreaming of rising stars in the hip-hop world. "As I sit back/Relax, crack jokes for a minute/I think about the up and comers/That could prolly get it/I might go to jail for fucking with Hell Rell/If he get ill/And pull on my ponytails," she raps on the track, on which she manages to sound funny, feminine and aggressive all at once. Lil' Kim, who was Biggie's protégé (similar in fashion to Wayne and Nicki, only Biggie and Kim were involved intimately), had also covered the song on her debut solo album, 1996's *Hard Core*. However, she had followed the original premise, naming famous R&B guys she wanted to "bed": "Babyface can pay da rent/And cook me five meals/Lil' momma got the whip appeal/What the deal on that Prince cat/He be lookin' kind of fruity but he can still eat the booty."

And 'Dreams '07' is not the only song connected to Lil' Kim that Nicki decided to redo; in what can be taken as another ode to the reigning "Queen of Hip-Hop," the ambitious newbie also included a remake of Kim's hit single 'The Jump Off' from her 2003 platinum album *La Bella Mafia*. Kim infamously quipped "I can make a Sprite can disappear in my mouth" on the track and, as if she could not get any more flagrant, on the remix she boasted "You thought the Sprite can was off the meter/Imagine what I do with a two-liter." In contrast, Nicki's version was light-hearted and full of boasts: "Mami ya flow sic/My flow's retarded/Cause you can say something/And you won't be sick/But uh I can't help it retarded chick/Cause my flow stupid, wheelchair bound/Take the small bus all year round." Nicki and Dirty Money even shot a DIY-type video for the song, with her performing around the city with a group of girls acting as if they were hanging out and having fun.

Playtime Is Over also featured Nicki's very first collaboration with Lil Wayne, entitled 'Can't Stop, Won't Stop'. A playful, bouncy cat-and-mouse jam sampling Young Gunz's Top 20 hit of the same name, the chemistry between Weezy (one of Wayne's aliases) and Nicki was notable and it would be the first collaboration of many to come. In 2011, Nicki tweeted about the song: "Haha! But then who can 4get my very 1st Weezy collab 'Can't Stop, Won't Stop'. ★gazes into the sky★ sings: memories don't live like ppl do".

Playtime gave the world a taste of Nicki's skills. Her emboldened rhymes and cocky performance style breathed new life into the female rap genre. Her confidence was fun and her words so clever, she was nearly irresistible to any lover of that brand of rap popularised by Foxy Brown and Lil' Kim years before. Furthermore, the hip-hop world was abuzz with talk of her being the next big thing and having the potential to take the throne from Kim, who, at the time, was working to rebound from her prison stint after serving 10 months of her year and a day prison sentence. (In 2005, Kim had been convicted on three counts of conspiracy and one count of perjury for lying to a New York Grand Jury about her friend's involvement in a shooting that took place outside the Hot 97 studios in Manhattan in 2001.) Kim's last two albums, 2003's *La Bella Mafia* and 2005's *The Naked Truth*, and 2008's mix-tape *Ms. G.O.A.T.* (an acronym for "Greatest Of All Time"), had been well received, but Kim was still struggling to regain the glory she had experienced during the mid nineties to the early noughties. And Missy Elliott, at the time the most successful female rapper, had not released an album since 2005. With the field wide open, Nicki honed in on her opportunity to make a name for herself.

And in her next project, she went even further with the shock tactics, subsequently widening her comparisons to a certain predecessor.

In April 2008, Nicki released her second mix-tape, *Sucka Free*, and the cover caused quite a stir. Nicki, squatting with her legs wide open in the photo, had recreated Lil' Kim's cover of her debut, *Hard Core*, only Nicki had added to the image, licking a lollipop in her version. This immediately ignited whispers that Nicki was simply following Kim's playbook for success, but Nicki's reasoning for the imitation was more than that. She told *Rock Me TV*: "Everything that I do, I see it as a marketing tool. You may look at that picture and think, 'Oh, she is being an exhibitionist.' I looked it as a way to draw attention and give myself a platform and say 'Hey, out with the old and in with the new.'"

Sucka Free, hosted by Lil Wayne, pushed Nicki's sex-fuelled but witty persona even further. She brags about her parts with gleeful abandon on 'Lollipop (Remix)': "I got that presidential cooch/When he sees it/he salutes/He makes my pussy sing/Ahhh/Like it's Mozart" and flaunts comedic flair without effort on 'Baddest Bitch': "I got an Austin Powers flow/I'm groovy bitches". Nicki remixed the Gucci Mane, Ludacris and Lil' Kim collaboration 'Freaky Gurl (Remix)' into the track 'Wanna Minaj' and she began to evolve as an artist by displaying a slight vulnerability on the song 'Autobiography', in which she opens up about the bitterness she felt towards her father after his attempt to burn down the family house while her mother was still inside. "They shoulda thrown the book at you/Because I hate you so much/That it burn when I look at you."

Nicki's effort on the mix-tape won her the Female Artist of the Year Award at the 2008 Annual Underground Music Awards in New York. Many of the things that she had been dreaming of for many years were finally coming true. She had two successful mix-tapes (which were also making her more money than she had ever made before), her fanbase was growing, her name was becoming increasingly recognisable and she had one of the most famous rappers in the world co-signing her abilities. And with the success of *Sucka Free*, she saw herself as the next female rap superstar.

"Anything that is great revolves and evolves, whatever you want to say. Nothing stays the same," she said to *Rock Me TV*. "I commend Lil' Kim. I was paying homage to her. I love Lil' Kim. But I think I have what it takes to fill her shoes. I think that, if anyone has the power to do it, it's Nicki Minaj."

And soon, she was about to show the world just how able she really was.

In 2008, Lil Wayne announced that he and his Young Money cohorts would set out on the I Am Music tour and he asked Nicki to join them as the show's special guest. Elated, she tackled each night of her first tour as if it were an arena-sized classroom. She was determined to learn all that she could with the purpose of becoming a better artist and also a more financially sound one. She looked at Wayne and the monetary success he had achieved; every night the raucous applause he would receive from the crowd of thousands made her want the same thing. "Why can't I have this?" she would think to herself. She decided to redirect her focus. "The tour made me hungry," she told MTV. "I was OK, but I wasn't focusing on the music." However, all was not OK with Nicki and she left the tour early. Because of her actions, Lil Wayne, disappointed at the direction she was taking as an artist, ousted her from the Young Money clique.

Nicki, now a free agent, began to record on her own, but something was missing. "I started to record by myself and I lost track of what I was doing and who I wanted to be," she told *Billboard*. She eventually put aside her pride and went back for a meeting with the man she had previously called her Sensei and, in appropriate mentor fashion, Wayne did not mince his words: she was the femcee getting everyone excited about feminine hip-hop again, but she had fallen off. "It wasn't until I linked back up with Wayne that he gave me this speech. He said, 'What happened? You were hot,' and it just hurt me so much. I wanted to prove to him that I was still hot. It hurt my ego so bad that I went back with a vengeance."

With the inspiration from being on tour, coupled with Wayne's brutally honest critique, Nicki went back into the studio and created the project that would help her finally secure a label deal.

The release of *Beam Me Up Scotty* in 2009 took the streets and industry by storm. She was already being touted as the future of female rap, but that mix-tape sealed the deal for many. While she still tackled some of the same topics as her predecessors, she did it with a boss-like confidence, which the hip-hop scene had not witnessed since Kim, but with a unique Nicki flair: her boasts did not seem dependent on the backing of a man. "I'mma need a couple of those Benzesess/I be out in China spending all them Yensess," she raps on 'Shopaholic'. And regarding money, well, she wasn't lacking in that department according to her blunt braggadocio in 'I Feel Free': "You know I pop, pop, pop like a pistol/And you know I keep my wrist lookin' like a disco". She gives label mate Canadian rapper Drake quite a run for his ever-growing money on the remix of his hit 'Best I Ever Had' by relating her connection to her fans as an intimate encounter: "When I hear those screams/I feel that they are living vicariously through me/That's why I put an S on my chest," she rhymes easily. But it's the explosive 'Itty Bitty Piggy' that solidified teetering fans and completely won over others.

Accompanied by a raw, ready-made freestyle beat, she wastes no time ripping into her opponents from the onset: "I was on the plane with Dwayne/You can call me Whitley/I go to Hillman/I am the baddest in the game/Excuse me honey, no one's in my lane." The song is a surprising retro-like romp reminiscent of eighties battle-rap femcees like

Roxanne Shanté. Nicki is rapping so swiftly, it's as if she has to pull an emergency brake at the song's end before she wraps up in an LA Valley Girl-esque tone: "It's like, I just single-handedly annihilated every rap bitch in the building... I don't know why you girls bother."

Due to her growing popularity and mix-tape success, a label bidding war grew up around her. But Nicki was not in any hurry. "I was not looking to get signed that time, anyway, because I would not have been able to negotiate the right deal," she told radio personality Jenny Boom Boom. "I don't jump at just anything. I am not bent off of money. You can't wave money in my face and expect me to just do anything. I knew this was going to happen in my life. I knew I was never going to work a nine to five again," she said.

Even though Lil Wayne had taken Nicki under his wing and virtually inducted her into the Young Money camp, he shied away from wanting to sign artists. Instead, he had decided to first look at executive producing albums. So, with his intentions unclear to her, Nicki decided the time had come to move forward with finding the right deal for her career. "I was so close to signing with Warner Brothers," she told The Breakfast Club. Then she received a phone call one night from Wayne that made things a little more interesting. "Yo, Nick! You not going to sign with Young Money? What's up?" he said to her. He was calling her from a basketball game and she could barely hear him over the deafening cheers in the background. The call took her by surprise. But she decided to be honest with him. "Well, I was not sure if you guys still wanted to sign me," she replied. He made it clear that the offer was on the table and she told him that she would get back to him very soon.

All the while, Irv Gotti, the founder of Murder, Inc. (now known as Inc. Records), who discovered Ashanti and was also largely responsible for rapper Ja Rule's superstardom, was also mentoring Nicki. She credits Gotti with helping her to avoid the typically horrific freshman deals that some artists can fall for. "Irv got me with top lawyers early in the game," she said to The Breakfast Club. "He called them up and told them, 'This girl is going to be big, please represent her.' I did not have the money to get with a big firm, but they agreed to rep me," she said.

With everything seemingly aligned for Nicki to win, Gotti was angered by her reluctance to move forward with Young Money. "'Are you crazy?'" she said he asked her. "I was so busy listening to what other people were telling me. They were in my head saying, 'Wayne ain't ever going to release your album if you sign with him,' and 'Wayne is not a businessman,'" she remembered. "It was then I realised that you have to make your own blueprint."

No longer listening to her peers, she began following her own instincts as well as paying attention to her subconscious. "I had a dream that I was on a boat. Everyone on the boat was like, 'It's time to go,' but I stayed on one side while everyone else went to this other place. Then, from a distance, I saw everybody rocking at this crazy concert. When I woke up, I said, 'If you don't go with Young Money, you will regret it.'"

Lil Wayne won out and in the summer of August 2009 he officially signed Nicki to the Young Money roster, in a deal that would reportedly see her retain the rights to her songs, merchandising, publishing, touring and endorsements. "I have to thank Lil Wayne for that [deal]," she told Jenny Boom Boom. "Even though I had buzz and everything, let's not forget who Wayne is. There are a million people out there who would love to be in my shoes. He believed in me so much that he gave me everything that I was asking for. It's a new time and a new day. I really wanted to own all of my stuff and I got it."

It had been a long and winding road but Nicki finally had a home. All of her hard work had paid off. She told The Breakfast Club: "Nicki Minaj made Nicki Minaj. I was paying for my own mix-tapes. I was doing shows four times a week then I would record and get DJs to host the mix-tapes. I got help from Deb [Deborah Antney, her former manager and mother of rapper Waka Flocka Flame] and I would meet other great people and they would help me. I created my own buzz."

But her success at that moment was not eclipsed by ego; she was well aware of what her story meant for other young women coming behind her. "To say I'm excited would be an understatement. It's validation. It's proof. It's empowerment. I represent every little girl in a hood near you," Nicki stated in an official Cash Money/Young Money press release. "To everyone that supported me two years ago when I was on underground mix-tapes and DVDs and to the people that only caught on two weeks ago, I say thank you. Be proud of yourself. You've given girls all around the world the permission to change the face of female rap."

Not wasting any time, Lil Wayne planned a Young Money compilation album featuring the acts he had signed up to that point, including Drake and Nicki, under the group name Young Money Entertainment. Everyone was in Miami to record the song, yet on the day Wayne scheduled Nicki to record her verse for the track, 'BedRock', she was nowhere to be found. Unknown to him, she had a previously scheduled show that she had forgotten about. She was still a new artist, building her career, and she did not want to break her obligations. When she returned back to Miami, she discovered that the boss was far from pleased with her absence: she was kicked off the song.

A couple of days later, Nicki made her way to Wayne's multi-million dollar South Beach mansion for dinner. He sent word that he wanted to meet with her. After having a relatively quiet dinner, at opposite ends of a very stately table, Nicki rose from her seat, approached him and started to perform the four verses she spent the last couple of days writing with the hope of him liking one enough to put her back on the song. "I thought that if at the end of the night he doesn't like any of my verses, I'm going to be very, very pissed off," she told *Vibe* magazine.

President Carter was a tough crowd of one. She kept on, rhyming: "Okay, I get it, let me think, I guess it's my turn/Maybe it's time to put this pussy on your sideburns." Not fully convinced, although he did crack a slight smile at the punch line, Nicki went for the jugular; the line that she was positive would get her back on the song: "I'm so pretty like/Be on my pedal bike/Be on my low scrunch/Be on my Ecko whites/He sayin' 'Nicki don't stop/You da bestest', and I just be comin' off the top asbestos!" Seeing his reaction, she asked if she could record it, and once he said "Yes", she literally ran out of his home to the studio and immediately laid it down. When he arrived to listen to her verse, he said, "Congratulations," she told *Vibe*. "You made [it on] the single." 'BedRock' was Nicki's first single as an official Young Money artist and went on to sell over three million copies. And Nicki went on to begin a surprising string of recordings that would soon secure her a place in the history books.

Nicki's impressive thread of guest features started in 2009 with an appearance on rapper Yo Gotti's '5 Star Bitch' (the explicit version of '5 Star Chick'). It was an interesting time for her because not only was she still learning the lay of the hip–hop land, she was about to film a video with Yo Gotti and Gucci Mane, which would be her very first time on a video set. Those on set would have never known. She delivered her lyrics with such animation – head bobbing, eyelash fluttering and funny faces – that she was unknowingly creating the style that would come to define her to the masses. While filming the video, she told *Billboard*, "My hands just went on my hips and I became like a doll. I had never done that before or planned to do it – it just happened. After that, I would go to shows and girls in the audience would do the whole '5 Star Bitch' dance. Afterward I thought, 'Maybe I'm on to something.'"

Soon, Nicki began to receive calls from established artists requesting her Young Money-flavoured rhymes to spice up their songs. R&B singer Robin Thicke was one of the first. Taking the advice of rap titan Jay-Z, he reached out to the then green raptress. "I was in the studio with Jay-Z and played the track 'Shakin' It 4 Daddy' for him and he told me I should get this female rapper named Nicki Minaj for the song," he told Andy Cohen on *Watch What Happens: Live!*. "So, I looked her up on YouTube and saw all of these amazing videos of her performing and I called her up."

Nicki was equally excited, not only that she had the chance to work with an artist such as Robin, but also by the fact that Jay-Z had recommended her for the song. "I had never met Jay at that point," Minaj says, "but he told Robin Thicke that if I did the song I should say, 'I be, I be, I be, I be, I be on that money shit.' So I took that line and just ran with it," she recalled to *Billboard*. "Does it get any better than that?" she said to intromagonline.com about Jay-Z's co-sign. "It really feels good when I think about it in that light." Although the song was never officially released as a single from Thicke's 2005 album, *Sex Therapy*, the two went on promotional rounds together, performing the song on BET's *106 & Park* and *Late Show With David Letterman* on CBS. Nicki was elated by how far she had come in only two short years.

And she wanted more.

Mariah Carey, in need of a remix for her single 'Up Out My Face', called Nicki, who was in a complete state of disbelief throughout the process. "Until I was physically in the studio with Mariah, I could not believe that I was making a record with Mariah," said an incredulous Nicki Minaj to *MTV News*. Carey reached out to the rapstress causing a stir around the industry, but it was not a stretch or an out-of-place move for the pop/R&B diva to elicit Nicki's talents, since she had established herself as a hip-hop collaborator back in the early nineties with 'Fantasy (Remix)' featuring the late Ole Dirty Bastard of Wu-Tang Clan fame. (Coincidentally, Nicki has referenced ODB at times in regards to her use of different-sounding voices in her music. Later, on the song 'Monster', she begins her memorable verse with the three words "First thing's first," a direct reference to ODB's line from the classic Wu-Tang Clan song 'Protect Ya Neck'. He displays the hyperactive flow that Nicki mimics when he raps: "First thing's first, man/You're fuckin' with the worst/I'll be stickin' pins in your head like a fuckin' nurse/I'll attack/ Any nigga who slack in his mack/Come fully packed with a fat rugged stack.")

Mariah Carey is recognised as one of the most prolific songwriters of her generation and she can traverse successfully between a big power pop ballad and R&B and hip-hop flavoured songs. Her lyrics (she has written the majority of her own songs throughout her career) are often similar in texture and rhythm to that of hip-hop records. 'Up Out My Face' finds Carey almost rapping: "If you see me walking by boy/Don't you even speak/Pretend you're on a sofa/And I'm on TV/You might see me on a poster/You might see me at a show/You won't see me for free/This ain't a promo". Carey's sophisticated comedy is a complement to Nicki's more curb-side but highly witty humour on the track: "Yo, Mariah, I was in a million dollar meetin'/He was cheatin'/All up in the church/He was sneakin' with the deacon."

Most A-listers working with lesser-known artists will often send in their track and both will then record separately. But Carey and Nicki recorded the remix together in a studio and the rapper was shocked at Mariah's down-to-earth demeanour. "She is so silly and funny; I thought she was going to be this diva," Nicki said.

By this time, Nicki had built on the sensation she sparked in the '5 Star Bitch' video (doll-like movements with hands on hips) and had decided to develop her brand. Carey, who co-directed the video for 'Up Out My Face' along with her husband, Nick Cannon, liked Nicki's idea of the two women appearing as Barbies trying to break out of giant boxes. Nicki admitted that, while shooting, Mariah jokingly told her: "[People] are going to say 'Oh, she is doing Nicki now,'" in reference to Nicki's Harajuku Barbie style. But Nicki didn't agree. "I told her that she has always had the doll-like persona so she goes well with Barbie," Minaj continued. "A lot of times, a more famous artist or a more popping artist will take from a younger artist but they will never give you credit or include you in it. She liked the whole doll thing, and she wanted to do it with me. We had fun and that's all that matters."

Even after filming the video, Nicki did not believe that it was actually going to be released. In her mind, she could not fathom how she, an artist without an album under her belt yet, could have a song and video with one of the most successful singers of all time. She told MTV: "I did not tell anyone that I was shooting a video with her because in my head, this video is not going to come out. There is no way I am going to have a video with Mariah Carey before I put out my own album. I was one of those girls that stood in the mirror and sang Mariah songs with my mother."

Despite her disbelief, Nicki knew it was a milestone in her very young career. "It was insane. She's a huge icon. No album out! Female. Rapper. Doesn't happen. That does not happen," she told *Vibe*. "I don't care how far back you look. I dare any hip-hop historian to tell me when that has ever happened. It doesn't. And I still don't know why it did."

Although the song was a breakthrough opportunity for Nicki, it was not a hit. It peaked at number 100 on the *Billboard* Hot 100 Singles Chart and number 39 on the Hot R&B/Hip Hop Songs Chart. Later, after becoming a chart-topping success herself, Nicki looked back on the collaboration with gratefulness. "I worked with Mariah and it wasn't commercially successful," she told *Complex*. "But I had fun and I made a real friendship with her. It was, obviously, a life-changing moment for me."

Well, whether she knew why Mariah called her or not, it did not matter; other major artists saw it as well, including Atlanta-based, multi-platinum rapper Ludacris. For his 2010 album *Battle Of The Sexes*, he wanted to explore life on Venus and Mars by trading a battle rhyme-like give-and-take between the best female rappers and himself. He called Nicki to appear on the original version of the album's hit single 'My Chick Bad' with him, which later included a remix featuring rappers Trina, Eve and Diamond, who was a former member of the Atlanta-based rap group Crime Mob. In the original video Nicki sports a pink wig (further evolving into her Harajuku Barbie character) and is wrapped in restraints with Freddy Krueger-like blades as fingers (she also switches to nice, regular, good-looking video girl, but wears a pink feather to link her clean-cut image to the mad one).

Ludacris says that he saw an instant similarity between himself and Nicki, which attracted him to her style. "She's an animated female and I'm an animated rapper myself," he told *Rap-Up* magazine. The chorus chants: "My chick bad/My chick 'hood/My chick do stuff that your chick wish she could," and Nicki dives in head first to prove just why she's the self-proclaimed "baddest bitch". She rhymes: "Yo, now all these bitches wanna try and be my bestie/But I take a left and leave them hanging like a teste/Trash talk to 'em then I put 'em in a hefty/Running down the court I'm dunkin on 'em Lisa Leslie/It's going down, basement/Friday the 13th guess who's playing Jason/Tuck yourself in you better hold on to your teddy/It's nightmare on Elm Street/Guess who's playing Freddy?"

Nicki's lyrical dexterity, intriguing looks and unselfconscious performance style began to quickly set her apart from the small pool of female rappers and put her on a par with the male ones. Her punch lines and willingness to look weird had not been seen on such a scale since Missy Elliott. "Every great rapper has a great sense of humour," Nicki told *Rolling Stone*. "I think that I obviously pull from Lil Wayne and people like Jay, [as well] as comedians like Larry David. He has a lot of sarcasm."

And the phone continued to ring.

Superstar entertainer Usher thought of Nicki when he needed a partner for his 2010 song 'Lil Freak', in which Usher basically tells Nicki that in order for them to have sex, she must recruit a few friends. And from the moment in the track's video that she steps into the industrial-looking elevator and ogles deliciously at the other ladies (stirring rumours of her being bisexual, which would continue to be a mainstay in her career), Nicki, donning an ebony and platinum Cruella de Vil-esque wig and black bondage and bandage wear, plays the role by the book. "[Nicki] played the part, but it was still her," director Taj Stansbury told *Vibe*. "If you really listen to her words in the song, you can kinda visualise her outfit."

Nicki was very excited about the video and compared it to one of her favourite movie franchises. "The video is freaky. And it's a great concept, a great story line. It felt just like one of the sequels to *Saw*. It was dope." In that series of horror films, the lead character, John Kramer, or "The Jigsaw Killer", leads his potential victims through a series of tests or physical challenges. Likewise, Nicki leads a group of impossibly beautiful women around the club, steering them to Usher as if she were Kramer.

Critics loved the collaboration, especially Nicki's contribution, with *The Guardian* describing her performance as equally humorous and ridiculous: "In some nightclubs there are girls who send up a flare for male attention by grinding against each other doing the sexy 'finger in mouth' pose. This is basically what is happening here, except instead of winding up in an 'are you looking at my boyfriend' fight, it's actually pretty funny and absurd. Why? Because Nicki uses Santa's reindeer as a metaphor for 'hos' and brings up *Everybody Loves Raymond*, that's why."

The video oozes sex and some critics, while liking the song, labelled both the lyrics and video NSFW (Not Safe For Work), including MTV writer Chris Ryan. "Usher pairs off with current queen MC Nicki Minaj, and the two glide over Polow Da Don's minimal bass beat," he wrote. "And what happens on the track should only take place between two consenting adults. Horrestly it's hard to find lyrics to reproduce without angering the gods of civility and good taste."

But talking to intromagonline.com, Nicki was revelling in all of the opportunities that were coming her way. "You know what part feels great? The amount of people that have reached out to work with me. I never thought in a million years that at this stage in my life I would be contacted by Mariah Carey, Robin Thicke [and] Usher," she said.

This was just the beginning of her success to come but she would have to brace herself for something not so joyful only a few days after the release of the 'Lil Freak' video.

Lil Wayne released his seventh studio album – the rock-tinged *Rebirth* – on February 2, 2010, almost exactly a month to the day he would have to report to jail for a weapons charge. In 2007, New York police had stopped and searched the rapper's tour bus outside of the Beacon Theatre after a performance. During the search, officers found a .40-caliber pistol they said belonged to the multi-platinum entertainer. He pleaded guilty and was sentenced to a year in jail. Wayne was the reason Nicki was a superstar. It was her talent that had gotten her to the top of the game, but it was his vision that had gotten her *in* the game. So for him to have to leave to serve jail time during this crucial period of Nicki's career-building was quite an emotional blow.

"I am a crybaby," Nicki told MTV when asked about Wayne's prison sentence. "He shouldn't have to go to jail. He's such a strong person. I emailed him the other day about something that I wanted him to do for me, and then I thought 'That was so selfish'. What is the mindset of someone going to jail who has never served that amount of time? I am always amazed at Wayne's dignity. You can't take away his confidence. He is like 'I am who I am.' He's a legend."

Nicki was clearly shaken by Wayne's absence but it did not stall her on her road to releasing her debut album. Through her many feature appearances on songs with established artists, she had built an enviable foundation from which to launch her first album, but talk questioning Nicki's ability to carry a song on her own had begun to bubble. Feeling the pressure to prove that she was the face of new millennial hip-hop, Nicki went into the studio with mega-producer Sean Garrett, who had crafted hits for a swathe of artists, including Beyoncé, Britney Spears, Usher and Enrique Iglesias. Garrett first made a name for himself by writing Usher's flyaway hit 'Yeah', which propelled Usher's album *Confessions* to sell 1.1 million copies in one week and over 10 million copies in the US alone. Garrett went on to write Ciara's number one hit 'Goodies' and 14 other number one hits in only seven years. He is considered by *Billboard* to be one of the best producers in music across the board (Jay-Z nicknamed him "The Pen" for his ability to write hits). It's no surprise that Nicki chose Garrett to co-produce her first solo song (along with English producer Alex da Kid), which would be the lead single from her debut.

A clear departure from her previous work, 2010's 'Massive Attack' caught many people by surprise, with its King Kong-sized jungle-like drum beats mixed with lighter Euro-synth sounds. After hearing the track in the studio, the Head Barb loved it. "It's very rare... You're not gonna get the song the first time you hear it," she told *MTV News*. "After the second or third time, you're gonna be like, 'Whoa, what is this?' It sounds nothing like anything that's out right now." She was excited about the track's futuristic sound and told MTV that she had chosen Garrett because he was the best to "illustrate Nicki Minaj" and that he understood her personality.

Garrett, known for his high energy and cocksure attitude, was equally excited to present his view of Nicki to the world. He told *Rap-Up*: "I just did Nicki's first single, featuring me. It's gonna be a fucking bomb. It's very, very explosive! It's a club banger. It's a lot broader than what people would expect her to come with. The record puts her in the game in a way that says she should've been here a long time ago. She has a real way of how she wants to do this. It's just gonna be a surprise when it comes. She just wants to make it as huge as possible."

The video, shot by legendary hip-hop video director Hype Williams, was a large-scale production deserving of Nicki's clearly broad ambition. It co-starred Kanye West's ex-girlfriend Amber Rose and featured the two ladies cruising through the desert in a pink Lamborghini. With a squad of Harajuku Barbies, a helicopter and Nicki also in the jungle, it was completely over the top.

She told *MTV News*: "I didn't want to shoot the typical new-artist vision. Thank God I have a wonderful label that stands behind me and my vision. It all came together. It's just beautiful – the clothes, everything. The ambience. It's for all the girls that like to play dress-up. They're gonna love this one... It's really fashion and beauty shots, and we're acting like we're doing something important. We wanted to make it pretty in the dirt. We wanted to have a very crazy contrast. I didn't want to do everything clean. I like the dirt. All that pink stuff looks even prettier in the dirt."

'Massive Attack' was leaked onto the internet and then officially released to radio shortly afterwards in April 2010. Reaching number 22 on the *Billboard* Hot 100 and only number 30 on the *Billboard* Hot Hip-Hop/R&B Chart, it certainly did not meet Garrett's nor Nicki's expectations. Garrett, sounding a bit defensive over the single missing the mark on the charts, told *Vibe* that people did not understand at that time that Nicki, as an artist, is beyond hip-hop. "'Massive Attack' was huge sonically, but I don't think it had the kind of radio success that she or I wanted," he admitted. "Nicki is a different type of artist. She is a pop icon, not just a rapper. I think the only people who don't know that are her fans." The blogosphere – full of fans and haters – went awry with a range of reviews. While one person on missinfo.tv wrote: "This shit is gonna BANG! Her 1st single is gonna be a MASSIVE ATTACK!", another respondent on nahright.com wrote: "I mean, I like that she is trying to do new, never before type shit, but this beat is just brutal on the ears."

Nicki was also disappointed; one listen to her verses and a watch of the video shows that she had put a lot into what was supposed to be her first single, and she has rarely talked about it since. In an interview with *Rolling Stone*, the writer notes that Nicki "pretends the song does not exist to avoid further embarrassment" and expresses that it was a very low point in her career. However, she has admitted that the situation was an example of her following her own instinct and passion, rather than doing simply what others expect of her. "It was important for me to do something not everyone thought I was going to do," she told *Vibe*. "People close to me have their preferences, their favourite Nicki thing, and I have to stand up sometimes and block out the noise." But, she also put a positive spin on the letdown of 'Massive Attack': "It was a good lesson to learn early on," she told *Complex* magazine.

A few months later, at the 2010 BET (Black Entertainment Television, a cable network in the US) Awards, Nicki redeemed herself. Although she had yet to drop an album of her own at that point, the girl from South Jamaica, Queens took home three awards: Best Female Hip-Hop Artist, Best New Artist and Best Group (with Young Money Entertainment). During her acceptance speech she thanked the person whom she says saw the vision for her career even when she did not. "This is for Dwayne Carter," she said, referring to Lil Wayne, who was serving his sentence for the 2007 gun charge at New York Rikers Island prison at the time. "He predicted this about a year ago. I was sitting there so mad that he was giving me a tough love speech, and I hated him at the time. Thank you so much for believing in me and seeing me sitting on a staircase rapping and for seeing something in me."

Emotional and overwhelmed at winning such significant awards so early on in her career, Nicki also gave props to rapper and Academy Award-nominated actress Queen Latifah, whom she said pulled her aside earlier in the day during rehearsals. "She gave me so much positive energy. It's so important right now for positive energy among women," Nicki said, most likely in response to the growing "beef" that was supposedly brewing between her and Lil' Kim and the negative comments made by other female rappers about Nicki's meteoric rise to fame. "I am fighting for women. I am not doing it for me. It's for all of us. Thank you to all of the female rappers that paved the way for me."

Unfortunately, Nicki did have not much time to revel in her big win at the BET Awards. The next day, the blogs were ablaze with accusations of Nicki lip-syncing her performances. Nicki was the busiest artist in the auditorium that night. Aside from gracing the stage on three separate occasions to accept the awards, she also performed three separate times. Clad in a second-skin black catsuit, she stormed the stage and performed her verse on the remix of 'Hello Good Morning' with Diddy (the all-conquering producer, formerly calling himself, among other names, Puffy, Puff Daddy and P. Diddy); she rocked out with rapper Ludacris, along with Mötley Crüe drummer Tommy Lee, performing 'My Chick Bad'; and then she joined DJ Khaled and a clan of other artists featured on the runaway hit song 'All I Do Is Win'.

Nicki was feeling proud of her wins and performances that night. She takes much pride in knowing that she is disciplined and works hard. Safaree Samuels, her hype man (a back-up rapper who supports the main rapper by bringing attention to their lyrics and interjecting with their own unique lines and actions to excite the audience), assistant, best friend, rumoured boyfriend and all-round constant counterpart, believes that she is one of the hardest working artists in the industry. "She is definitely focused. Everything is straight up dealing with beats, dealing with the label, dealing with other artists," he told *MTV News*. "She is on top of everything, more than a regular artist." And according to Nicki, she is just as hard on herself as she is everyone else. "I push people around me but I don't push anyone more than I push myself," she told *Rolling Stone*. "I tell people all the time, 'You want to work for me? You have to give 250,000 per cent,' because when I'm in the booth, I don't half-ass it. I demand perfection from everyone around me and if you can't live up to that, then bye-bye."

Because of her personal dedication and hard work, it truly bothered her that people thought she was miming. Hip-hop is built on authenticity, raw improvisation and the super-charged electricity of live performances, so when an MC is accused of faking anything, it strikes right to the core. Nicki, now an avid participant in social media, took to Twitter to defend herself to the people that mattered most: her Barbz and Ken Barbz. "U could hear me in the auditorium but apparently not in TV land. Shout out to the sound guy," she tweeted to her hefty legion of Twitter followers. And she added a little recourse: "They say it'll be fixed when it re-airs."

While Nicki was proving her worth onstage, she was already winning on the *Billboard* charts. Her song 'Your Love', featuring a sample from Annie Lennox's 'No More "I Love You's"', was leaked on the internet and then radio picked it up. The pint-sized rapper was at first livid. "I was not planning on putting the song out at all. Somebody told me it was online. And I was like, 'No way, no way in the world that song is out.' I went and listened to it and was really upset. It wasn't mixed, it wasn't finished, it wasn't anything – I wasn't gonna use it at all," she told MTV. This was especially embarrassing since 'Massive Attack', the single she originally thought would anchor her album, was DOA. She was angry, humiliated and frightened. Confiding in Drake, she told him, "This is going to ruin my career."

But she could not have been more wrong. The label mixed the track and released it formally to radio on June 15, 2010. Nicki filmed a video (co-starring actor Michael Jai White) where she's dressed as a geisha and fighting another girl with a samurai sword for White's affections. It's Brandy & Monica's 'The Boy Is Mine' meets *Kill Bill*. The single became a gigantic hit and went to the number one spot on the *Billboard* Rap Songs chart, Nicki becoming the first female rapper to achieve the accolade since Lil' Kim and 50 Cent's 'Magic Stick' topped the chart in 2003.

Later that summer Nicki introduced the world to another side of her ever-growing persona. The track and video for 'Bottoms Up', a bouncy collaboration with R&B heart-throb Trey Songz was released on July 27, 2010 and became an instant hit.

Songz thought of Nikki for the track just days before recording it while he was in Los Angeles for an awards show. "I hit Nicki and [told her] 'Man, I've got these two incredible records, I think one of them is gonna be my first single, and I need you to do it. Can you come this weekend? Can you come down?'" he told MTV.

Mainly an ode to drinking and partying, Nicki made the song an event. At this point, her fans were becoming familiar with her alter egos. They knew Onika and Nicki already. There was "Barbie", who is very sweet and soft-spoken in her attempts for perfection. But on 'Bottoms Up' the world was treated to the zaniness of Roman Zolanski, the part of Nicki that is brutally honest and unapologetic.

Roman rhymes: "I'm wit a bad bitch he's wit his friends/I don't say 'Hi', I say 'Keys to the Benz'/Keys to the Benz? Keys to the Benz!/ Mother fuckin right yeah weed to the 10/If a bitch try to get cute I'mma stomp her/Throw alotta money at her then yell fuck her/Fuck her, fuck her, then yell fuck her/Then I'mma go and get my Louisville slugger".

Nicki says that she worked on the verse for days because she thought Trey was going to think she was crazy. She was especially concerned over this gem: "Yellin all around the world/Do you hear me? Do you like my body?/Anna Nicki/Rest in peace to Anna Nicole Smith/Yes, my dear, you're so explosive/Say hi to Mary, Mary and Joseph/Now bottoms up and double my dosage." Not only does she pay homage to former model and reality TV star Anna Nicole Smith (who died in 2007 from a fatal mix of prescription drugs), but she also tells Smith to say hello to Biblical entities Mary and Joseph (Jesus's parents) and Mary Magdalene (widely regarded as a prostitute who became one of Jesus's closest friends and disciples, Jesus having cleansed her of her sins).

With every guest feature, Nicki grew more and more confident with her skills and especially with herself. She allowed her personal style to breathe and flourish, despite the fact that she was still a bit self-conscious about the schizo-flow of her rhymes. Nicki retreated for a few days and contemplated the verse before sending Trey the finished project. "I kept on hitting [him] like, 'I'mma have it done today.' I think I did live with it for, like, three days because I was changing it up, I couldn't get it," she admitted to MTV. But then, all of a sudden, something just hit me. I was gonna take [the Anna Nicole Smith part] out because I was like, 'Trey is gonna think I'm crazy.' Roman is very spastic. Roman is crazy and Roman is weird and Roman doesn't care."

While Roman gives Nicki the freedom to do whatever she wants, whenever she wants, without consequence, Nicki, at this point in her career, could only dream of such luxuries. Only moments before, the now famous rapper was cruising around Queens in a used white BMW that she had bought with money saved from the several thankless jobs she was ultimately fired from. Now, she found herself living in a new luxury apartment in Los Angeles, being courted by music moguls (Diddy) wanting to manage her and buying her mother a house.

She had also become a fully-fledged leader of her own movement: as the Head Harajuku Barbie, she commands an army of Barbz, whose breasts she signs with Sharpies, and Ken Barbz (the iconic doll's arm candy boyfriend), who love her every move. Gaga has her "Monsters" and Nicki came up with the names to personalise her relationship with her own audience, whom she hates to call fans. "That word makes me feel like I am on a different level than the people that love me. I call them my 'Barbz' and 'Ken Barbz' because we are one. They go through the same things that I go through. They feel the same damn way I do. They cuss people out the same way." But, all the same, she had become someone to look up to.

Nicki was also teetering on joining a new world: that of pop music. With her background, it made perfect sense. She had spent four years studying acting and being exposed to all types of cultures, tastes and perspectives while at LaGuardia. She was no longer rapping on the street corner, so it was a natural progression that her music would follow suit. It was no coincidence that she and label mate Drake were fast becoming the hottest new kids on the block. Both were the antithesis of what male and female rappers were supposed to be. "At one point, you had to sell a few kilos to be a credible rapper," she told *Rolling Stone*. "Drake and I are embracing the fact that we went to school, love acting, love theatre, and that's OK – it's especially good for the black community to know that it's OK."

During the spring and summer of 2010 while working on her debut album, which would finally define who she was as an artist. Nicki was facing a lot of pressure because of the expectations. She told *Vibe*: "You got people saying 'Oh, that might be too pop for you,' or 'That might be too dance for you.' I just started meditating on what makes them say that. I think people say those things just because of the past."

And she may have been right.

Her predecessors, most notably Lil' Kim and Foxy Brown, achieved success with genitalia-soaked rants backed by hood beats, perfect for the clubs and Jeeps. Lil' Kim soared slightly above the fray with some mainstream chart success and was embraced by the establishment, however she – and Foxy – fell prey to their own devices. Always rapping about sex, pushing sex with their barely-there outfits and talking about sex in interviews, the two rappers paralysed their careers with an overindulgence in sex and sexuality. The same had happened to the Queen of S&M (sex and money), Madonna, in 1983 when she faced a trifecta of failure with the book *Sex*, the movie *Body Of Evidence* (portraying a woman accused of killing a man with sex) and the album *Erotica* all under-performing (although *Sex* went on to become a collectable). No matter how much they may love you, if you stay in the same place, the fans will eventually tire and move on. And worse: the competition will level you.

"The female rappers of my day spoke about sex a lot," Nicki told *Vibe*. "And I thought to have the success they got, I would have to represent the same thing, when in fact I don't." There are plenty of YouTube-able moments out there that Nicki now regrets – especially the *Sucka Free* mix-tape cover recreating Lil' Kim's pose and her loose talk about sex. "In the beginning I felt very controlled," she told *V* magazine. "When you're a new artist – especially when you're a female – everyone thinks they know everything. Everybody wants to be Daddy and feel some empowerment or joy when they can tell a female what to do."

However, when one thinks of feminism, Nicki Minaj's name is not the first name to come to mind. Writer C.J. Fontaine believes, "If [Lady] Gaga is exposing the public to high fashion and art then Nicki Minaj is a caricature of feminism. I do wonder if the only feminism we are willing to accept comes teetering on high heels, flanked by high-pitched giggles, donning a miniskirt. Welcome our Beta version (training wheels mandatory): she is charming while evasive and if needed she bites back, with wit and a smile."

Nicki may not deliver feminism in a blatant Gloria Steinem on steroids kind of way, but her brand of female empowerment is there. And in between the growls and screams of "It's Barbie Bitch," the HBIC (Head Barb In Charge) has a message: if not for all women, but definitely for herself. "Well girls are multifaceted, but women artists stifle themselves, or are stifled by others who tell them that you can only be one thing and you can't change from that thing – that's all you are," she stated to *V*. "Starting out, I can't remember what it was that I had to look like per se, but I felt boxed in."

The fall of 2010 proved that there was no such box that could contain Nicki's irrefutable talent. While she was putting the finishing touches to *Pink Friday*, her long-awaited, much speculated about album, Kanye West released a song that he was recording for his upcoming album *My Beautiful Dark Twisted Fantasy*. The track included appearances from Jay-Z, Rick Ross, Bon Iver and Nicki, who had no idea Jay-Z was going to be on the track (her life was coming full circle; Jay-Z co-signed her for her first collaboration with a major artist and now she was rapping with – and outshining – him on the same track). "I did not know that Jay was going to be on [the song]," she told New York DJ Angela "Angie" Martinez. "Or else, I probably would have been too scared to get on it."

Entitled 'Monster', the collaboration was an eerie track, reminiscent of Michael Jackson's 'Thriller' in mood, and featured its powerhouse performers relating their own experiences to feared monsters. Jay-Z compares himself to a host of horrific characters: "Sasquatch, Godzilla, King Kong, Loch Ness, goblin, ghoul, a zombie with no conscience," he states on the track. Despite being the freshman in the crew, Nicki came out like an upperclassman. Spewing lines like "Let me get this straight/Wait I'm the rookie/But my features and my shows 10 times your pay/50k for a verse, no album out/Yeah my money's so tall that my Barbie's gotta climb it," the 5'1" rapper soon towered over all, male and female.

Just weeks earlier, during a radio interview, West had declared that Minaj was the "scariest artist out right now", and he went even further, "She has the "potential to be the number 2 rapper of all time," behind Eminem.

However, although West had asked Nicki to be on the track, since he had such belief in her talents, he was not initially impressed with her verses. "It was the first verse submitted for the song. I had a verse already and Kanye and I did not really love it and then he pushed me to go in. Kanye brought that out of me. He was like, 'What do you want to say?' So, instead of writing a rap, I wrote page after page of what I wanted to say and then 'Monster' came out of those words."

Critics praised the track, especially Nicki's lyrical prowess and her jumping from verse to verse, changing voices and personas seamlessly. Rick Ross joined in on the praise fest: "Nicki Minaj earned my respect as a lyricist," he told *Rap-Up* magazine. "Before that day she was a great entertainer, but for me to get in the studio with my own two eyes and see her write her verse, I knew that was gonna be one of the greatest verses of this year."

In fact, all those that were on the fence about her skill as a rapper were silenced with the 36 bars she delivered on 'Monster'. Now Nicki knew one thing for sure: the world was ready for *Pink Friday*.

Chapter 3

Barbie's About To Pop

It was an early Tuesday afternoon in September 2010, a few weeks before Nicki Minaj would make history on *Billboard* with a record number of songs on the chart at once and release *Pink Friday* to great success. But that day Nicki Minaj was struggling. Not the same struggles she had only recently risen above – to name a few, being disrespected by male rappers in New York City, especially her hood of Jamaica, Queens; finding difficulty in believing in her talent; getting fired from dead-end job after dead-end job; signing a record deal only to find that she'd have to constantly prove herself and outwit the accusations of her using another female rapper's career as her blueprint. Nope. None of those. Those concerns were tired. Rather that day, Nicki Minaj, the first lady of Young Money Records, was struggling with the notion of going pop – not in the sense of losing it; rather going POP! in the same vein as Britney Spears (who she greatly admires) and Lady Gaga (who she thinks is a little bananas).

This would seem like a First World dilemma to anyone, especially to a burgeoning star. In just three years, with the help of some mega-selling mix-tapes – and mega-watt rapper Lil Wayne popping off about her skill as a rapper every time the golden grills that are his teeth parted – she had sky-rocketed from a New York nobody to a round-the-clock buzzed-about female MC working alongside several superstar "somebodies", such as Mariah Carey, Christina Aguilera, Usher and Ludacris, all of whom wanted the new-fangled fire that Nicki unwaveringly brings to each and every track she breathes on. Nicki set the streets aflame and established that the long endured drought of skilful female rappers had officially come to an end.

In fact, many at that time were whispering (but not too loudly, for fear of speaking too soon or having the body of Lil' Kim fall from the sky on top of them) that Nicki Minaj would be the new Queen of Hip-Hop (*Rolling Stone* crowned her with the moniker back in 2010 when she didn't even have an album out). But, the funny thing is, hip-hop was not her concern; it taught her, raised her, trained her and sharpened her – it wasn't going anywhere. Rather Nicki had gotten a taste of the sweet nectar that flows freely (but is not free) from the mainstream. "It definitely has happened organically," Nicki said over the phone from Los Angeles (where she moved to from New York), while still recording tracks and tweaking songs for her debut album (which was at that point being touted as a major event).

Only in America: a poor girl from Queens becomes a rap superstar with no album to call her own, and at the same time chafes inwardly over the possible perils of a pop splash. "People just started coming to what I was doing," she continued to say in explanation of her then situation. "I did not [seek out] these choices, these choices found me. Five years ago, I really could not see all of this in a crystal ball. I knew that I wanted to make it. I always had faith in myself and I never took no for an answer." The irony of her life was not at all lost on Nicki. She's as clever in real life as she is on wax. The choices may have found her, but just know that the Trinidadian beauty had calculated them. "I knew that my career would finally reach pop culture," she said easily.

A declaration that presumptuous from an artist with a career in its infancy would typically soar past the risk of ridiculous; however, hearing the words directly from Nicki herself, the claim seemed perfectly normal. Maybe it had to do with the fact that *Pink Friday* wasn't about to be her true first album, but actually her fourth.

In the hip-hop world, the mix-tape has become a non-official album, and it can transform unknown artists into celebrities overnight. Nicki's Young Money label mate Drake released his mix-tape *So Far Gone* in 2009 and, due to its inexplicable popularity, he has since been able to re-release it as an official EP, whereupon it debuted at number six on the *Billboard* Albums Chart, selling over 73,000 copies in the first week and eventually going on to sell almost 700,000 copies, all this despite the original mix-tape being available for free download. Nicki's three mix-tapes, *Playtime Is Over*, *Sucka Free* and *Beam Me Up Scotty*, have served as her first three albums; they made her money and enabled her to tour clubs around the country (where fans rap along to every word).

"The typical new artist does not have as much history as I do. People have seen me for the last three years. They cannot compare the experiences I have gone through," she said in an almost whisper. Where was the usual endless hoard of energy that her audience had come to expect? It is usual to listen to any one of her alpha-female verses and end up exhausted from the attempts to follow her lead as she breathlessly travels from persona to persona, replete with differing voices, each character so distinct. So it was startling to hear such a calm, reserved and poised woman on the other end of the receiver.

And it was because, in that moment, she was Onika Maraj, the girl who handles the fallout and business of her much more famous and successful sister Nicki. "People have read about me and heard me for three years [before my album]. People [have] got to learn me." And there seems to be many layers underneath her look, a Skittles bag explosion of Tokyo-inspired get-ups and cartoon-like rapping style. Some have the vision and see it. Others not so much. "She has a lot of doubters," rapper Ludacris said. "But the people who say negative things or fear her don't understand her."

But at that point in Nicki's career it wasn't just her haters that were confused, but her many fans, particularly those that had spotted her rhyming on *The Come Up* video, the loyalists that had been downloading her music since *Playtime Is Over* and especially those converted by the tour de force flow she revealed on the claptrap 'Itty

Bitty Piggy' from *Beam Me Up Scotty*. This conundrum brought Nicki back to her pitchfork in the road: "Hip-Hop Hooray" or "Pop Goes The Weasel"?

The single 'Your Love' had opened the door to the possibility of Nicki Minaj Pop Diva. As well as hitting the top spot in the Rap charts, breaking long-held records in the process, it had debuted on the *Billboard* Hot 100 singles chart at number 51 and the following week it had darted 25 positions to number 26 (the song ultimately peaked at number 14 on the Hot 100 and numbers four and one on the R&B/Hip-Hop and Rap charts respectively). The song's success had been a surprise to many, not least to Nicki Minaj herself. It was never supposed to be a release, period. In common with Usher's 2004 mega-hit 'Yeah', which had never been intended for release but was leaked and went on to propel his album *Confessions* to multi-platinum status, 'Your Love' had met with the same fate. Initially, Nicki was horrified. She knew the song was far from complete and was not in single-release shape. However, the public thought otherwise. "'Your Love' was a miracle song," she said. "I did it two and a half years ago. It leaked. Radio got to it. They started playing it. I would never have put that song out. I had left it to die. It took on a life of its own. I am a lot edgier than that song but it was a moment in time. I can't be mad at that."

Indeed, it was nothing to be mad at. The originally intended first single from *Pink Friday*, 'Massive Attack', had virtually tanked, and many critics noticed the stark difference between the two songs. *Entertainment Weekly* stated: "OK, her first single was a dud. But Nicki Minaj is slicing the competition to pieces with her second try." *Billboard* declared that the song introduced a "new brand of hood majesty".

Loaded with an undeniable charisma, a quixotic style and now a pop hit, Nicki's name wasn't just mentioned in the same sentence as Lil' Kim: she was hot on the heels of Lady Gaga. And those close to the emerging star already knew that her ambitions were more aligned with becoming the Queen of Pop rather than the Queen Bee. She told *Vibe* magazine, "I have to invent something, to show that a girl can rap over any kind of beat and still be hip-hop."

When asked if she would ever consider a collaboration with Gaga, she said, "I think it would be a freaking zoo! It would be crazy and it would probably shut the world down for a couple of days. I have never spoken to her."

Surprisingly, though, the artist Nicki said she admires most is not some hip-hop titan of the past, but a pop princess with just as many personal problems as albums sold: Britney Spears' phoenix-like rising from the ashes of what was once her party and paparazzi-plagued life has been a source of inspiration to Nicki. "She is a Sagittarius too. I saw her go through so much in the media. I kept thinking that she was going to commit suicide," Nicki said. "I was thinking that there is no way that this woman could continue to function that way. Paparazzi were around her house 24 hours a day. She could not go to 7-Eleven without being followed and every late night show was making fun of her. When I saw her bounce back like a freaking queen, I was so impressed. You can't keep a good bitch down. When you have something inside of you, people can only take it from you if you let them. She would not allow people to take it from her. I respect her for that."

After 'Your Love' had propelled Nicki into the pop stratosphere, she began to experience a shift in her life that Spears had been dealing with for over a decade. "Before [the pop success] I was just doing whatever I wanted to do. Saying what I wanted to say," she says. "I did not really think about the future when I was doing "Underground Nicki". I was not thinking about how my interviews would do and how they could change people's views of me."

Several of those interviews must make her cringe: from insinuations about liking girls to comments about her genitalia. She told *Rock Me TV*: "I love to cook. My 'box' (slang for female genitalia) is Top 10, but my cooking is number one. I cook a mean kingfish. If you like seafood, besides eating me, you can eat that. [But] it's not enough to make you cum on yourself." She now looks back on such interviews with regret. "I wonder, 'Why did I say that?' Or 'Why was I acting like that?' At the time, I was just being organic and doing whatever I wanted. I did not make any really calculated decisions in the beginning.

Now, of course, I do. Now, I am kind of considered mainstream. So, there are things that I need to figure out. I do have to think a lot of things out now."

Her musical character – outspoken, unpredictable, aggressive – gives the impression that Nicki is impetuous and rash. But actually, she is thoughtful and calculated. In a time when an entire generation of twenty-somethings – dubbed "Millennials" – were either suffering from post-college confusion or wandering through a minimum wage existence in search of their "Ah ha!" moment, this twenty-something and her "Barbie" movement had already arrested the attention and adoration of the world. She may have said and done things prior to her success that don't gel well with her current incarnation, but they were said and done with the ultimate intention of establishing herself and standing out in a world not particularly generous to or respectful of female rappers. Nicki looked to the successful rappers who came before her – Foxy Brown, Lil' Kim – and she simply mimicked their overtly sexual ways, before she realised that she didn't have to. But, by 2010, because she had moved into another realm of stardom, she had to make more sacrifices.

"Yeah. But you know what? You have to sacrifice fun for money. I would not want to have fun and be broke. Would you? Do what you have to do. It's no different than being in corporate America. If you really want to be the president of the company, you are not going to wear jeans and sneakers, unless you started that company from the ground up. If you want to work your way to the top, you may wear a suit and tie every day and then when you get to the top, you can let your freaking hair down and do whatever the hell you want to do. But you do play by certain rules when you want to get to the top. Anyone who tells you any different is just lying. As artists, we are free, but we have a certain awareness of where we want to go and this game has rules."

Nicki had to play by the rules, but at that point in her career some of those rules deeply annoyed her. While she was still a novice in most industry observers' eyes, she was no stranger to the necessities for and requirements of being an artist. She'd been giving interviews since 2007, on home-spun video blogs and hosting outlets, but she had recently gone through media training (when an expert media specialist teaches a client how to handle themselves in front of the press) and had started to grace the cover of magazines, as in *Vibe*'s June/July 2010 issue. But in this age of social media expediency, when viral videos generate overnight celebrities and Twitter can transport an artist from Main Street to Madison Avenue, everything new becomes old hat very quickly. And it's no different for rising rap stars with a predilection for pink.

"[I hate] doing interviews with people that do not know anything about me," Nicki said. But she wasn't being difficult or demanding; she was being real (in as much as someone living and working in a world fuelled by popularity can be). She had come to realise that, even though artists (particularly new ones) need the support of the media to further their careers (and recruit more Barbz and Ken Barbz, undoubtedly), she did not have to do it all on someone else's terms. "I can kind of get the sense when I am interviewing with someone who has done no research on me and is just going to ask me the same generic question over and over. I don't like it," she stresses. As she started seeing mainstream hits, Nicki was encountering the mainstream media, and many journalists were certainly not clued up on her rise to stardom: "I am tired of answering, 'How did Lil Wayne find you?' I am tired of answering, 'How did you get your name?' I am tired of answering, 'Where were you when you first met Wayne?' All of those questions make me go in the past. I want to talk about what's current. But, I do understand I do have to explain some things for people to get to know me. I have to answer those questions as if it's the first time I have ever answered the question."

Nicki has talked before about how she was the class clown in school and, with her majoring in theatre in high school, it should come as no surprise that she is an expressive conversationalist – not gregarious (there is a difference), but she is not talkative just for the sake of it, or she doesn't limit her interviews to mere minutiae in order to hide or avoid the substance (which many celebrities are guilty of). In contrast, Nicki is articulate. She delivers exactly what she wants to say in the manner and feeling that she has chosen. That does not mean, however, that she has grown accustomed to opening up to complete strangers outfitted as journalists. "I am still a little cautious. But I happen to be a very open artist by nature," she says. "I think I always give a lot more than the average artist does in interviews. So, I am used to it. It's because it's a part of my personality to have a conversation and to really speak and to allow a person to get inside of my head. But, even for me, it gets to be a bit much sometimes. Especially me, being a female, you may wake up on the wrong side of the bed and you don't want to answer a sexual question, and personal questions."

The Queens-bred rapper accepted the parameters of the game because she wanted the world to know who she is. "Unfortunately, it is a rule that I cannot change, if I want to get into important magazines. If I want everyone to know me, then I have to be aware that there are some people who have never heard of Nicki Minaj. It's not that I don't like those rules, it's just, as an artist, it's something that you have to get used to. I don't want people to think that just because you are an artist, you can do anything you want and just fly to the moon and you're in a private jet and you are buying Giuseppe Zanotti shoes. It's a job, just like everyone else puts in work when they go to a nine to five."

In her new nine to five, Nicki no longer encounters irate customers, but it does involve an at times hard-to-please boss: Lil Wayne. She and the dreadlocked word slinger clash at times, primarily over the direction of her career. "Wayne wanted me to stay more 'hood' and he did not want me to start doing 'pop' music. He felt that I should stay in the rap lane and that I would be more of an asset in hip-hop because there were so few females [then]. He did not want me to do any singing because he felt that it would take me out of the lane that he felt I was strongest in."

Wayne tells her what he thinks, but he is not a micromanager and he allows the artists signed to Young Money Records to journey down the path they ultimately choose. Plus, he's smart enough to know that he cannot tell Nicki what to do with her music. "Wayne knows that I will do a little of both and express myself," she said of their compromise. Just as she was clever enough to avoid signing a dreadful, albeit typical "360 deal" with Young Money, Nicki is in creative control of her career. "I always do whatever I want to do when it comes to music."

This is an advantage point not many artists, and nary any female hip-hop artists in the past, have enjoyed. Nicki approaches her career with a populist eye: she looks to her fans to see what they want from her. "I put it out and allow my [fans] to decide if they like [what I am doing] or not. And then I go from there," she says. But, Lil Wayne did have a voice in the Barbz-ocracy. "There were a lot of things that he said to me that were beneficial," Nicki admits. "He told me to keep myself hip-hop and my lyrics hip-hop. I look back on that now and I am very thankful."

The First Lady of Young Money records is also grateful to Wayne for taking her out on her first tour, which was a turning point in her career. "Being on tour with Wayne gave me the 'eye of the tiger'. I wanted to perform in those huge venues and for people to know my name and my songs and have them sing with me. It made me feel like, 'Yo, what is preventing me from having what Wayne has?'"

Amid her moments of introspection during the 2010 phone call, Nicki also reflected on the moments of contention between her and Wayne. One such disagreement ended up with her abandoning the tour halfway through. "I left the tour then and worked on my mix-tape. I realised that if I were not supplying people with product then they would never love my music or me. I would hear people say, 'I am still on the fence about Nicki Minaj. I just need more.' So, I said 'I am going to give you more. A lot more.' And that's what I did."

And, like rap legend Kool Moe Dee rapped many moons before her on his classic 'I Go To Work', Nicki Minaj did just that. Her unrelenting work ethic paid off and established artists began to take notice of the rising hip-hop star. R&B singer Robin Thicke became her first major collaborator outside of the hip-hop sphere. Thicke had been thoroughly impressed with Nicki's magnetism and diversity. "She could do dance, she could do hip-hop, she could do street, she could do gutter. She can do whatever she wants," he told *Vibe*. However, Thicke acknowledged that being a prodigy is both a blessing and a curse and because Nicki can turn her hand to so many styles with ease, it's hard for her to settle on one thing, which also prevents her listening public from digging in. "She has to find her thing," Thicke continued. "It's hard to know what to do when you can do anything."

With all that she has accomplished so early on, Nicki feels she should receive some credit for the hard work that her climb to the top has required. And because her style is so left-field of what the world has come to expect from female rappers, she had experienced push back. "They were basing those opinions on the way that I look. If I were wearing baggy jeans and a Yankee fitted cap, then I would be loved by the masses and the hip-hop culture. But when you are a girly girl and you're taking beautiful pictures, people's first instinct is to hate.

"Hip-hop has a lot of jealousy. If you look a certain way, people seem to judge you a lot more. If you walk around as if you don't care how you look, people are less intimidated. If you see a girl come onstage and she looks like 'I don't care what you think about me, I am confident,' that makes people insecure. If you come out in baggy jeans and a hoodie, then they feel like 'I am secure enough to be around this person.'"

Because she is confident in her skills, Nicki ackowledged that the resistance was just not her problem any longer. "I know that I put in my work lyrically," she said easily. "There [are] absolutely no reasons for anyone to still be on the fence about me unless [they] are jealous and intimidated. If you were not jealous and intimidated you would give me my props for breaking the record for [the first] female topping the *Billboard* Hip-Hop chart in eight years, for having three BET Awards with no album out, for being the first female rapper to do the MTV pre-show with no album out, for getting on songs with Jay-Z, Wayne, Kanye, Drake and holding my own. Those insecurities are not my problems; they are someone else's."

Being a freshman attending the senior prom, Nicki definitely caught the attention of the entire school, yet, despite her obvious skills and flair, many people at that point in her career were still not convinced. From haters leaving blistering remarks questioning everything about her life to celebs still looking at her with a raised brow, Nicki was feeling it all. Sandra Denton, better known as Pepa from the legendary rap duo

Salt-N-Pepa, told *Vibe*, "She reminds me of Lil' Kim. Bold and you know… but to me she has not learned the message yet."

And Nicki has received criticism from other female rappers, which she says has bothered her gravely, but that she had learnt to accept. "I used to lose sleep [over that]," she says. "I used to be sick. I used to stop eating. I just don't care any more." Before she resurrected interest in female rappers, while she was still working for her own platform, she says that she paid appropriate respect to the ladies that came before her. "I walked around kissing everyone's feet for two years. I paid my dues. If you don't get it, goodbye."

But what if hip-hop in general doesn't get it? Does she have an obligation to the culture? "Hip-hop made me," she said quickly, during the same phone interview. "I could never turn my back on the culture. [While] working on *Pink Friday*, I was very conscious about not straying from the hip-hop audience. I don't want to be one of those artists that forget their roots. I will always be Nicki Minaj: Female Rapper. So, even if I add slashes to my title later on like actor, shoes salesman, I will always know that I owe that to hip-hop."

Yet, the rapper felt that the responsibility was two-fold and that hip-hop must respect her ambitions as an artist; in the same way it was holding her accountable, she was refusing to allow it to constrain what she knew lay within. "[I cannot] be suffocated by the hip-hop culture. I want the culture to be aware that there are people in the culture that are not so black and white. I am somewhere in the grey area. Hip-hop and me, we have to make a compromise. Hip-hop is going to have to accept me for who I am and I am going to have to remember that hip-hop is where I came from."

And Nicki managed to live up to that promise with her appearance on Kanye West's 'Monster', which reminded fans why they fell in love with her, while also helping her to achieve the respect of an entirely new legion of admirers. She recorded an undeniable marvel of a guest appearance; but those otherworldly verses did not come without labour. "No one [else] was on the song; it was just my verse at first. I felt pressure because I was on a song with Kanye and I wanted to impress him," she admits. "I just wrote what I felt at that time and it happened to be meaningful stuff to me. The hook, saying that I am a monster, brought all of it out of me. I wrote the song twice and the second time, it became it a miraculous verse. To be honest, I never love anything that I do. I thought it was dope, but I did not think it would get this reaction. I heard it after it was mixed and mastered with Jay and Kanye on it, and that's when I fell in love with it because it was so creative."

Nicki is known for her strong work ethic in the studio. She doesn't like to waste time or spend lots of time playing around. Multi-platinum producer Swizz Beatz, who worked with Nicki on *Pink Friday*, said he was shocked by her behaviour in the studio. "She would sit in the corner with her notepad," he told E! "Some people write on scraps, she had her own little neat writing book. I was impressed to see how organized she was with her craft." Nicki admits that her creative process is a lonely one. "I get a beat. Then I start vibing to it. I play it for a couple of days, and just see what comes to my head," she said. "Then I start jotting stuff down and I will write my chicken scratch over on a clean sheet of paper. Then I will go in the booth and record."

Ask Nicki if she is a perfectionist and she will agree 100 per cent. In fact, she'll say, "Absolutely." But the reason she seeks perfection has nothing to do with her ego. "When I was little, I wanted to change my mother's life and I always felt like if I were really, really perfect, I would become rich and famous and I could help my mom," she said in the same phone interview, her voice softening as she spoke, almost as if she was imagining the austere childhood homes in which she grew up in both Trinidad and Queens, witnessing her mother's struggle to support the family. And it's not only music and performances that she makes sure are beyond excellent, it's the entire Nicki Minaj aesthetic. "When it comes to music, I always feel like there is so much riding on every verse and every song and fashion choice and every little tidbit – if I mess up then there is a possibility that I will not be able to fulfil my childhood dream of making sure that my mom and my family are good. I think psychologically that is why I am a perfectionist."

Nicki and her mother, Carol Maraj, are extremely close. And the rapper has kept her word, buying her mother a house and taking care of her. But, after a while, with cash flow no longer an issue, Nicki says her mother got a little carried away with spending and the role of parent and child was momentarily reversed. "I was spoiling my mother and she lost a sense of reality. I had to sit with my business managers and come up with a plan and put my mother on an allowance. I had to show her that this is not to be taken for granted." Many rappers have had hit songs. Some have achieved mainstream success and have made lots of money. But, very few have actually retired from music with their finances intact. Nicki is learning from the mistakes of her predecessors. "You cannot live like you don't have a care in the world," she said. "God forbid that there is a rainy day; you want the people you love to be taken care of. I definitely have to set parameters for my family and I have to have those uncomfortable conversations with them." Those conversations were inevitable. Nicki went from being a waitress at Red Lobster in the Bronx to a millionaire in a short amount of time. Yet she trusts her family unwaveringly. "My family would never try to take advantage of me. I take care of my immediate family. Maybe in the next few years, I will add a few more to that list," she laughed.

In fact, Nicki Minaj laughs a lot. "I was the person that everyone came to [in high school] to lighten up the mood. I can find humour in anything," she says. "We can hear the worst news ever and then start cracking up laughing. It's not that we are mean people, we are able to step out of situations and look at it in a different way than the average person."

She loves jokes and adores quick-witted people. "I am very intrigued with sarcasm. I love it. I love people that use lots of sarcasm. When I hear someone who uses lots of sarcasm, they strike me as an intelligent person. I love dry humour." It makes sense, then, for her to admire Larry David, the creator and star of HBO's hit series *Curb Your Enthusiasm*. She also loves the in-your-face crass of *Martin* and the acid tongue of a certain officer of the court in the afternoon. "When I just need to be gut-busting laughing on the floor, it's *Martin*. When I want to think and be amused and super-excited mentally, then it's Larry David's *Curb Your Enthusiasm*. I also love Judge Judy. I love dry humour. I love the 'it factor' in a joke that a lot of people don't get. I love that type of stuff."

But the good-time girl was all about her career at that time: "I don't do anything outside of work right now. It's all work related. Even when I laugh and have positive moments, it's work related. In a few years, I will be able to loosen my grip. Right now, there is no recreational time for me. People email and [text] me all the time, asking, 'Can we go to the movies or Six Flags?'

In fact, she had recently managed to find time to take her little brother, her nieces and nephews to the adventure theme park and she was able to have a great time, even though the crowds eventually recognised her, despite her attempts at dressing down. "I took [them] to Six Flags Great Adventure and we had a water-gun fight in the front of the venue," she said. Her love for her younger relatives was apparent in the noticeable lift in octave as she spoke. "People were beginning to crowd around and ask 'Is that Nicki Minaj?' I looked a hot mess, but I did not care. I love the time I spend with my little brother and my nieces and nephews. I love the purity of their thoughts. I make them sing and dance for me and I tape them and take pictures of them." Did they know that their sister and auntie is a celebrity? "They get it that I am a celebrity, but, I did not want them to get it so soon," she said. Even though Nicki has wanted and worked for fame since before attending the famous LaGuardia High School, her family did not follow her path. Therefore, she tries to shield them from it as much as possible, but it still inevitably seeps into their lives. "I took them bowling, and we could not bowl because all the kids wanted to take a picture, and I could not tell the kids no. So, I had to say to them, 'I am going to take these pictures, then can I have a little time with my little brother and nieces?'"

Her kindness to fans is two-fold: she knows without them she could be just another young girl running food orders in New York. However, the well-being of her family will always come first. "[Another time] my brother was 12 years old, we were in a store and people started coming in to stare at us. Even though I had security, he started taking on that role and taking on more than he should. I wanted him to shop and have fun, but he was standing at the door, seeing who was looking, being cautious, seeing if we were in danger."

Family and friends are very important to Nicki Minaj. And now that her life has completely metamorphosed into an existence with notoriety and money, they are even more important. "My friends mean the world to me. I don't make lots of friends," she said. And with her new focus, it is near impossible for her to start new friendships and, surprisingly, she is not really the sociable type anyway. Even before Nicki Minaj was born, Onika Maraj was never a party girl. And now, she does not like being around people who thrive off the "velvet rope life". "To be honest, I have such tunnel vision [with my career]. I don't really go out in recreational types of atmospheres. My friends are very down to earth. I don't like going out and being flashy and being seen. I don't like the hoopla when I am around people that I love. They are people who don't need to be in the spotlight and they are cool with us doing something low-key."

In the same way that she worked hard for her mother, Nicki feels a sombre obligation to help those around her that she loves and were supportive of her when she was struggling to make it as an artist. "When your life changes, you feel a little guilty. You struggled with them and you know how it is to struggle. You definitely feel an obligation to get these people out of the hood and give them a shot. That's actually one of the things that really weighs heavily on my heart every day." Even more so, according to the rapper, she not only worked to achieve her dreams, but she also wished for the opportunity to be in a position to bring up those around her. "When you 'make it', you are not doing it for yourself, you are doing it for so many other people. You become the breadwinner for so many other families. And it's a good thing. That's what I wanted. I would pray that I would be in a position to help my family and friends and that's what God gave me. He gave me what I asked for."

Nicki has even been able to hire one of her best friends and, like she had to do with her mom, she has had another "conversation". "I have a few friends. My best friend in the whole world is "Tee-Tee". I don't get to see her much. I live in LA now and she lives in NY, but when I tour she will come on the road as one of my assistants because I want to be around her. She came on the road before and I think she was missing her boyfriend and it was affecting her work. I had to have a real talk with her. She got it and she understands. She and I are so close; there is nothing that can come between us."

Beyond her bestie, as she grows in stature as an artist and as a brand, she wants to help women who come behind her. "I feel [an] obligation to employ women so that they are making their own money and calling their own shots," she said. "A woman should play the role of boss in this business. I definitely want to create those opportunities when I am in a position to do that."

Nicki may have a few girlfriends, but the majority of her life is spent around men. That's the occupational hazard of being female in the hip-hop industry; it's a testosterone-sustained world, where women seem to thrive behind the scenes, but very few have succeeded on the stage and definitely not in the way Nicki is right now. "I always had girlfriends, but when I started doing music, it all changed. When I started rapping, I wanted to be around guys who were rapping because I could challenge them. When I would rap with guys I would push my pen harder. Even with my team now, I am usually only speaking with guys every day, whether it's my assistants, or Baby, Slim and Wayne [at Young Money]. I don't think it's a bad thing," she says. And anyone following her pictures in magazines, watching her television appearances or reading articles about her, would know about Safaree Samuels. He's the guy who is always at her side, serving multiple roles in her life. "I hang out with SB," as she calls him (short for his stage name, Scaff Beezy). "He is also my business partner, my assistant; he has a million different jobs. He is my hype man as well. We have been friends for about eight years. We met in NYC when we were both doing music and we were trying to do a group together. He was a dancer and he was very silly and he did not care if he looked stupid. So, when I went solo, I was like, 'You should be my hype man!'"

Nicki is comfortable with being friends with males and although she has created and leads the Barbie brigade, she gets along better with guys overall. "Sometimes I think it's easy to deal with guys because they are less emotional," she said. "They give me a free pass because I am a girl and they allow me to express myself in a bitchy way at times and they don't take it personally. The next day, we are back to normal and kicking it like nothing happened. Girls tend to hold grudges a little longer and I am in a fast-paced environment and I don't have time for that. I am on the go."

However, Nicki's energetic personas have only served to strengthen her female fanbase and increase the already staggering support she receives from the gay community. She acknowledges that she represents the qualities that gay men adore. "Gay men are attracted to over-the-top aggressive females, because that's who some of them feel they are inside. If you see someone doing and saying the things that you would yourself, it inspires you. When you meet someone, and you're like 'I have the same views and I feel the same way', that's an automatic bond, it bonds you and that person. Gay men are very artistic and very dramatic. When you take a female artist that is iconic, they usually are very artistic and dramatic. That's why you will have gay boys impersonating those women because it speaks to the heart of who they are inside."

Gaga has also intimated that the gay community is the reason for her phenomenal success. "The turning point [in my career] was the gay community," she told *MTV News* in 2009. "I've got so many gay fans and they're so loyal to me and they really lifted me up. They'll always stand by me and I'll always stand by them. It's not an easy thing to create a fanbase."

Nicki feels that her fans understand her best. In her mind, they are extensions of what true friends should be. "They really get me, stand behind me and that's all people want out of a friend. They are my friends." And, at that point in her career, she was betting on her BFFs allowing her to explore and experiment while she figured out the pop thing. "They know that I am going to make mistakes. They don't love everything that I do, but they allow me to make mistakes and are not super judgmental."

Despite what we've been taught about the iconic doll Barbie and her eternal quest for the perfect life, underneath the clothes, beyond the body and forget the homes and cars, Barbie is still just a girl. She has insecurities. Ken pisses her off at times. Other girls hurt her feelings. But, she presses on and supplies the smile that makes her fans happy.

Similarly, Nicki Minaj is just a girl with a dream that has finally come true. She is a girl who is learning and growing every day as a person and an artist. She has made mistakes. She will make more. And, just like Barbie, the world would either leave her on the shelf or buy her.

Fortunately for Nicki Minaj, they would choose the latter.

Chapter 4

Something Like A Phenomenon

Nicki Minaj's breakout appearance on 'Monster' was the perfect set-up she needed for the upcoming release of her album. It silenced the naysayers who were constantly doubting her, gained the rapper new fans and strengthened her existing ones. Plus, having two hip-hop juggernauts like Kanye West and Jay-Z co-sign your skills did not hurt either. "Jay-Z and Kanye don't record records with just anybody," DJ Clue told E!. "If you get in that lane, the rest of the world is going to accept you in a big way." Before the world even noticed, Nicki wanted the attention and respect of those around her; she had always worked for the respect of her male peers – both publicly and secretly. When she was just a girl hanging with the guys that were aspiring rappers in Queens and wanting to jump on their tracks, but getting offers to sing their hooks instead, she was working for respect. But it was not until she realised that she needed to be whomever *Nicki* saw fit to be that she soared. "When I first started rapping I felt like I needed to be someone," she told Wendy Williams. "Everyone was telling me to be this way, you are from Queens, so be hard. And that was never really me and that's not who I wanted to be. So, when I changed the people that were around me, I started being free. I have always been animated, I have always been crazy, I studied theatre and I wanted to put that into my [music]."

It was Lil Wayne who encouraged Nicki to explore the various sides of her personality and pour that into her music. He gave her advice that he had taken for himself. Reportedly, he was signed to Cash Money Records at the age of nine and began contributing songs to the label at 11 years old. In 1995, at 15, he experienced success as part of the group the Hot Boys and later as a solo artist with a few adequate records, but it was not until Wayne's 2004 album, *Tha Carter*, that he experienced breakout success. The album was the last project produced by Cash Money's in-house producer, and the first on which Wayne debuted a new delivery style he'd been perfecting on eight mix-tapes released prior to the album. It seemed like an inhumane amount of recording for mix-tapes and guest appearances – thus building buzz. Before the successful release of *Tha Carter* (which has gone on to become his signature franchise with three sequels as of 2012), the label execs baulked. "The label said, 'Oh, no, no, stop,'" Cortez Bryant, Wayne's manager at the time, told *Rolling Stone*. "But... his status was actually growing because of all the things he was doing outside of studio albums. He said, 'Trust me – I've got this, I've got a plan in my head.'"

Years later, and now head of his own label imprint, Young Money, Wayne instituted a similar plan for Nicki. By the fall of 2010, she was experiencing the height of hype, featuring on a whopping 13 singles, including songs with such stellar artists as Rihanna, Christina Aguilera and Jay Sean. During this period, artists just wanted a piece of Nicki. "They all wanted the hottest rapper on their tracks and if you wanted a female rapper, who are you going to go to: there's only Nicki," Safaree Samuels told E!. "That door was so wide open she just knocked that door down and killed every feature she did."

With the success of the two very different singles – 'Your Love' and 'Monster' – Nicki needed to build on both in order to have an explosive release week for her debut album, *Pink Friday*. She and her team did two things: firstly, they released 'Right Thru Me', a ballad-like, romantic confection roaming on Katy Perry's pop turf, which served as the official second single for the album; and, secondly, they leaked 'Roman's Revenge', a heat-seeking battle rhyme led by Nicki's alter-ego Roman Zolanski and accompanied by Eminem and his popular – and psychotic – alter-ego Slim Shady.

'Right Thru Me' revealed a different side to the burgeoning artist. In the Diane Martel-directed video, Nicki appears in a way that is more unusual than her typically technicoloured costumes. Sans the Pixy Stix-shaded wigs and outrageous antics, she is in a T-shirt and jeans, with black, wavy long hair and rapping and singing about a relationship. Plus, she was finally able to exhibit the acting chops she had been referring to in almost every interview she did where she was asked about her tenure at LaGuardia High School as a drama student.

On the 2010 MTV documentary special *Nicki Minaj: My Time Now*, cameras followed Nicki as she prepared for the release of her album; and, one day, they filmed behind the scenes of the shoot for the 'Right Thru Me' video. Nicki and French model Willy Monfret (starring as her boyfriend in the clip) are seen in between scenes working with an acting coach. Nicki takes acting very seriously and considers herself an actress before anything else. "Acting is very important to me," Nicki told MTV. "I am an actress first. I don't want to be a rapper turned actress. That is not who I am. To me, it would be a slap in the face of every teacher and actor I have ever worked with if I make a mockery of the craft."

In 2009, Nicki made her independent film debut in super low budget film *Stuck On Broke*, an urban street drama set in Atlanta and co-starring rapper OJ Da Juiceman. She filmed the movie while living in Atlanta and after having toiled for so long on the streets as a rapper, and, at the time, still grinding to make it, Nicki felt a sense of homecoming when filming this indie. She was finally utilising the skills she had trained in at LaGuardia. And Nicki acknowledges that her thespian ways will always be part of her performance; it is almost impossible to separate the two in her eyes. "When you spend so many years of your life onstage doing theater, its hard to take that out of everything you do," she said in an E! Network documentary on her life. "And it's fun!"

'Your Love' found her jonesing over a guy that everyone wants, while in 'Right Thru Me' she's not fixated from a distance, but rather in a full-blown relationship. "It's a really, really pretty song," Nicki told *Entertainment Tonight,* anticipating the single's release. "It's just really insightful but in a very conversational kind of way. She showed romantic vulnerability for the first time in her music, and admitted: "The song to me is very, very personal. I haven't spoken about an authentic relationship since I've come out." Nicki was giving the audience an alternative to the usual material trappings found in most hip-hop songs. "Not everybody is rich, not everyone likes jewellery, not everybody likes playing dress-up," she continued, "but everyone has been in a relationship at some point in their lives, so when you hear a relationship song you react." And react the audience did. The song climbed to number three on the *Billboard* Rap Songs chart and number 26 on the *Billboard* Hot 100.

In complete contrast, the second part of the planned attack on the charts, 'Roman's Revenge', was leaked to continue the street momentum that 'Monster' had provided her several months earlier and prove that the verse on Kanye's hit was not a fluke. "There was another voice in me, that I wanted to speak," Nicki told E! "When I was about to wrap *Pink Friday,* there was a beat I had from Swizz Beatz and I wanted to go buck wild on it."

And Nicki wanted the number one rapper on the track. She was apprehensive about asking Eminem to join her on the album, but emailed him anyway. And she was surprised that he responded. She told MTV: "We went out on a whim and put it in the air like, it'd be great if he would collaborate with us. I remember I kept talking about it, and I thought, 'It can't hurt.' I sent him one record, and he didn't love it. He just said, 'Can you send me something that's a little more me?' I sent him an email and thanked him for just having enough respect. Sometimes people don't respond. He had the respect, at least, to treat me like a peer."

Much has been said about Nicki's piercing lyrics on the song. Her alter ego, Roman Zolanski, was not merely making an appearance this time around, rather this was his tour de force. She has described him as her zany, gay-boy alter ego who is liable to say anything. "Roman is so flamboyant, so outspoken, so open, and, you know, creative," she told *Out* magazine. With verbal jabs like, "Look at my show footage, how these girls be spazzin'/So fuck I look like gettin' back to a has-been?/ Yeah, I said it, has-been/Hang it up, flat screen/(Ha ha) Plasma," it was inevitable that people would assume that she was jabbing at Lil' Kim. In most of her interviews, she denied that the song was directed at the Queen Bee, but during her appearance on *The Wendy Williams Show*, while the Young Money powerhouse didn't admit the lyrics referred to Kim, she did not deny it either, "They know who I am talking about," she told the chatty host coyly. "When you put out records, only the guilty ones think you are talking about them."

Nevertheless, building on what she had achieved with 'Monster', the song helped elevate Nicki into the coveted group of premium hip-hoppers, a group that would usually rarely even allow a female at the table, no matter how many alter egos she may have. She is aware of where her hard work has taken her. "It's been so hard to get in that boy's club," she quipped to Wendy Williams. "They don't really let a lot of people in there." Laurieann Gibson, Nicki's choreographer and Lady Gaga's former creative director (she helped to create Gaga's stage persona), agreed: "The way she delivers that rap is so full of fire and so much attitude... Not everyone can deliver a 'Roman's Revenge'. So, when you hear her on that track, she's separating herself from ever being duplicated." (Three months after the release of 'Roman's Revenge', Nicki released a remix featuring Lil Wayne.)

Nicki's debut album, *Pink Friday* (the title being a play on "Black Friday", the term used to describe the Fisk/Gould scandal, a financial crisis that hit the United States on September 24, 1869), was a fantastical blend of rap, R&B and pop delivered via her now trademark hyper-charismatic and schizophrenic rhyming style. It was released on November 22, 2010, moved forward from the original date of November 23. Going head to head with Kanye West's album *My Beautiful Dark Twisted Fantasy* (both artists appear on each other's albums), it was considered a clash of the Titans to some and an act of audacity on the part of Minaj to others. Even though it was her debut album, the label believed that Nicki was established enough to go head to head with the hip-hop/pop titan. To Nicki, the day was about more than her and Kanye. "It could never be a bad thing," she told Connecticut's Hot 97.3. "The stars will align on that day, it's been a very long time since we had a powerful week in hip-hop. It's not about who sells the most in the first week; it's about hip-hop culture and making an insane impact."

West's album debuted at number one, selling 496,000 copies and putting Nicki into the number two slot, with unit sales of 375,000, heralding in her already history-making career. However, there were critics of the album, including Debra Antney, the mother and manager of rapper Wacka Flacka Flame and former manager of Nicki. Antney has been credited with helping Nicki rise after her days with Fendi at Dirty Money Records. However, their working relationship came to a stop after Nicki's lawyers sent a cease and desist order to Antney regarding her work as Nicki's manager. This occurred before *Pink Friday* was released. After the album dropped, Antney did not mince words about her former client's debut. "It's *terrible*. I like some stuff, but she went too left. I don't think people were ready for her to come [out with pop]," she told Vibe.com. "When I had Nicki, I really wanted her to sing. That's why I took her for training cause Nicki loves singing, but she kept saying to me, 'Deb, I can't do it yet because people won't understand.' And that's why the [rap] mixture was done to introduce them to all of Nicki. I think [*Pink Friday*] was very disappointing to a lot of her fans. She didn't need a lot of [the] features. That was one of the biggest things like... you gave people so many features, give them you now. Nicki could be so much better because – outside of anything that people say – she's very multi-talented. I really wish that she would learn to be more of an *artist*." Despite the outpouring of praise for 'Roman's Revenge', Antney saw it as a disappointment. "I didn't particularly care for ['Roman's Revenge'], but when Eminem came in I liked it. He *made* the song. [Nicki] didn't have to go there with [Lil' Kim]. My view on that is that she came too far to go back that route. And Kim does not even have to go there," she continued to tell Vibe.com. "There are no comparisons to them. Some things are best left unsaid. The whole thing is stupid. People had to learn to love Nicki – that's how the door opened up. It wasn't about Kim or Foxy or any of the rest of them. So I was just a little disappointed [by her album], but if she likes it, I love it."

In spite of Antney's disapproval, Nicki's star continued to soar. In October 2010, at the tender age of 27, Minaj became the first artist in history to clock-in seven songs at one time on the *Billboard* Hot 100 chart, an achievement that no other artist has ever accomplished in the 52-year history of *Billboard*, which is regarded as the Bible of the music industry; its charts are read and revered like a weekly Ten Commandments. The songs included 'My Chick Bad' with Ludacris (she and the Atlanta rapper were nominated for a Grammy for this song in 2011), Lil Wayne's 'Knockout', Trey Songz's 'Bottoms Up', Usher's 'Lil Freak', Sean Kingston's 'Letting Go (Dutty Love)', Jay Sean's '2012' and her own single 'Your Love'. Not only did each of the songs chart well, collectively they brought in over $4.3 million in sales ('Your Love' made over $756,000 before the video was even released). Nicki was as blown away by the accomplishment as everyone else. "Having seven joints on the *Billboard* Hot 100 from a female rapper has never been done," she told E! "I don't know how it happened but it did."

Pink Friday boasts equally aggressive and feminine sensibilities – displaying a woman fighting to establish her independence ('Did It On 'Em') while also fearlessly laying her insecurities on the table for all to see ('Here I Am'). It also served notice to the world about whether she would remain "Street Nicki" – as popularised on her street classic 'Itty Bitty Piggy' ("Flyer than a kite I get higher then Rapunzel/Keep the snow white I could buy it by the bundle/Step your cookies up for they crumble/Don't be actin' like the Cardinals and gone fumble)' or become the burgeoning 'Pop Ingénue Nicki', evidenced on her first two official singles, 'Your Love' and 'Right Thru Me'. The track 'Dear Old Nicki' summed up the inner conflict she faced: 'You was the braveheart/You stole Wayne heart/You never switched it up/You played the same part/But I needed to grow/And I needed to know/That there were something inside of me that I need to show".

The album became the second-highest selling debut in female rap history, behind Lauryn Hill's *The Miseducation Of Lauryn Hill*, although that album was not technically classified as hip-hop. "Interesting. Lauryn sold 422,000 in the 1st wk w/Miseducation! That album wasn't categorized as Hip-Hop/Rap under genre. So Pink Friday under the

'Hip-Hop/Rap' genre has the highest selling first week from a female in HISTORY. #cheers," Minaj tweeted on December 1, 2010 to her millions of followers. "The previous holder of highest 1st week sales for a female RAP album was missy elliott's 'under construction' with 260K. I am in the company of 2 amazing groundbreaking women & for that, I am beyond grateful. S/O to Lauryn and Missy," she continued.

Bryan "Baby" (sometimes "Birdman") Williams, who heads the Cash Money label to which Young Money belongs, proclaimed Nicki's first week out of the gate a milestone and praised her as an artist. "It's cool, it's been 10, 15 years since anybody did that. I love her. I got the utmost respect for Nicki because she is a hard worker and she is dedicated and she's smart, she's intelligent and she's a student of this shit," he told *XXL* magazine. "Nicki's gonna keep growing. She has that mindset and what she is reaching for is high in the sky, so you're going to keep seeing Nicki grow."

And grow she did. After the numbers posted, the new "Queen of Hip-Hop" devoted herself to continued hard work with the album. "I feel like I gave birth to my baby, now I'm gonna teach it how to walk and how to talk and spoil the baby," she told *MTV News*. The subsequent releases from the album all soared in the charts. Following up on the the success of 'Your Love' and 'Right Thru Me', 'Moment 4 Life' (with Drake) hit number one on the Rap chart and went platinum; 'Did It On 'Em' peaked at number four on the Rap chart, also going platinum; 'Super Bass' – arguably her biggest hit to date of writing – soared to number three on the *Billboard* Hot 100 and sold three million copies in the US, another three million in Australia and one million in New Zealand; 'Fly' (with Rihanna) went to number nine on the Rap charts and was certified gold in both the US and Australia. Furthermore, to round off what was a record-breaking album release, *Billboard* announced that 'Super Bass' was the first rap single to crack the Top 5 since Missy Elliott's 'Work It' in 2002 and only the eighth in rap history to even chart on the Top 100. The only other female rappers to crack the *Billboard* Top 10 are Lauryn Hill (1998's 'Doo Wop (That Thing)', Da Brat (1994's 'Funkdafied'), M.I.A. (2008's 'Paper Planes') and Lil Mama (2007's 'Lip Gloss').

Consequently, 'Super Bass' made the biggest impact of the album in the States and around the world. During an interview at Nashville radio station 107.5 The River, country music star Taylor Swift requested that the DJ play 'Super Bass' and shockingly recited a verse from it on air. "I've been listening to it on repeat," Swift confessed, "and I really freak my friends out because I can recite every single lyric to the rap." Swift's co-sign of the song introduced it to another audience.

And Nicki was excited. In a radio interview with Los Angeles radio station 102.7 KIIS FM she said: "Taylor Swift did her little interview about 'Super Bass' and [it] took off in the States with the people sort of knowing it... it's just really uncanny how all that stuff happens... We didn't plan it like that."

There is no way Minaj could have planned any of the remarkable, and sometimes magical, things that occurred in her life during this time. But, with *Pink Friday* going multi-platinum worldwide, her hard work, determination and Barbie ambition had turned her into a phenomenon.

"Damn *Billboard*... I mean I'm winning but I am still bored," Nicki spits on Birdman's single 'Why U Mad?', in reference to her major successes on the *Billboard* charts but her ability to remain unfazed by the hype of it all. However, her *Billboard* reign continued in February 2012, as her second collaboration with DJ and producer David Guetta, 'Turn Me On' from his album *Nothing But The Beat*, climbed to number four on the Hot 100 chart. Nicki's identity as a pop star solidified more and more with each risk-taking venture she embarked on that snatched her out of her comfort zone. "I can't front, I just thought she was going to be the new female MC that none of these other female MCs can touch," Lil Wayne gushed about Nicki to *MTV News*. "But now, she's blossomed into a megastar with this new attitude and this style."

Nicki's growth and confidence as an artist are apparent in the controversial video for 'Turn Me On', with Guetta, who usually promotes a dancefloor democracy in his promos, where everyone is equal and humanity rules. With Minaj, he took a decidedly different approach and the raptress' influence is stamped all over it. We see the Grammy-winning DJ as a mad scientist in a steampunk society full of machinery and manufactured human dolls, with the Head Barb being his main creation. "I wanted to come with a new story, with a new concept and something maybe a little more artsy in terms of creation and a little more crazy too," he told *MTV News*. "It's a little more risqué. I don't know if everybody's going to love it. I don't know if it's going to make me sell records, and to be honest, I don't really care. I wanted to have a video that is a piece of art by itself." Guetta has sold over three million albums and 15 million singles worldwide and has produced hit records with superstars such as Usher, Kelly Rowland and Fergie, but it was the Queens-bred rapper who nudged him to take a different direction visually.

Lil Wayne had also recognised Nicki's vision and independence and not only did he admit that she was a megastar-in-the-making, he took it a few steps further. "Now when I talk to her, I just tell her, 'Do what you do, baby,'" he told *MTV News*. This admission was astonishing; and not for the conceit, but rather for what it meant historically.

Since the dawning of the popular and successful female rapper, a woman rocking the mic has almost always had a man engineering every aspect of her career, much like Geppetto manipulating Pinocchio. The Real Roxanne and Roxanne Shanté enjoyed hits in the mid eighties with their contributions to the Roxanne Wars, a series of records created in answer to U.T.F.O.'s (Untouchable Force Organization's) 'Roxanne, Roxanne'. Brooklyn native the Real Roxanne (Adelaida Martinez) was the sole creation of Full Force, U.T.F.O.'s producers. She met two members of U.T.F.O. in a Brooklyn mall and was later recruited by Full Force to take on the persona of "Roxanne" after the first girl, Elease Jacks, had not worked out. In stark contrast, Queens rapper Roxanne Shanté (Lolita Shanté Gooden) was a member of DJ Marley Marl's legendary Juice Crew, and when U.T.F.O. unceremoniously dropped out of a planned concert date the Juice Crew was promoting, Shanté offered to record a diss track to the group as the character in their hit song. Entitled 'Roxanne's Revenge', the 1984 song became a major hit, selling in excess of 250,000 copies in New York alone.

Brooklyn's MC Lyte enjoyed success with her rough and tumble 'as hard as the boys' persona, but because she was affiliated with the male duo

Audio Two (Milk, one half of the group, was her brother), she was given an unspoken, but acknowledged, pass to play with the boys. New Jersey rapper Queen Latifah, who was to go on to become a huge star in the music and film industry, came up under the Native Tongues crew, which included A Tribe Called Quest, De La Soul and the Jungle Brothers (all male acts). Salt-N-Pepa broke barriers and were arguably the first female rap darlings of MTV, but their relationship with Svengali-like producer Hurby "Luv Bug" Azor, who crafted most of their early hits, including 'Push It', was the reason for their initial success. They were the first female rappers to go platinum, but a few years later in the mid nineties, Da Brat, bolstered by super producer Jermaine Dupri, scored a hit with 'Give It 2 You' from the album *Funkdafied*, which sold in excess of one million copies, making her the first female (solo) rapper to go platinum. Soon thereafter came the ultra-fem one, two punch of Lil' Kim and Foxy Brown, who both (particularly Kim) ushered into hip-hop a new wave of never-before-accepted female über-sexuality – before these two women, MC Lyte was rapping in oversized clothes with work boots , rapping that she needed a 'Ruffneck'. Lil' Kim and Foxy, attached to the Notorious B.I.G. and Jay-Z, respectively, were groundbreaking. But, no matter how much acclaim Lil' Kim received, the rumour mill churned that Biggie was writing her rhymes and teaching her how to rap (the same was whispered about Jay-Z and Foxy).

Therefore, for Lil Wayne to plainly state that he did not need to add sugar to the Minaj mix to sweeten it was unprecedented. Kim was always considered Biggie's underling, whereas Nicki is Wayne's colleague. "Nowadays, rap is about who you actually are," Wayne told E! "This is who she is and it's interesting. Her personality overall wins the attention of everybody. She has broken the mould of what an artist should be."

In the beginning, Wayne would give her guidance in the studio, but now things have changed, he told MTV. "I used to be able to go into the studio and say, 'Nah, don't say that, don't say that.' You know, 'That was better.' Now, [it's more like] do what you do, baby. I don't have a clue about what you're doing right now, but it's working, do it.'"

Another superstar who also liked what Nicki was doing was Britney Spears. The pop star chose the femcee to open for her Femme Fatale Tour in 2011, which made perfect sense. Nicki had already proven her crossover appeal with her first two singles and this was a fantastic opportunity to prove her show-womanship to a larger, more mainstream artist. Her set was a little more sophisticated than when she had opened for Lil Wayne. "I wanted my set to be more than an opening act," she told MTV. "I didn't want to do a lot of colour. I wanted to tone it down, [be] sort of, you know, futuristic and all over the place... but cagey and epic. I always like to raise the bar for myself, and that's what I did. I think it's important to give people what they paid for."

And Nicki's fanbase transcends race, gender and age. "That tour was such a melting pot of music, with those kids in the suburbs who grew up listening to Britney Spears *and* the kids in the hood loving Nicki," said industry videographer Jabari Johnson. The mixture of people who attended the shows shocked those on her team. "I think the youngest fan I have seen is like eight years old and it goes to college-aged women," said Day Hill, Nicki's former make-up artist. "It goes beyond all demographics. Whatever she eats, drinks, wears and says, they have it before we all know."

"I don't really expect them to know all the records, but I guess it just kind of transcends all genres of music at this point," Nicki added.

Nicki was making moves in the mainstream world that few other hip-hop stars had achieved before her. "You are definitely not seeing a hip-hop artist connect with other pop artists [on this level]," said DJ Diamond Kuts, her tour DJ, "Unless you're Jay-Z." Candi Clarke, one of her closest friends since childhood, was completely blown away by her friend's appeal and accomplishment: "Sometimes, I am still in shock," said Clarke to E! "I am like, 'Is that really my friend?' But Minaj would soon make friends with people who were more than familiar with outdoing expectations.

In November of 2010, Nick Minaj appeared on *Jimmy Kimmel Live!* and after leaving the theatre, she was bombarded with screams from a legion of fans and paparazzi that had been waiting more than five hours or more to catch a glimpse of the diminutive powerhouse. She graciously signed autographs and posed for pictures with her Barbz and Ken Barbz. One of them shouted out a question and Nicki's answer now seems prophetic. "Nicki, who do you want to work with next?" asked the fan. "Madonna," she said without hesitation.

Two years later, Nicki's wish – and even more than she could have expected – came to fruition. Madonna invited Minaj to guest on the single 'Give Me All Your Luvin'' (along with rapper M.I.A.), which was the first single from Madonna's highly anticipated 2012 album *MDNA* (Nicki also appears on the track 'I Don't Give A'). The three performed 'Give Me' during Madonna's much-lauded 2012 Super Bowl halftime show.

"Meeting Madonna changed my life. Working with Madonna changed my life. Rehearsing with Madonna for two weeks changed my life," Nicki told Ryan Seacrest. "When you look at these amazing women, you have to realise that a lot of work goes into this. I, for the first time, refused to go to any parties. This performance was it and this is the first performance that I'm proud of in my entire career. I saw how much Madonna sacrificed and how much she rehearses and rehearses and rehearses and rehearses."

Along with performing with Madge during the most-watched event around the world, Nicki's appearance on the track 'Give Me All Your Luvin'' led to her joining the rarefied ranks in Madonna's Popdom occupied only by two other first-name-only blonde pop bombshells: Britney and Christina.

Both Spears and Aguilera, respectively, shocked the audience at the 2003 MTV Video Music Awards when, clad in lingerie-esque wedding gowns – *à* la Madonna's legendary 1984 performance of her classic hit 'Like A Virgin' – they slithered onstage and eventually lip-locked with the Queen of Pop. The kisses, especially the one between Britney and Madonna, sent shockwaves around the world.

On a smaller scale, but no less spectacular in principle, while shooting the video for the Madonna single, Nicki was celebrating her 28th birthday on set when the unimaginable happened: Madonna shared a birthday kiss with a very shocked Minaj. "In the presence of greatness.

MADONNA," Nicki tweeted. "OH MY f'ingggg Gahhhh!!!!! MADONNA jus kissed me!!!!! On the lips!!!!!!! It felt sooooo good. Soooo soft!!!! *passes out*"

A couple of months later, when asked about the incident, Madonna 'fessed up. "It was her birthday and it was actually the end of one of those long days of shooting and we were all giving a birthday toast to her. After a few sips of champagne, I kissed her," the iconic singer confessed during an interview with Anderson Cooper on his daytime talk show.

There were critical mumblings about the transparent nature of Madonna's invitation to Minaj to collaborate on the first single from her album *MDNA*, which was largely considered a comeback (or, in some circles, a make or break venture) for the 53-year-old superstar. But Madonna told Cooper of her genuine admiration for Minaj and M.I.A.: "I listen to Nicki Minaj. I love her," Madonna confessed. "They're cheeky and unique and they have individual voices and they're not conventional pop stars, and I really admire them both. I wanted to collaborate with both of them on my record because I'm a big fan of their music, but also I like their independence."

Minaj's courage as well as her outlandish personality and equally wild wardrobe selections have also led to comparisons being draw between her and another huge pop star: Lady Gaga. (The year that Nicki first hit the Grammy red carpet, Gaga had arrived on the crimson runway only moments before in a giant opaque egg, which she called a "vessel", created by acclaimed fashion designers Hussein Chalayan and Nicola Formichetti.) Fans of both artists are literally begging for a collaboration between the two. "Of course, I would love to work with Gaga," Nicki told hollywoodscoop.com. "She is so iconic. I don't know when that would happen or if it would happen, [but] that would be a dope experience."

While the two outrageous stars share an obsessive love for their fans ("They are all of the kids in school that everybody makes fun of," Nicki told *Vibe*, "all of the weird kids, the artistic kids, all the bad ones. And I love that, because that's who I was"), some critics believe that Gaga and Minaj's outlandish costumes and equally wild behaviour is borderline circus-like, the ladies serving as ringmasters to their audience of sing-along fanatics. But underneath those simple (and lazy) comparisons lies a more substantial and commonsense explanation: both learned early on in their career that the type of fame and success they witnessed while growing up – the stadium-sized superstardom of Madonna, Michael and Prince – was achieved by creating characters fuelled by exceptional talent and an intense appreciation for fame. And both rookie superstars are playing characters, while also remaining true to themselves.

But, while Nicki respects Lady Gaga, she was starting to get a little frustrated with the comparisons and she didn't want to be known as "The Lady Gaga of Hip-Hop", especially when that's hardly her mission. However, she can see a definite similarity between the two of them. "We both do the awkward, non-pretty thing. What we're saying – what I'm saying, anyway – is that it's OK to be weird," she told *Blackbook*. "And maybe your weird is my normal. Who's to say? I think it's an attitude we both share."

No matter what the comparisons, it is clear that Nicki Minaj is staying true to herself. "Nicki isn't like any other female rapper," said Baby. "We knew she had the goods when Lil Wayne signed her. She's not a female rapper – she's a pop star who happens to rap."

Chapter 5

Off With Her Head

Michael Jackson was a thief. The most celebrated artist of all time, with 1982's *Thriller* the biggest-selling album in history, the self-proclaimed King of Pop "borrowed" many of the moves he made famous in his 'Billie Jean' video from world-renowned choreographer/director Bob Fosse, whose direction of Liza Minnelli in the film *Cabaret* garnered him an Oscar. In 1974, Fosse performed a number called 'Snake In The Grass' in the little-known movie *The Little Prince*, and his outfit (all black with white socks and spats) and dance moves are almost identical to those featured in Jackson's 'Billie Jean' and in the singer's now legendary performance of the song on the 1983 television special *Motown 25: Yesterday, Today, Forever* (the routine featured his first recorded "moonwalk"). Jackson would also go on to receive the Bob Fosse Award for Best Choreography in 1997 for his short film *Ghosts*.

More recently Beyoncé spoke of the fact that she and her choreographers "referenced" many of the dance moves from the Fosse-produced 'Mexican Breakfast' – performed by Fosse's wife, Gwen Verdon, in 1969 – for the video for her 2008 global mega-hit 'Single Ladies (Put A Ring On It)'.

Artists are inspired by other artists and Nicki Minaj is no different. Endless comparisons have been made between her and Lil' Kim; some justified, others ridiculous. Most are simply lazy. Nicki has said that she has sufficiently applauded the career of Lil' Kim and paid her respects. Arguably, if it were not for the blueprint crafted by Lil' Kim and her Svengali the Notorious B.I.G., aka Biggie Smalls – that of a sexy feminine MC with a hyper-masculine flow – the Nicki Minaj model of today may not even exist.

Some believe Lil' Kim inspired Nicki, others believe the Young Money mistress completely plagiarised her style and, still further, a large sect of Nicki's fans adamantly deny any connection between the two raptresses. And let's not forget that many of Nicki's younger fans would have no knowledge of Lil' Kim's place in the hip-hop pantheon: they barely remember a time when hip-hop's nest was ruled by the Queen Bee. However, for anyone, especially Nicki's biggest supporters, to know Lil' Kim's story – the quintessential rise and fall – is to understand (and appreciate) Nicki even more.

It was Thursday August 3, 1995, and a typically hot, late summer's night in New York. But inside Madison Square Garden, at the 2nd Annual Source Awards, it was even hotter. Many hip-hop fans remember that as the night Death Row Records founder Suge Knight called out Diddy (then known as Sean "Puffy" Combs) for getting "all up in the videos" instead of being a behind-the-scenes CEO of his record label, Bad Boy Records (originally Bad Boy Entertainment). This diss officially ignited the East Coast-West Coast beef, which would have rappers from both New York and Los Angeles spitting derogatory comments at each other and making threats of violence on wax and in real-life scenarios. Rappers Tupac Shakur and the Notorious B.I.G. were the de facto leaders of the West and East coasts respectively. And the rap war would ultimately end in tragedy for Tupac and Biggie: the latter was murdered in September 1996 and the former was murdered in March 1997.

However, that night Biggie was on cloud nine. He stormed the stage with his group Junior M.A.F.I.A., which consisted of several of his childhood friends from Brooklyn. It was the group's first big performance and the crowd responded well, but the Garden erupted when the 5'3" force of nature Kimberley Denise Jones, going under the stage name Lil' Kim and the sole female in Junior M.A.F.I.A., took to the stage with her verse from 'Player's Anthem'. That night "Big Momma", as she was known in New York circles, officially became the Queen Bee. With her even and robust voice and tough-as-nails bravado, Kim successfully managed a previously almost impossible first for a female rapper: she connected equally with both men and women. Petite, cute and in possession of a grimy, straight-off-the-block flow (reportedly due in part to the writing skills of B.I.G.), Kim succeeded in gaining the attention of the guys; they unabashedly rocked her music in their Jeeps and entertained thoughts of getting her into their beds.

But Kim also managed a delicate vulnerability, which appealed to female hip-hop fans. She was the little Brooklyn girl from around the way who went on to rock arenas around the country with the man everyone was touting as the greatest rapper to have ever grabbed a microphone. She rapped about sporting the labels that urban pop culture was obsessing over in the logo-plagued nineties: Versace, Moschino and Christian Lacroix, among others. Women loved her confidence and style, but publicly baulked at her mostly profane lyrics and self-titled Queen Bitch moniker. However, in private, they applauded her lack of self-consciousness and sexual freedom. After all, Kim was only giving voice to fans whose fantasies had to be locked away in most cases.

After the runaway success of Junior M.A.F.I.A.'s hit single 'Get Money', which featured Lil' Kim and Biggie, Kim released her 1996 solo album, the multi-platinum *Hard Core*, and soon became a fixture not just in the urban world, but also in the mainstream market. She was snapped sipping Champagne with Donatella Versace in Italy one day and hanging out with downtown designer Marc Jacobs the next. Her sexed-up image was splashed all over covers of magazines, from the hip-hop-fused *Vibe* to the mass-market focused *Nylon*. Kim's household name game was on the rise. Her purple one-shoulder jumpsuit – which exposed one of her breasts with only a sparkly pasty covering her nipple – was a head turner at the 1999 MTV Video Music Awards. While presenting an award with her, Diana Ross, the iconic singer, marvelled at Kim's bravery (or lack of shame) and touched the exposed breast in wonder. The Brooklyn girl had made it.

But soon things began to change: most notably, her appearance.

In 2000, Kim would peak with the release of her second album, *The Notorious K.I.M.* Despite the (minimal) success of her next two albums, she would fail to achieve the mass success she craved. Biggie's death in 1997 and her unfortunate entanglement in the shoot-out at a New York radio station, resulting in her perjury prison stint, both contributed to the stall. However, most critics and even some fans point to Kim's apparent addiction to plastic surgery as the reason behind her downfall. Her drastic change in appearance was indicative of what she craved most: to look like a Barbie doll. During her rise, Kim went from hanging with her Brooklyn brood of hoodlums to skipping around the world with Pamela Anderson Lee and sporting blue contact lenses. She and her fans began referring to her as the "Black Barbie" (dressed in Bulgari). All of a sudden her breasts were bigger. Her nose was smaller. Her cheeks more pronounced. Her lips poutier. Her chin narrower. And she eventually stopped making music and was largely absent from the music industry. However, as a testament to her legend, her disappearance from the rap scene left a gaping hole for several years. Many attempted to fill the pop culture void she left – most notably Philadelphia rapper Eve, with her platinum albums, TV show and clothing line – but to no avail.

Enter Nicki Minaj.

During an interview with *Rock Me TV* early on in her career – before the contracts were signed with Young Money and way before any media training – the host asked Nicki "What do you think of Lil' Kim?" Among a few things, she expressed her love for Kim, but she felt she could "fill her shoes" and that it was now time to be out with the old and in with the new. She said all of this with a smile. Her boastful language, which stood out against a backdrop of the usually steely, yet mostly polite, artist's veneer in press interviews, could be attributed to poor advice from her management team, her going along with the hip-hop battle ethos, or that she simply did not know any better, or, for that matter, care.

Being that Nicki is the most interesting and transformative female in hip-hop today, her meteoric rise shocked many of the female MCs that she grew up listening to, and even idolised to a certain degree, and she has received a fair share of resistance, push back and, well, just plain ole' hate from other female rappers (there aren't even enough relevant ones to form a substantial sorority). Yet in interviews, she would shower her peers and Lil' Kim with praise, mentioning, in particular, how the Queen Bee had motivated her and influenced her style. However, after a while things took a turn. Nicki has hinted that she tried reaching out to the other well-known female rappers as her star began to rise, but it was futile. "I see this as a great opportunity for every female rapper," Nicki said to *Vibe* magazine. "But I don't feel like they're appreciative, so I'm done. I used to do it for everybody and now I don't. It's sad, though, because people take the fun out of it." Her tone and sentiment are remarkably different from her speech at the 2010 BET Awards when she loudly proclaimed that she was fighting for all the women in the hip-hop game.

Both Kim and Nicki have told different versions of the origins of their issues and they have told them to the same woman: Angie Martinez. Martinez is widely known as "The Voice of New York" and an appearance on her afternoon show on Hot 97 is considered a privileged must-do for both new and veteran artists.

Angie became a breakout artist in her own right in 1997 when Lil' Kim offered her a guest spot on the song 'Not Tonight (Ladies Night Remix)', which went on to become one of the biggest singles of the year, selling over one million copies and garnering two Grammy nods. With Martinez's stature in the industry and with the knowledge that all of New York and, subsequently, the country would be listening to her show, it is no surprise that both Nicki and Kim decided to open up to her about their squabbles, and open up they did.

In November 2010, Nicki Minaj was the exclusive guest at Angie Martinez's Hot 97 VIP Lounge, an event series in which the host invites a popular artist to be interviewed and also perform in front of a live audience of their fans. Nicki arrived in Nicki wear: straight blonde wig with bangs and pink tips, lime green sleeveless top, green Daisy Dukes over electric blue leggings. She walked onto the stage to deafening applause and cheers and then proceeded to talk about how hectic her life had become with all of the success. Soon the talk turned to her perceived nemesis. In the same breath, she admitted her love for Kim while also issuing a warning of sorts, saying she had begun to hear rumblings among industry people that her fellow rapper was talking about her. But Nicki says she refused to believe it until she heard it from Kim herself. That is, until one day she had a short conversation with Lil' Kim's old rival, nineties hip-hop rapper and former Jay-Z protégé, Foxy Brown. "I ran into Foxy Brown one day and she was like, 'Why you bigging up Kim all the time in interviews? She does not like you," Nicki said.

But the young Minaj refrained from taking the rumours as fact until she got a confirmation from the rap legend herself. A short while later, while on the nationwide tour with Lil Wayne, Nicki was relaxing backstage in Wayne's dressing room when Lil' Kim walked in. Anxious to either confirm or squash the hearsay, Nicki walked across the crowded dressing room and approached the elder raptress. "Hi Kim, are we OK? Do we have any problems, because I have been hearing things," Nicki told a slightly startled Kim.

"Oh, no, we are all right. We are cool," said Lil' Kim before she shuffled out of the dressing room.

However, speaking to Martinez, Nicki said she soon began to realise that things were less than all right. A war of words ensued on the airwaves, on blogs and in magazine interviews, which was, initially at least, one sided.

Just days before Nicki's interview with Angie, while making an appearance at Pure Nightclub in Queens (Nicki's home turf), Kim, full of bravado, declared in a chest-poked out, King-Kong-ain't-got-shit-on-me way: "I'll erase that bitch's Social Security number." As if that were not threat enough, Kim (who had not released an album since 2005) added that there was no need for her to bring out new material because in a possible battle with Minaj, "I'd kill that bitch with my old shit."

While speaking to Angie that day at the VIP Lounge, it was clear that Nicki only discovered Kim's rumblings when the press started confronting her about their "beef". "She just really jumped out the window," she said of Kim, as the audience burst into laughter. Revealing her confusion as to why the elder raptress was upset, she continued, with slight exasperation: "I respect you, I love you, and I have said it in every interview time and time again. But if that's not good enough for you then it's something deep rooted in you. It's not Nicki Minaj."

Being that Angie and Kim were friendly from sharing a spotlight in the heyday of nineties New York, it was no surprise that the Queen Bee stopped by Angie's show that same afternoon. Wearing a blue baseball cap with IRS stamped on the front (IRS being the entertainment company that Kim had launched), Kim sat down and immediately got to business. Addressing the court of public opinion in the matter of Lil' Kim vs. Nicki Minaj, she skipped her defence and went straight to her closing arguments.

"Once she got with Wayne, I could see that this girl was inspired by me," Kim almost whispered into the microphone. Her slightly high, still Brooklyn-brushed voice sifted through the airwaves, tinged with the confidence of the 22 year old who had dropped the instant classic *Hard Core*, but mixed with the confusion of a now thirty-something woman fighting to maintain her relevancy in a brave new (hip-hop) world.

Lil' Kim left her filter at home that afternoon. In a remarkable show of actual concern, she admitted to having followed Nicki's burgeoning career, despite the fact that she herself was a hip-hop legend. "People think that Kim is such a big icon, she's Hollywood, [so] she doesn't know what's going on in the street. I am always on the internet, I saw [Nicki] coming up. [I also] saw her rapping saying, 'All you chicks in the game for 10 years need to sit down.' I thought that was disrespectful," she said. Kim insisted that she knew Nicki's thinly veiled mix-tape verses were aimed at her, but says it did not bother her... at first. "She started saying things that were directed at me and another female. I was not automatically going to dislike her, because I know oftentimes females coming up in this game are misguided." Kim then went on to say that she dismissed Nicki's initial potshots because Slim, one of the owners of Nicki's label Young Money, was a friend and he reached out to her. She says that he even paid for studio time for her to record and requested that she do a duet with Nicki. In another act of surprising vulnerability, Kim admits that she accepted the offer because, well, her career needed it.

"I had not been doing music for a second. So, I looked at [Nicki's] buzz as a way for me... to come back in. I went over there. I was getting ready to be allies and in their family. As a businesswoman, this would be good for people to see me with her and for her it would be good for people to see that I was willing to rock with [her]. I don't have any beef. Beef is serious. They was like, 'I wanna do a record with you,' and I was like, 'Let's do it.' In my eyes, I needed the exposure, as far as music is concerned. And Baby promised all of these things; we are going to do a big video and all of that. We did the record and they put it out."

According to Kim, the record was released on iTunes, but after people began commenting that the original Queen Bee was superior on the track, Nicki's camp pulled it. However, if one searches the regions of the internet, two other tracks featuring the two immediately surface: the first a remix of Gucci Mane's 'Freaky Gurl', on which both pop off hardcore porn-grade verses, and the second a track called 'Everywhere We Go', which was produced by Deric "D-Dot" Angelettie at least two years before Nicki's debut album. D-Dot was a successful Grammy-nominated producer and had once been captain of Diddy's production team, the Hitmen, which wrote, produced and remixed hits for the Notorious B.I.G., Jay-Z and LL Cool J, among others. As an artist, he created the character "the Madd Rapper" – an MC who essentially used comedic swipes and observations to complain about the success of the rappers dominating the charts at the time. It was all in jest. His 2000 album, *Tell 'Em Why U Madd*, featured a fresh-off-the-street 50 Cent and a young producer he was mentoring at the time named Kanye West. According to him, he informed Lil' Kim right after she was released from prison in 2006 and right before she appeared on *Dancing With The Stars* in 2009 that she should work with the up-and-coming Nicki. "I was like, 'There's this new bitch that's about to be hot, you might want to fuck with her,'" he told *Vibe*. "Nicki came to the studio and did the verse with me. She hadn't even met Kim. [Lil' Kim] said 'Cool, when you put Nicki on it send it back to me.' I sent it back and she never re-did a new verse."

While the incident seems to have sparked the supposed "beef" between the two femcees, its exact origins are still foggy. Whether or not it is due to Nicki pulling their original record from iTunes or Kim simply refusing to lay down verses on the D-Dot record, it all depends upon whom you ask. But, as Lil' Kim told Angie Martinez, Nicki could have squashed the whole ordeal with one simple act. "If she would have addressed me, maybe it would not have gone this far. She is a very contradicting creature. We could be in this game together. She just wanted to be in this game by herself. I have proven that I don't need to be out there by myself. I have done records with all of the female [rappers]."

Many other hip-hop artists have also weighed in on the situation. Diddy, who was instrumental in launching Lil' Kim's solo career (along with the Notorious B.I.G.), was at one time very close to her, appearing on her debut single from *Hard Core*, 'No Time'. Furthermore, after the death of Biggie, her former lover, Kim leaned heavily on Diddy, who also executive produced her second album, 2000's *The Notorious K.I.M.* Biggie was more than the greatest rapper on Earth to Kim and their crew; he was their world. She and Biggie had met when she was a clerk at Macy's and he'd worked with her to develop the raw potential he saw in his little "shorty". Although he went on to marry R&B singer and fellow Bad Boy Records artist Faith Evans, Biggie still remained close to Kim. His sudden death at the hands of an anonymous gunman was a major blow. All had collapsed and Diddy was there for her. They went on to make hit records, such as the club classic 'It's All About The Benjamins', on which she famously rhymed, "You wanna rumble with the bee, huh? Bzzzzzz!"

However, in the early months of 2011, snapshots of Diddy and Nicki Minaj began to pop up in the blogosphere. One night, paparazzi captured the twosome walking hand in hand as they exited Hollywood hotspot the Guys & Dolls Lounge and the rumour mill went into overdrive. Reports of a new hip-hop power couple began to buzz about, but Nicki quickly shot them down. "Can I just say, I hold everybody's hands! I hold my bodyguard's hands! No [I'm not dating him]," she told MTV. And the self-proclaimed Barbie wasn't lying;

truth was, Diddy had begun co-managing or "consulting" her career in the several months leading up to the release of *Pink Friday*. And this was no surprise to most insiders; Diddy is known for his knack for eyeing talent and even more so for his almost super-human ability to remain relevant in a genre where careers experience moments, not marathons (along with his simultaneous rise up the rap-ranks with Lil' Kim, he famously dated pop/R&B behemoth Jennifer Lopez at the height of her ascension to superstardom). And in this case Diddy's praise was poured like an uncapped street hydrant. "Nicki Minaj, she's definitely one of the great ones. She has a long way to go," he told MTV, "but you know how we recognised LeBron [James] was a great one, Tiger [Woods] was a great one, and Kobe [Bryant] was a great one? Nicki is up there. Her story has just begun."

His former bad girl Lil' Kim was none too happy. She was loyal to the man whom her lover and mentor had called his best friend and teacher and had supported him while he was on trial for weapons and bribery charges in 2001 (he was acquitted of all charges). In essence, she was staying true to the Brooklyn ride or die chick (a woman who stands her ground and supports those she cares for when they are in need) she was brought up to be. And now Diddy was rocking with her nemesis.

She expressed her disappointment to MTV personality Sway Calloway on the *RapFix*: "I'm bothered by his actions, because I rolled with Puffy to the bitter end, and still would have rolled with him. [He] never came to see me in prison, not one time. He didn't write me a letter. He didn't say, 'Here's a number for Kim to call,' not one time... The only problem I had with Puffy is that you see this girl [Nicki Minaj] taking shots at me... Even on [Puffy's] own record she took a shot at me... and you didn't stop that? If this was me years ago, if it was somebody he was working with or had a relationship with and he got money with or whatever, he would be like, 'That can't go out!'"

The diss song Lil' Kim was referring to was the remix to 'Hello Good Morning' by Puffy's group Diddy Dirty Money, onto which Nicki jumped. Her opening bars can easily be taken as swipes at Kim's position in the rap world. "I came up in it a little bit self centered/But did I kill a Queen..." Nicki rhymes on the track.

Nicki gives a side eye to the competition while performing at Philadelphia's Power 99 FM's Powerhouse concert at the Wells Fargo Center.
BRIAN HINELINE/RETNA LTD/CORBIS

Before the Technicolor wigs and outrageous rhymes, a young Onika Maraj visits New York's famed Coney Island.

Getting ready to take over the world, Nicki smiles for the camera back-stage at BET's Rip The Runway 2010, which she co-hosted. WALIK GOSHORN/CORBIS

Black Eyed Peas leader will.i.am and the Head Barbie land their spaceship and takeover the stage at the 2010 MTV Video Music Awards pre-show in Los Angeles. KEVIN MAZUR/GETTY IMAGES

Hot Headed: A blazingly red-wigged Nicki commands all the attention at the legendary Hot 97 Summer Jam concert in the Meadowlands in New Jersey in 2010. WALIK GOSHORN/RETNA LTD/CORBIS

A Pink Homecoming: Nicki attends the Lil Wayne Welcome Home Party hosted by Cash Money/Young Money Records. CHRIS GORDON/CORBIS

Sandwiched between Drake (the one that wants to marry her), and Lil Wayne (the one that signed her) at the IMP Entertainment and Steve Marlton Worldwide Allstar Event at Siren Studios in Hollywood in 2011. TODD WILLIAMSON/WIREIMAGE

A Day in the Park: Nicki grins on the set of BET's *106 & Park* New York City in 2010. JOHN RICARD/RETNA LTD/CORBIS

Clockwise from top left: Kanye West gives a head to toe approval of Nicki while performing; the raptress' much talked about derriere; exciting label mate Drake; proclaiming girl power with Rihanna: all at the 2010 Hot 97 Thanksgiving Thank You Concert at Hammerstein Ballroom in New York City.

Bejewelled Barbie: Nicki lights up the red carpet at the 2010 American Music Awards in Los Angeles. HUBERT BOESL/DPA/CORBIS

Channelling Marge Simpson and the Bride of Frankenstein, Nicki arrives at the 2011 Green Auction: A Bid To Save The Earth at Christie's in New York. BROADIMAGE/REX FEATURES

Working Girl: Nicki snaps a picture with Young Money President and rapper Mack Maine and Cash Money Records co-founder and rapper Birdman at the Cash Money Records 2011 Pre-Grammy Awards Party at the Lot in West Hollywood. AMY HARRIS/ZUMAPRESS.COM/CORBIS

The young lioness makes an appearance at the Oscar de la Renta Show during Spring 2012 Mercedes-Benz Fashion Week in New York.
KRISTIN CALLAHAN/REX FEATURES

Backstage at the 2011 American Music Awards double fisting her wins.
STARTRAKS PHOTO/REX FEATURES

Nicki leads her dancing Barbz during her set on the 2011 'I Am Music II Tour' at Palace Of Auburn Hills in Auburn Hills Michigan.
CHRIS SCHWEGLER/RETNA LTD/CORBIS

Nicki shuts down the red carpet in Givenchy at the 2011 Grammy Awards at the Staples Center in Los Angeles.

When Diddy appeared on the popular Funk Master Flex Show on Hot 97 later that same year he explained his side of the story. "I love Lil' Kim no matter what's going on, no matter what's being said. Kim definitely has a responsibility for my success," he easily admitted to Flex. "Me working with Nicki Minaj has nothing to do with going against Kim. When Kim works with other producers, when she raps with other artists, I'm not getting upset. It's not a problem. I think a lot of us who have been here for a long time have inspired a lot of people. We have motivated a lot of people, we have touched a lot of people in a certain way. We have been those cats that people aspire to be. I wouldn't be around Nicki if I ever heard [anything] negative said about Kim. I've never heard [anything] like that." He went on to say, "If they want to do things and be MCs? That's they business. I'm not with no negativity. I'm not with no beef and I love both of them." And in response to Kim's charge that Diddy allowed Nicki Minaj to diss her on the remix to his record 'Hello Good Morning', he had to hand it off to hip-hop. "When it comes to just being an MC, that's when I gotta stand back," Diddy explained.

Nicki's second album, *Pink Friday: Roman Reloaded*, hit the charts in April 2012, with the rapper releasing 'Stupid Hoe' as a promotional single. In the same vein as 'Roman's Revenge' (with Roman leading the charge once again), the song's lyrics tear into her subject with delightful abandon: "I get it cracking like a bad back/Bitch talkin' she the queen when she looking like a lab rat/I'm Angelina, you Jennifer/Come on bitch you see where Brad at!" And the chorus rings like an evil playground taunt on repeat: "You a stupid hoe/You a you a stupid hoe/You a stupid hoe/You a you a stupid hoe." It's not had to see the connection to Kim.

Bangladesh, producer of *Pink Friday*'s 'Did It On 'Em', believes Nicki should stop with the diss records. "She should leave [the beef] alone. It's just keeping Lil' Kim relevant. It makes it look like you're concerned about it or it's on your mind when you're addressing it." Some in Nicki's camp knew about the song, but not its theme. "I knew the title of the record, but I didn't know she would be taking shots at anybody," said Diamond Kuts, Nicki's DJ and 'Stupid Hoe' producer, to *Vibe*.

"That was a surprise. I don't know if she's looking at it to benefit her. She's just doing what she feels."

While making an appearance on the late-night show *Watch What Happens Live*, Lil' Kim commented on the song, when asked about it by host Andy Cohen and guest, television personality William "Willie" Geist. "I guess you are a stupid hoe if you have to make a song called 'Stupid Hoe'," she deadpanned.

When a new rapper emerges, the one and only objective is to become known. And the best way for people to notice you, in a sea filled with look-alikes, clones and wannabes, is to gun for the one in the top spot. And with MCing being one of the four pillars of hip-hop culture (along with DJing, graffiti and break dancing), Nicki's and Kim's battle-rap spat was certainly not the first of its kind.

In 1999, 50 Cent was the new kid on the block. His debut major label single, 'How To Rob' (produced by the Trackmasters), consisted of the Queens rapper mouthing off ridiculously witty lyrics, stating how he would rob an entire laundry list of artists, from Lil' Kim and Jay-Z to Whitney Houston and Will Smith. He may have been joking, but only a few years later he would re-emerge with the gargantuan hit 'In Da Club'. Up to that point, hip-hop artist Ja Rule had been the hitmaker of his time – his collaborations, which often featured him singing with artists such as R&B singer Ashanti and Jennifer Lopez – were massive chart toppers. However, 50 Cent started a smear campaign against rapper Ja Rule which called the rapper out for his constant "singing". That and his own meteoric rise to the top essentially "robbed" Ja Rule of his career although, ironically, 50 Cent would later take to singing on his own records.

More recently, in 2011, Nicki's Young Money brother Drake found himself in a similar situation when the more senior (and less popular) rapper Common included a vague quip about his being sick of MCs singing on records on his single 'Sweet'. Then, on the remix to 'Stay Schemin'' with Rick Ross, Common abandoned the ambiguities and took aim squarely at the chart-topping Canadian: "I'm taking too long with this amateur guy/You ain't wet nobody, nigga, you Canada Dry." Drake replied indirectly via Twitter: "Platinum! Now THAT's Sweet!"

Then at a Las Vegas show, he spoke about the "beef" directly: "I might sing, but I ain't no b★tch. If Common got something to say, say it to my face."

The "beef" between the senior Kimberly Jones and the junior Onika Maraj was therefore just another day in the hip-hop hood. DJ Clue, a producer and popular disc jockey in New York, certainly believes that the situation between the two is overblown. "I don't think there is any 'beef', he told E! "Women are territorial in any aspect, whether it's men, music, status, money and [over] who's prettier. I think it's more of a competitive thing."

But not all female rappers feel threatened by other female rappers. Miami rapper Trina, who scored big hits like 'Nann Nigga' with Trick Daddy and 'Here We Go' with Kelly Rowland, and was a long-time on-off girlfriend of Nicki's boss Lil Wayne, had one of the more balanced perspectives on the situation. "I feel that Kim is an icon. What she has done for females in hip-hop, it's done," Trina told VladTV. "I don't think Nicki wants to disrespect her. I don't think this is something that needs to be." Trina, who has five albums under her belt and was part of the movement of female rappers who scored hits throughout the nineties, believes that all artists have an expiration date of sorts in the top spot and that it's a natural occurrence of musical evolution for the new generation to rise and take over. "For everybody that has been a part of our genre, we have all had a successful run of 10 years; that's a long time. Nicki is the new generation of female hip-hop. She saw an open space and lane. No one should be mad," she continued. Furthermore, she thought it admirable the way Nicki had come in and wrestled her way to the top. "It's a male-dominated industry; you have to damn near pull out the guns and knives to stay afloat in this game. Give Nicki her platform to do her thing. There is enough space, money, clothes and hair and jewellery for everybody."

50 Cent, who collaborated with Lil' Kim on the hit song 'Magic Stick', acknowledged that the writing was basically on the wall and that it wasn't anyone's fault. "Obviously [Nicki] is inspired by Kim," he told radio personality Lady La. "There are not a lot of female artists that you can make reference to."

But another one of Kim's collaborators feels much differently. Prodigy, one half of the veteran hip-hop duo Mobb Deep, who enjoyed the mega hit remix of 'Quiet Storm' with Kim, admitted that the blame ultimately lies at Lil' Kim's feet. "I like both of them, [but] I think that Kim should have been working a little more and not using the Nicki Minaj thing to come back," he also told VladTV. Speaking quite honestly and seemingly with no bias, Prodigy went on to say that he thought Kim should never have stopped making music. "If Kim would have kept going and put out another album and another single, then she would have been all right. But me as a fan, I see Lil' Kim pop off for many years and then take a break. Kim never should have come at [Nicki] like that. She should have shown her love for her and did songs [with] her and toured with her."

The major complaint from everyone on #TeamKim is that Nicki Minaj swagger-jacked Lil' Kim; that is, she stole her style, part and parcel. And according to Prodigy, who knows a thing or two about hip-hop (his group Mobb Deep have sold over three million albums and have partially credited with bringing East Coast rap back from the brink of extinction in the nineties) and beefs (he was infamously involved in a war of words with Jay-Z), everyone needs to change their way of thinking when it comes to music today.

"We fail to realise that these days, there is no such thing as biting or copying somebody's style. There is nothing new under the sun. You can be unique or add your own flavour to it, but you are not doing anything new," he continued to VladTV. "I think with Kim, she thinks that Nicki is biting her style with the hair and the way she is carrying herself. Kim has to realise that those rules are gone. It's all about who is doing it best and what you are doing now. At the end of the day, I like them both. But, it's all about who is working and who is not."

Nicki Minaj has never denied Lil' Kim's influence on her career. There is honestly no way she really could, even if she wanted to. She recreated Lil' Kim's infamous spread-eagle pose from the promotional picture for Kim's album *Hard Core*. She remade Kim's hit 'The Jump Off' and filmed a video for it. She began to sport the candy-tinted wigs that Kim first featured in her 1997 'Crush On You' video. And like Kim, Nicki's early raps were hyper sexual.

But then something funny happened on the way to the mainstream: Nicki changed. She stopped rapping about sex. There were no longer verses dedicated to the power of her genitalia – a long-running and seemingly necessary theme for a female in the Lil' Kim lane to find success in the male-dominated hip-hop world. But in 2010, in an interview with *The Guardian* before the release of *Pink Friday*, Nicki was teetering on what her image was going to be, swaying back and forth between sexy and non-sexy.

"I've switched it up and just tried to show people a whole different bunch of sides to me. I would be lying if I said I don't like to look sexy. But then there are some days when I don't want to look or feel sexy. So it just plays into how women are so multifaceted. Men don't understand that because they wake up and they're the same person, unless you're a Ken Barb and you can understand the girls." She goes on to say, "It's weird because I feel most comfortable when I'm covered up. I think that's the biggest misconception – that in order for me to be sexy I have to make sure my boobs are out." Well, with the release of the album and the subsequent videos, the world saw a Nicki Minaj focused on tight flows and biting lyrics expressing her place in this world, not the size of her breasts. "I went above and beyond to prove that I could not talk about sex and not talk about my genitalia and still have a successful album," she told *Vibe* in 2012.

And, although Nicki took on the role of Barbie, instead of becoming a carbon copy of the iconic doll, she created the more accessible and more global character of a Harajuku Barbie. In this way, Nicki took it a step further than Lil' Kim. Rather than simply applying Barbie's celebrated Euro-beauty to her own Afro-Caribbean features, she went gangsta, creating the character whose every move is followed daily by over 10 million people on Twitter. A comparison of the Queen Bee and the reigning Queen of Hip-Hop is one of imitation *and* vision. Nicki surveyed what had been done, built on it and made it her own.

According to Sarah Todd, contributing writer to the popular blog Girls Like Giants, the two stars share one commonality in this area:

"…both Lil' Kim and Minaj use Barbie as a means of allying themselves with girls and girl culture. In Barbie's world, clothes, exciting careers, and Malibu dream houses take precedence over Ken, who is doomed to be a helmet-haired afterthought… when Lil' Kim and Minaj call themselves Barbie, they're appealing to a female fanbase."

It's hard not to agree. What better way to make yourself equally attractive and attainable to girls all over the world, of all races and ethnicities, than by aligning yourself with what is seen as eternally young and beautiful? However, what has been even more brilliant about Minaj is that she managed to take the power of Barbie and own it without ousting anyone, especially the boys. Todd agrees. She writes: "Since boys who play with dolls tend to get stigmatised in our culture, Barbie has traditionally been a toy that girls play with by themselves or with other girls. [Calling] her fans Barbz and Ken Barbz… has the effect of both de-fanging some of Barbie's harmful elements (if everyone's a Barbie, then everyone's beautiful) and empowering Minaj (she names her fans after herself)."

On her hit 2003 single 'The Jump Off' (featuring rapper Mr. Cheeks) Lil' Kim memorably declared her status long before Nicki appeared on the scene: "Black Barbie dressed in Bulgari/I'm trying to leave in somebody's Ferrari," she rapped. But, of course Lil' Kim cannot take all the credit for the "Black Barbie" image; Mattel issued the first African-American Barbie line in 1980 (along with the first Hispanic Barbie doll). And since then, via Kim and Nicki, more hip-hop artists have followed suit.

The popular French rapper Reine du 93, a Cameroonian who began rapping at the age of 11 and is now making a lot of noise, albeit with a knotty, Euro-gangsta-like sound, calls herself Black Barbie, while in the States another young New York native has thought of adopting the doll's image. Harlem native Azealia Banks, who went to the same school as Nicki and broke out in 2011 with the song '212', told *GQ* magazine: "It could just be that we were both inspired by Lil' Kim. She did her thing with it, but I was kind of going to do a little bit of that same thing, with the characters, the pink and the Barbies. I wrote a song called 'Barbie Shit'. I was thinking, 'I'm going to be black Barbie, that's going to be my thing.' Then all of a sudden [Nicki came out being Barbie]! I was like, 'Fuck! This is way too coincidental!'"

And quite humbly, Nickmajesty did indirectly admit to taking from Lil' Kim's groundbreaking style during her interview with Angie Martinez. "We all take from each other. There is nothing new under the sun. When you see Gaga, you see Madonna," Minaj said easily. "[But], the same way [Kim] opened doors for me, I can now open doors for her."

At this point in Nicki's career, it's clear that whatever blueprint she may have had was merely a springboard to the unparalleled success she now enjoys. Rapper Trina believes that Nicki is in a class of her own right now. "[She] challenged herself to not be boxed into just hip-hop or do one kind of music, which is exceptional," she told *Vibe*. "She is already living in the pop-rap space."

"She's in a space of her own." Derrick "EI" Lawrence, vice president of Cash Money, told E! "Of course, at the top, people are going to take shots at you... The crown is heavy and it's on her head."

Chapter 6

God Gave Me Style

Mention the name Nicki Minaj and most people think of her colour-blasted sense of style as much, or sometimes more, than her pop-hip-hop blend, which has commanded the music charts globally since the release of *Pink Friday*. During the spring/summer shows at New York Fashion Week in 2011, without effort Nicki was the main attraction at every designer's show she attended. Backstage at the Oscar de La Renta show, she posed for pictures with singer/actor Justin Timberlake, wearing magenta eyeliner, black tights and leopard-print Mary Janes topped off with a *Romper Room*-ready lion headdress. She tweeted to her then six million followers (she now has in excess of 12 million): "Oscar is a very handsome man. So is Valentino. Tell y'all about the collection in a bit." On another day she was seated front row next to *Vogue* editor-in-chief Anna Wintour at the Carolina Herrera show, sporting a sixties blonde beehive wig and an outfit covered in multi-sized rainbow pom poms with green tights. Not quite the attire expected of an A-lister taking up precious front row real estate, but that was the point.

This was all new for the girl from Queens who once rhymed "Ed Hardy" (the mid-level priced Christian Audigier-produced apparel line featuring the imagery of tattoo artist Ed Hardy) with "party" in 'The

Jump Off 07' and proudly sported extremely oversized denim and no make-up back in high school. "I was dressing in Tommy Hilfiger baggy shirts and Boss jeans, but then I met a [girl in school] who dressed like a tiny lady – pantsuits, heels, lots of make-up. I thought she was larger than life," she told *Vogue* magazine. "She once did my make-up – I had never seen myself made up before. I didn't want to wash it off; I felt like I had one day to live this fantasy of being a glamour girl."

Glamour is a very real – and consistent – aspect of Nicki's life today. But, as with every other part of her now much more complicated existence, she is exploring fashion on her own terms. In the film *The Devil Wears Prada*, fashion editor Miranda Priestly (played by Meryl Streep and supposedly based on Wintour), making an observation about the world outside of fashion, turns to her assistant and whispers: "Everyone wants to be us."

Well, Nicki Minaj begs to differ.

"I'm not impressed to be in that world," Nicki told *New York* magazine. I'm in my own world. I think sometimes the fashion world isn't even about clothes any more; it's about this 'in' crowd, and I am not into that."

Anyone looking at the newsstands would disagree with Nicki. Since 2011, the rapper has graced the covers of at least 35 different magazines including coveted titles such as *V*, *Elle*, *W*, *Cosmopolitan*, *Allure* and *The New York Times* style magazine *T*. The rapper would also appear in the March 2012 issue of *Vogue* looking like Marilyn Monroe meets *Avatar*, covered in blue body paint and wearing a sexy, low-cut crimson dress. Nicki may not feel an affinity with the fashion scene, but it definitely has an obsession with her.

But Nicki is insistent on maintaining her individuality. She learned from making the mistake of relinquishing her personal tastes to the opinions of photographers and fashion editors. "I always yell at the magazines when they tell me what to wear because they do not know my brand like I do," Nicki told host Terrence J while making an appearance on *106 & Park*. "Sometimes they look at me like, 'You're a new artist, we're going to tell you what to do,'" she said.

She told *Vibe* magazine how she learned trial by fire in the fashion world: "I kept on being told, 'This is what we want your hair to look like and this is what we want you to look like,' and it stifled my creativity. I was talking to a photographer and he said, 'I like your everyday looks so much better than when you do photo shoots for magazines.' And I was like, 'So do I, you're absolutely right.' When they do that, it's a timeout. I have to go to the side and speak to my team and then we figure it out. They never forget me when I leave." Consequently Nicki decided early on that, although she is grateful for the chance to be in the publications, her appearances must show who she is as an artist and a person. "I've made up my mind that when you see a Nicki Minaj magazine cover from now on, it's really going to reflect me and it's going to be something that I creatively had a hand in."

Nicki may not be moved by the contemporary fashion world, but it would appear that she has been influenced, knowingly or not, by several past musical figures, all of whom are hugely creative, highly stylised and moving individuals. From an eighties British cross-dresser to a nineties hip-hop fireball, each of them shook the world – including the Nickiverse – with their unrestricted style.

Cyndi Lauper

Nicki Minaj wanted to go blonde at the age of 14 because of Cyndi Lauper. "I wanted blonde highlights, but the beautician said, 'No, you have to get your mother on the phone,' and I was just crying and begging," she told *New York* magazine. "I've always been experimenting. Cyndi Lauper's videos – that's what intrigued me."

And it wouldn't be long until Nicki Minaj finally met her idol for the first time, at the 2011 Grammys. The young rapper, dressed in a head-to-toe Givenchy leopard-print jumper, was surprised to meet the eighties pop icon and gushed to the cameras about Cyndi's influence on her style and career. Two months earlier, on December 5, 2010, Nicki Minaj had hit the stage with another pop phenom, Katy Perry, and performed Cyndi Lauper's classic 1983 hit 'Girls Just Want To Have Fun' for the VH1 special *Divas Salute The Troops*. For those familiar with the trajectory of Nicki's career, the performance made sense. Nicki may have begun as the cute and lusty Lolita, but over time her style has become less about sex and more about sass and, well, fun.

That evening, the Young Money rapper commanded the stage in a platinum blonde asymmetrical wig, a colour-bombed miniskirt and skyscraper high heels. Rewind to the early Eighties and you may find Cyndi Lauper in an outfit of a similar nature.

It's clear that Lauper is an influence on the rising star and what an appropriate one she is. Not only did Lauper shake things up on the *Billboard* charts, she influenced the world around her.

Cyndi Lauper was born in 1953 in Queens, New York (the same borough where Nicki was raised). Her parents, Fred and Catrine, divorced when she was young, although her mother did not stay single for long; she remarried, but divorced again soon after. Her volatile family life did not deter Cyndi's musical ambitions; at age 12 she picked up a guitar and taught herself to play as well as write songs. An extremely creative youngster, Cyndi searched for multiple ways to express herself. Unconcerned with fitting into any mould, she dyed her hair multiple colours and began sporting chaotic clothing choices – unknowingly setting the stage for what was to come in her later life.

Cyndi attended a public high school with a curriculum centred on the arts (much like Nicki's alma mater LaGuardia High School) and then went to college in Vermont to study art at 17. After returning to New York, she sang in a couple of bands, working several odd jobs in between. Then, in 1981, Cyndi was finally discovered. Critics around town began to take notice of her skilful, multi-octave voice. One night at a New York bar, she met a guy who would soon become her boyfriend, her manager and the person who would secure her a record deal with the label Epic Records, which would distribute her 1983 debut solo album, *She's So Unusual*. After the release of the album, Cyndi Lauper's life would never be the same again.

But the road from contract to concert was a difficult one. Even today the record industry has but a handful of notable female songwriters and producers and in 1983, the notion of a female, especially a brand new artist, having creative control over a record was not welcomed warmly. Lauper was given songs to record and, disliking them, she would rewrite verses. Her first single is a prime example. When she was presented with 'Girls Just Want To Have Fun', it was not the same record that it became for the world. According to Cyndi, the original lyrics involved pleasing a man; instead, she flipped the scene and made it a female anthem that resonated across cultures. MTV placed the quirky video in constant rotation and it ultimately became a gigantic hit, and has since become an eighties classic.

Cyndi's second single, 'Time After Time', soared to the number two spot on the *Billboard* Hot 100 chart. It has since become a classic, a transplant into the Great American Songbook, and has been covered by over a hundred artists (interestingly, Cyndi and Lil' Kim performed a mashup of the song and Kim's street hit 'Lighters Up' for the televised Nelson Mandela 91st birthday celebration in 2009).

Lauper stirred up a bit of controversy with her third single, 'She Bop', which included suggestive lyrics about masturbation. But this didn't detract from sales; it went on to become her most successful international single, after 'Time'. With her fourth single 'All Through The Night' also reaching the Top 10, Lauper became the first female to have four consecutive *Billboard* Hot 100 Top 5 hits from one album. Lauper's 1986 sophomore album, *True Colors*, also went on to spawn the number one hit title track and two further hits.

Over the course of her career, Cyndi has become an icon for the gay community and still makes appearances around the world at gay pride parades. In 2010, she launched the Give a Damn campaign with the mission of bringing awareness to discrimination against the LGBT community. The same year, Cyndi Lauper teamed up with Lady Gaga for the MAC Viva Glam lipstick campaign, with the proceeds going to the MAC AIDS Fund (Nicki Minaj and Ricky Martin starred together in the same campaign in 2012 to raise money for HIV/AIDS awareness and research in Latin America).

Cyndi continues to release music (her eleventh album, *Memphis Blues*, was released in 2010), remaining relevant through reinvention – not in the way Madonna has done with constant image transformation, but in a way that has worked for her, whether she's crafting instrumental and blues reinterpretations of her pop songs (her *Memphis Blues* collection was the biggest-selling blues album of 2010) or travelling the world representing the various causes that are important to her. As much as Cyndi's popularity initially caught on like wildfire, due largely to her unpredictable and carefree style, her staying power grew out of her sincerity and smarts; she was the witty New York girl with an attitude and a dream, which is, of course, not too far removed from Miss Minaj herself.

Missy "Misdemeanor" Elliott

Nicki Minaj is grounded but otherworldly. She's cute, but frequently grimaces. She's determined to challenge the notions of what's expected from a girl. She raps furiously over hyper-kinetic beats, but switches to singing a chorus effortlessly. She's known to rap with sound effects and in various voices. Nicki shares these traits and abilities with another female rapper who came before her and set the stage for the supernova success she's experiencing now. She has clearly been a major influence, not only on Nicki's free-to-be-wild style and futuristic flow, but also in the manner in which she continually breaks down doors in the industry, often seeing them crush her male counterparts. Instead of making uncomplicated comparisons to Lil' Kim, people would be more successful and, better yet, on point to compare Nicki to Missy Elliott – an out-of-the-box rapper/singer, with a passion for the futuristic, a love for odd videos, a habit of rapping in different voices with sound effects and doing all of this while dripping in attitude. Before Nicki bum rushed the *Billboard* Hot 100 with 'Super Bass', Missy had been the last female rapper to crack the pop Top 10 with the irresistible 'Work It' in 2002.

Melissa Arnette Elliott was born in the waterfront city of Portsmouth, Virginia in 1971. She is the only child of Patricia, who worked at the local power company, and Ronnie, whose career as a Marine took the family to North Carolina.

Melissa was an outgoing child; most considered her to be the class clown, and she delighted in the label. Schoolwork was another story; she had little interest in it, even though an aptitude test placed her two grades ahead. However, from the age of four, it was clear that her real love was performing. Speaking to *The Guardian*, she revealed that whenever someone asked her what she wanted to be, she would always respond with one word: "superstar". "I never saw anything else, never dreamed of doing anything else." But with no one to take her far-fetched dreams seriously, her creativity lay dormant for many years.

Melissa's home life was plagued with domestic abuse. At eight years old, a teenage cousin molested Elliott repeatedly until a relative discovered it almost a year later and put a stop to it. "Each day he wanted me to come to the house after school," Elliott told VH1 in an episode of the series *Behind The Music*. "It became sexual, which, for me at eight years old, I had no clue what that was, but I knew something was wrong. Being molested... it don't disappear. You remember it as if it was yesterday."

Furthermore, she witnessed the daily abuse of her mother at the hands of her father. "My father was very abusive, and it was hard for my mother at first to leave because we had depended on him for so long. Sometimes you kind of get adjusted to getting that beating." This continued until she turned 14 and her mother plotted their escape, whereupon they left for good.

In the early Nineties, an era in American musical history ruled by new jack swing – a sound created by producers Teddy Riley and Bernard Belle that merged R&B, dance-pop and hip-hop – Missy came into contact with a producer, also from the South, who was on the cusp of it all: DeVante Swing, creator of the hugely popular R&B group Jodeci. DeVante signed Missy and her friends, who had formed a girl group, to his label DeVante's Swing Mob Records, naming the group Sista in the process. He went on to record an album with them.

During this time, Missy also wrote and performed on an eight-year-old Raven-Symoné's debut single, 'That's What Little Girls Are Made Of' (Raven had found fame as a child star on *The Cosby Show* and *Hangin' With Mr Cooper*), and she also brought her neighbourhood friend, who was also a music producer, Timothy Mosley, to meet DeVante, who would give the rookie producer the name Timbaland.

Unfortunately, Swing Mob folded, Sista's album was shelved, and all of the acts went their separate ways – except, that is, for Missy,

Timbaland and another soon-to-be-famous rapper Ginuwine, who would all go on to make major noise in the industry.

In 1996, Missy and Timbaland joined forces to produce the majority of the late R&B singer Aaliyah's second album, *One In A Million*, which spawned the still memorable hits 'If Your Girl Only Knew', 'Hot Like Fire', '4 Page Letter' and the title track.

Also in 1996, Missy was asked by a then-named Sean "Puffy" Combs to rap on a remix he was producing for a rising R&B star at the time. The song, 'The Things You Do' by Gina Thompson, showcased Missy's truly original flair and raised her star quotient even higher. Her verses on the remix were considered groundbreaking at the time. No other female rapper had ever possessed her verve and energy on wax. With explosive energy, she fired: "You ain't ready, for Puff Dad-dy/Beware, how dare he make the remix so deadly/Pizzzow! Gomer be my Pyle like Sha-zam/Hee hee hee hee how, hee hee hee hee hee hee how!"

Missy's quick delivery and cartoon-like wordplay hit the radio waves and music video shows like a UFO landing. Puffy saw her as the female answer to British-born rapper Slick Rick who, with his playful storytelling rhymes and off-the-wall humour, became a star with the classic song 'La Di Da Di', with Doug E. Fresh, and then a hip-hop legend with his solo album, *The Great Adventures Of Slick Rick*, which yielded the hit 'Children's Story'. Rick bounced between different voices to portray various characters in his songs. Similarly, Missy made use of high-pitched inflections, an array of dialects and even the traditional African-American church-based call and response technique in her music.

In 1997, while writing, producing and performing for other artists, Missy somehow managed to record and release her first solo album, *Supa Dupa Fly*, led by the insanely original single 'The Rain (Supa Dupa Fly)' and just as innovative a music video, which saw the rapper donning an inflatable trash bag, worn as a one-piece, topped off with a jewel-filled headpiece (styled by June Ambrose who served as the fashion advisor). The video took the hip-hop world by storm and made Missy *the* female MC to watch; she commanded attention because here was a female rapper with an interesting flow and a quirky and original style. Despite her obvious talent, she didn't take herself too seriously, with her character-driven voices and her lyrics drenched with video game effects: "Beep, beep, who's got the keys to my Jeep? Vrroooom."

Missy was unlike any female rapper at the time. For one, she was hardly near a sample size; she did not wear barely-there clothing or rap about explicit sex. Instead of relying on her body to push her music, she leaned on a mix of sci-fi and eighties-like abstract visuals in her videos and comedic observations about love, relationships, partying and everyday life in her songs. Diddy tried to sign her to his all-powerful Bad Boy Records, but Missy, being the innovator she is, went to the more mainstream Elektra Records – in a move surely strategic on her part – and not only won a solo deal, but secured her own label imprint to which she was signed and could sign other artists.

Missy would go on to win five Grammys, release five more albums and sell over seven million records. She is the only female rapper to have six albums certified platinum and she has tentative plans to release a new album in 2012.

Missy's goal was to bring humour, fun and sheer entertainment back into hip-hop and it is for these reasons that she was one of the few popular female rappers to accept Nicki Minaj from the very beginning. Most female rappers could not comprehend Nicki's sudden emergence onto the scene, but Missy didn't care where she came from; she recognised Nicki's talent from the moment the new girl on the block started bubbling on the streets. The career Elliott has established for herself she built on going left when everyone else was looking straight ahead, which enabled her to empathise with and appreciate Nicki's diagonal and zigzag movements all over the industry. She and Nicki shared a common vision and she knew it: "She reminds me of myself, the way she says whatever she wants however she wants on record, like riddles or funny shit," Elliott told *New York* magazine.

Missy's endorsement of the rising rap superstar was potent. She and Lil' Kim were widely known to be good friends, so for her to back an artist accused of borrowing rather too heavily from Kim's career was significant. This was not a failing, no-longer relevant artist trying to grasp on to the fast-rising coattails of the latest luminary; this was the most successful female rapper of all time, giving props to the girl with the machine-gun flow and schizophrenic voices.

What goes even further to explaining Missy's support for Nicki is that both females come from homes with abusive and violent fathers, and each has stated that one of their main motivations for success was to be able to provide for their mothers. But Missy's connection to Nicki is essentially a very simple one in Elliott's eyes: "Nicki makes rapping fun again," she said. And if anyone knows fun in hip-pop, it's Missy Elliott.

Boy George

If the eighties is known for its stylised icons, then Boy George, with his colourful shock of dreadlocks and cross-dressing tendencies, complete with full make-up, is as much a face-to-remember from the highly influential decade as Michael Jackson, Madonna, Prince and Cyndi Lauper.

"I love the way he dressed, " said Nicki Minaj of Boy George, "and his music too." Those two elements are what made this working-class Englishman, born George Alan O'Dowd to Irish parents, such a marvel even before his eventual worldwide success in the early eighties. His androgynous tendencies began as a child; with four brothers and one sister, he is quoted as saying he often felt like the "pink sheep" (he was an early Ken Barb!). As such, he created an image that he could rely on and that made him stronger amid the testosterone-fuelled energy in his household.

But his extreme behaviour and garb made it nearly impossible for him to function in school, and he was soon expelled for his eccentricity and adversion to authority. Now, out in the world and in need of a job to support himself, George worked odd gigs as a farmhand, hat maker and a make-up artist for the Royal Shakespeare Company, which proved to be a great training ground for his later career. During this time, he also frequented Billy's nightclub, becoming one of the leaders of the Blitz Kids, a group of teenagers that included Steve Strange, Marilyn and Leigh Bowery (all of whom became pop stars in their own right) who, like George, were heavily into the punk-androgynous look popular at that time. But when the club's owner started regular David Bowie and

Roxy Music nights, the group quickly became bored and set off to break the mould.

Transferring their allegiance to the more elitist Blitz Club in Covent Garden, London, the group unwittingly created what was to become known as the New Romantic movement, which was fuelled by their flamboyant style, attitude and love for New Wave music.

The manager of the now legendary British group the Sex Pistols, Malcolm McLaren, noticed George's influence and offered him a slot in the group Bow Wow Wow to assist the lead singer, Annabella Lwin. However, much to Lwin's chagrin, George's irresistible stage presence and charm overshadowed her. Armed with more confidence and – more importantly – an audience, George formed his own band, Sex Gang Children, but they soon dropped that curious moniker in favour of the name Culture Club, which referenced the group's remarkable and socially uncharacteristic diversity: an English-Irish cross-dressing lead singer (George), a Jamaican-Brit guitarist (Mikey Craig), a Jewish drummer (Jon Moss), and an English keyboardist/guitarist (Roy Hay).

Culture Club was signed by Virgin Records and released their debut album, *Kissing To Be Clever*, to international acclaim. The album went to number five in the UK and number 14 in the US and spawned the singles 'Do You Really Want To Hurt Me?', 'Time (Clock Of The Heart)' and 'I'll Tumble 4 Ya', all three becoming Top 10 hits, making the freshman group the first since the Beatles to have three Top 10 hits from a debut album in the US.

The shy and awkward boy from England was nowhere to be found; Boy George had arrived and there was no turning back. Teenagers all over the world became enamoured with his bombastic style and cool, blue-eyed soul/pop. He quickly became an international household name and the group's second album, *Colour By Numbers*, released in 1983, surpassed the success of its predecessor. 'Church Of The Poison Mind', 'Miss Me Blind', 'It's A Miracle' and 'Victims' were all major hits, but it was 'Karma Chameleon' that solidified the group's, and especially George's, place in the pop pantheon.

Boy George went from strangely dressed soul singer to heavily worshipped pop prince and the entire world wanted a piece of him.

He was even asked to provide vocals for Band Aid's worldwide hit single 'Do They Know It's Christmas', which was recorded in 1984 by a mainly British and Irish set of pop stars to aid in Ethiopian hunger relief and became Christmas number one that same year. (This effort would inspire stars of the American music industry to embark on the 'We Are The World' project the following year.)

Sadly George's immense success as a hit machine (he wrote or co-wrote all of the group's songs) and the pressures that came with it led him to drug addiction, which he would continue to struggle with for many years. George's drug use, his soured relationship with drummer Jon Moss and the less than impressive sales of Culture Club's third and fourth albums led to the group's break-up in 1986. George released several solo albums and even enjoyed a Top 5 R&B hit with the song 'Don't Take My Mind On A Trip', produced by Teddy Riley, who was riding high on the success of his new jack swing sound. Despite several troubling episodes and a stint in prison, George reinvented himself as a hugely successful dance music DJ and continues to perform around the world today.

Nicki acknowledges that George's music and dress have influenced her, which is evident in her cavalier attitude towards the fashion and music worlds and in her refusal to conform to the way others believe she should approach her career.

Grace Jones

Nicki Minaj's single 'Girls Fall Like Dominoes' is a pro-feminist pop romp in which she claims that she is hot enough to steal fans from the greatest male rappers (playfully name-checking her mentor Lil Wayne and labelmate Drake) and skilfully name-dropping some of the most revered women in music today and pop culture in general, including one of the most bold of all: Grace Jones. Nicki raps, "Hit up Grace Jones and tell her I said 'Strangé'," in reference to the name of the fierce fictional model she portrayed in Eddie Murphy's 1992 movie *Boomerang*.

It's no surprise that Nicki references Grace Jones. Jones is perhaps, outside of Diana Ross, the most iconic black woman of the seventies and eighties, blending both fashion and music to totally unique effect.

Born Grace Mendoza in Spanish Town, Jamaica in 1952, Jones' parentage was not a reflection of who she was to become. Her mother was a politician and her father was not only a preacher (gasp!), but a Pentecostal one, practising in the division of Christianity that is not only charismatic, but its members believe in "speaking in tongues", during which they praise and worship God in an unknown or unintelligible language. No one could have predicted that their only girl (they had two sons as well) would go on to embrace the secular world in such a way that her name now invokes the hedonism of the late seventies and eighties New York party scene.

But Grace knew she was meant for more. Her father uprooted the family from the Caribbean and they moved to upstate New York where Grace attended Syracuse University in 1965 and studied theatre (the same path as Nicki had taken); she also studied theatre at a community college before finally heading to New York to pursue a career in modelling. At almost 6' tall, with Afro-Caribbean ebony skin and strong features, she was meant to marry the camera and eventually landed in Paris. Parisian photographer and illustrator Jean-Paul Goude took the newly arrived bombshell under his wing, the two having a personal as well as a professional relationship (they share a son).

Jones achieved success as a model and a singer in Paris, which took her back to New York where she signed a record deal with Island. Between 1977 and 1979, she released a trilogy of disco albums: *Portfolio*, *Fame* and *Muse*, all three brilliantly produced by Tom Moulton, one of the geniuses of disco. Jones' star exploded. She became a permanent fixture on the New York club scene, a virtual mascot for the now mythical mega-club Studio 54 and a muse for the "God of Pop Art" Andy Warhol. Jones found success with the singles 'Slave To The Rhythm' and 'Pull Up To The Bumper', and in movies as well (she starred in almost 20 movies, including a role as the memorable villain May Day in the 1985 James Bond flick *A View To A Kill*).

Despite her phenomenal success as a singer and actress, one thing overshadowed it all: her outrageous and unpredictable style. In the late seventies, she adopted a severely androgynous look. Taking on a hyper-masculine façade, Jones cut her hair into a square cube (the style, known as the "flat top fade", would later prove popular among young black men in the mid eighties, and because all that was old is often new again, the style re-emerged with nineties hipster-retro kids). She wore abstract blazers with major padding on the shoulders and because of her Amazonian build and crazy costumes, a scandalous (and of course false) rumour that she was a man began to spread. Ironically enough, she would become an icon for gay men, the community being a major contributing factor to her fame, much like Nicki's Ken Barbz are for her today. In 2012, Jones performed during England's Diamond Jubilee concert, celebrating the 60-year landmark of Queen Elizabeth II's reign. While singing her hit song 'Slave To The Rhythm', the 64-year-old singer hula-hooped throughout the song and it never fell once, to the excitement of the crowd and fans around the world watching. Jones has adamantly remained an individual and pushed for her fans to be the same. Nicki encourages the same from her fans around the world.

Lisa "Left Eye" Lopes

TLC was once the biggest girl group in the world. With their living-out-loud chromatic costumes, funny, brash, and always relatable lyrics, the three girls took the world in their R&B/hip-hop/pop grasp and did not let go until they had sold over 50 millions albums. Singers Tionne "T-Boz" Watkins and Rozonda "Chilli" Thomas were joined by Lisa "Left Eye" Lopes, who rapped about enlightenment, female empowerment, personal faith and also sexuality to complement TLC's anthems. Left Eye's cleverness lay in her ability to take the themes of the song a step further in hopes of generating something beyond a great beat and melody.

Everything about Left-Eye was over the top, from her clothes and rhymes to her interviews and relationships. "There's a thin line between genius and insanity – and I always get labelled as being the crazy one," she famously said in an interview. Because of both Left-Eye's and Nicki's larger-than-life persona, commitment to individual style, original rapping technique and fearless attitude, comparisons are likely and warranted.

Music mogul LA Reid, who signed TLC to LaFace Records, his and

Babyface's record label, in the early nineties, recognises the similarities. "I see a little Left Eye in [Nicki Minaj]," Reid told *The Hollywood Reporter*. "There are certain female artists [today in which] you can see the influence of TLC and that time."

Nicki Minaj is known for her out-of-the-box style and there was no person more left field in the mid to late nineties than Left Eye. Unfortunately, many say that Left Eye's personality oftentimes overshadowed her talent.

Lisa Nicole Lopes was born in Philadelphia in 1971, the first of three children born to Wanda and Ronald Lopes, Sr. By the age of five, Lopes' career choice was locked down; her parents gave her a toy piano for Christmas and, even though it was not a true instrument, she taught herself to play it properly. Furthermore, to entertain her younger siblings, she would concoct wildly imaginative stories and read them aloud, which no doubt helped her to develop her spoken rhythmic flow. Lopes' knack for music was passed down from her father, a musician who played multiple instruments, who was supportive of Lopes' musical ambitions and gave her constant encouragement. Performing at open mic nights around Philly – and winning at times – bolstered Lopes' confidence. She eventually left home in 1990, moving to Atlanta.

After meeting Michael Bivins of R&B group New Edition fame, who commented to her that her left eye was bigger than her right (and it made her unique and beautiful), her stage name was born. A year later, she formed a group called Second Nature with "T-Boz" Watkins and another girl named Crystal Jones, although they soon changed the name to TLC, which represented the first initial of each of the girls' nicknames). However, Jones dropped out and the group's manager Perri "Pebbles" Reid (then married to LA Reid), remembered Rozonda Thomas, who was a backup dancer with another group on LaFace and they added her to the mix. In order to continue with the group's name, Left-Eye christened Rozonda with the moniker "Chilli" and the future supergroup was born.

TLC's kaleidoscopic clothing (they attached condoms all over their outfits to promote safe sex, Lopes wearing one over her left eye) helped skyrocket their 1992 debut album, *Ooooooohhh...On The TLC Tip*, to multi-platinum status with three Top 10 hits. Their second album, 1994's *CrazySexyCool*, would be their magnum opus: it became the first album by a female group to be certified diamond, with over 10 million copies sold. The album also won two Grammy Awards for Best R&B Album and Best R&B Performance by a Duo or Group with Vocals for 'Creep'. But despite their success, the group was forced to file for bankruptcy claiming to not have received a fair amount of money from their contract.

Furthermore, Lopes made international headlines after setting fire to her then-boyfriend's (Atlanta Falcon player Andre Rison) sneakers in his bathtub, which caused the home to burn down.

TLC went on to record another album, *FanMail*, in 1999, which would be their last release together. In Honduras in 2002, Lopes was killed in a car accident while she was driving. She had recorded a solo album before her death that charted well in England but failed to find success in the US. Aptly titled *Supernova*, and including songs like 'Head To The Sky', 'The Universal Quest' and 'A New Star Is Born', Lopes was clearly on the path to truly cementing her individuality. "She was a true hip-hop star," producer Jermaine Dupri told MTV. "She was the star out of the group. She was the one who would curse on TV. She had the tattoos. You could not expect the expected. When you see Lisa, you could expect something from her. That is the gift she carried."

Her unpredictability and natural penchant for theatrics, innate understanding of hip-hop and pop music and different musical personas (she was going by N.I.N.A. before her death) not only invite comparisons to Nicki Minaj, but they have people wondering what might have been.

Lauryn Hill

When Nicki set out to become an artist, she originally wanted to sing, somehow ended up studying acting, and is now a superstar rapper who incorporates her singing voice into her music along with biting rhymes. If this trajectory sounds familiar, it should. It's almost exactly the route Lauryn Hill travelled to become a superstar – and so much more. Nicki has talked about her idolising Hill since she started giving interviews.

Hill's now classic debut solo album, *The Miseducation Of Lauryn Hill*, "was the soundtrack of my life when it came out", she has said. The album, released in 1998, was an extreme gust of fresh air at the time of its release. Hill, a founding member of the hip-hop outfit the Fugees, had become a beloved figure with her smart and swift rhymes and melodious vocals and her remake of Roberta Flack's timeless 'Killing Me Softly' from the Fugees' multi-platinum album *The Score*. (With over 14 million sold worldwide, *The Score* was the biggest selling hip-hop album ever until Eminem joined the party.) With her entry into the solo arena, Hill had cemented her reputation as a class act.

Lauryn was born to Valerie (a school teacher) and Mal (a computer programmer) in South Orange, New Jersey on May 25, 1975. Both of her parents were musically inclined; her mother played the piano and her father was a singer, and they played records from their soul music collection constantly in Lauryn's childhood home. Her brother, Malaney, also played saxophone, among other instruments, so growing up in such a musical family was an invitation to Lauryn to pursue a career in show business.

But the road was a little rocky at first. When she performed on the Amateur Night portion of the popular eighties and nineties show *It's Showtime At The Apollo* at the age of 13, a nervous-looking Hill began to sing her own interpretation of Smokey Robinson's 'Who's Lovin' You?'. Initially garnering some boos from the crowd, the persistent youngster belted her way through, earning the crowd's applause and their respect by the end of the track.

When Hill graduated from high school (which she attended with friend, actor Zach Braff of hospital sitcom *Scrubs* fame) she met Wyclef Jean. With Jean and his cousin Pras Hill, the threesome formed The Fugees, and after their double platinum 1994 album, *Blunted On Reality*, the group became international superstars. Hill was the breakout star, with fresh-to-death rhymes that blurred the lines between street and scholastic. Later 'Lost Ones', a scathing, hard-edged rebuke to Jean, kicked off Hill's solo journey, becoming the promo single for *Miseducation,* with the lead single from that album, 'Doo-Wop (That Thing)', becoming a major hit on both sides of the Atlantic.

Hill also became a recognised fashion plate; rocking everything from Balenciaga to Banana Republic, her style was a mix of high-end luxury and effortless bohemian. Furthermore, her acting skills were never forgotten. She was offered a role in the first installment of the film adaptation of *Charlie's Angels*, but turned it down (Thandie Newton took the part), as well as rejecting a part in the Brad Pitt and Julia Roberts movie *The Mexican*. These surprising decisions would be an indication of what was to come. In 2000, Hill disappeared from the music scene, with the exception of sporadic shows around the world and a small tour in 2011, during which audiences were infuriated by her tardiness. In some cases crowds waited for up to four hours for her to appear onstage (in her apology to Atlanta fans, she tweeted about the "make-up" concert she wanted to give them and quoted the Head Barb herself: "I had to come back. I'm HERE and excited for the opportunity to do what should have been done the last time. Starting off on the wrong foot can always be easily rectified by putting another foot down, especially in a 'monster shoe' (Nicki Minaj quotable). Come again!"

According to DJ Rampage, who tours with her around the world, Hill is a fan of Nicki's music. *Vibe* magazine asked Rampage if Lauryn Hill was intrigued by any new artists and he replied: "There are moments when we're taking a break from practising and just talking about things, and I remember this one time she mentioned hearing Nicki on the radio. I believe the track was 'Roger That', and she started reciting some of Nicki's lyrics and her ad libs. It was obvious to me she was feeling her stuff."

Nicki was excited to hear about Miss Hill's return the stage. "It's like, freaking, I want to bow down and kiss her feet," she told rapradar.com. "I think everyone in my generation, we look at her as a freaking, and I hate to say this, because it sounds kind of blasphemous, she's almost a godly-type of creature. It's not human. So the fact that she's doing stuff and performing, I think that it's a great day and I've always loved her and I still love her." Like Hill, Nicki can travel between multiple worlds that satisfy her various creative interests.

Having Hill recite Nicki's music is another full circle moment for the once struggling Minaj. When she was a no-name rapper in New York trying to get a deal, some industry execs and producers would scoff at her melding of rap and singing, one telling her, "Nicki, you are no Lauryn Hill." Now, that same person may be telling some other female rapper just starting out: "You are no Nicki Minaj."

Gwen Stefani

Nicki Minaj is the self-proclaimed Head Harajuku Barbie. But she wasn't the first superstar to lay claim to the wonderfully colourful Japanese style, Gwen Stefani having already done so in 2004.

Born on October 3, 1969 in Southern California, Stefani became obsessed with musicals, such as *Evita*, as a child. Her parents encouraged her to take vocal lessons and by high school she was performing in shows (including another of her childhood favourites *The Sound Of Music*). She joined the punk rock band No Doubt shortly after leaving school and the group went on to have numerous hits and sell millions of albums. Before Nicki commandeered her own army of Harajuku Barbies, the California girl had already adopted the electric fusion of styles displayed by the girls hanging out at Tokyo's Harajuku station.

In fact, when No Doubt took a hiatus and Stefani decided to record a solo album, there were two things that she knew would influence the sound, look and overall texture of her project: eighties era Madonna and those Harajuku girls.

Stefani's first solo album, 2004's *Love. Angel. Music. Baby.*, was a radio programmer's dream. Sweet and impossibly melodic, her dance-pop ruled the airwaves with hits like 'Rich Girl' and 'Hollaback Girl' taking centre stage. When the time came to tour, Stefani travelled with her Harajuku Girls troupe, which danced and sang backup. Showing her obsession with the style, after launching her incredibly successful fashion line L.A.M.B. in 2003, Stefani extended the collection into an accessories line in 2005, which she named Harajuku Lovers. Coincidentally both artists appeared on individual covers for the *Elle* magazine March 2011 Music Issue, which celebrated women in music, and both continue to pay homage to the Harajuku girls that have informed their colourful style.

Britney Spears

In October of 2010, Nicki Minaj told this author that she admired Britney Spears because of the strength that the pop singer displayed during her "dark period", during which the paparazzi was chronicling every waking second of her day, culminating in Spears shaving her head, losing control of her finances (to her father) and losing custody of her children (to their father, Kevin Federline). Nicki says that Spears' resilience and ability to make a comeback after such a turbulent time truly impressed her. And as Nicki has become a mainstream maven herself, surely Spears' virtual takeover of the pop music scene from the late nineties to the mid noughties was a source of wonder and awe for a then-teenaged Nicki.

Born on December 2, 1982 in Mississippi and raised in Louisiana, Britney Spears burst onto the music scene in 1999 and became an instant sensation. The singer is credited with resuscitating the "teen pop" genre, and was Madonna in reverse: young, comely, but simply wanting for nothing but a return on her investment, as was evident in the sweetly sexual worldwide phenomenon '...Baby One More Time'. Initially at least, she was a girl pushing her sexuality just enough to capture the attention of the world. Sound familiar?

Nicki had already transformed herself from a hyper-sexualised street rapper (in the vein of Foxy Brown and Lil' Kim) into an artist veering ever closer towards pop stardom. In Spears, Nicki saw what could be; but in Madonna she saw what she wanted to be.

Madonna

In 2010, Nicki first admitted in passing (to a paparazzi cameraman) that she wanted to work with the legendary star Madonna. Then, in the summer of 2011, while appearing on the popular ABC show *Good Morning America*, host Robin Roberts asked the rising star who she would like to work with next – again, she name-checked the pop icon.

Eventually her boldness and consistency paid off and resulted in her recording two songs for Madonna's 2012 album, *MDNA*, which led to her performing with the pop legend during the Super Bowl halftime show that same year.

Madonna Louise Ciccone was born in Bay City, Michigan on August 16, 1958. Her parents, Silvio Anthony, a design engineer for General Motors, and Madonna Louise, raised six children and were staunch Roman Catholics. When Madonna was five, her mother died of breast cancer at the age of 30, and Madonna retreated inwardly. But not long after, she fell in love with dance and, after high school, she attended the University of Michigan to study the art form.

The young Madonna soon set her eyes on New York, dropping out of college and, as the now mythical story goes, flying to the Big Apple (her first ride on an aeroplane), hopping into a cab for the first time, telling the driver to take her to the centre of it all and ending up being dropped off in Times Square with $35 in her pocket.

Madonna took a job as a waitress, whereupon she became a dancer and eventual singer in several bands before scoring a record deal, which she did in 1982. Her debut album, *Madonna*, did not experience immediate success, although her first single, 'Everybody', was a dancefloor hit (interestingly, the record sleeve did not include a picture of Madonna and her pop-R&B sound led many DJs and consumers to believe that she was black, until she convinced the label to allow her to shoot a low budget video). It was not until her third single, 'Holiday', released in 1983, that Madonna cracked the *Billboard* Hot 100.

Madonna's style during this time was just as important as her music. Her rebellious Lolita look of lace tops and dresses over leggings, with black rubber bracelets piled high on one arm and layers of jewellery around her neck, caused a worldwide fashion revolution. Soon everyone wanted the Madonna look – except that it was not hers to give.

In fact the iconic look can be attributed to French designer and stylist Maripol, who styled the singer on her first two albums. She also created the wedding dress Madonna dons on the cover of her second album, the 1984 mega-hit *Like A Virgin*, and a line of clothing and accessories called "Maripol for Madonna" was sold as merchandise during the tour.

Never mind how it came to be, the look and its mass response saw the beginning of "the Madonna Effect" on pop culture, and came to be the first of her constant reinventions in her efforts (with potent success) to remain relevant. "Pop" is instant and fast-moving; it has a high turnover and if one remains static for even a moment, the competition will wipe you out. Madonna recognised this early on in her career, and her ability to stay relevant is the key factor behind her dominance of the pop industry over nearly four decades.

Nicki has said she admires Madonna's work ethic, but it's the constant movement that she relates to most. In just a few short years, Nicki has introduced several alter egos, countless styles of dress, innumerable wigs and an impressive catalogue of hits so far. Instead of the $35, Nicki began with a DVD appearance and has not looked back ever since. Surely, Madonna, who is still making music and movies, would not either.

Nicki Minaj is a character, a product that Onika Maraj has created over several years who has both confused and entertained her fans and the music industry. Although her style is most certainly her own, the influence of these artists who went before her is clear to see and some would say they helped to pave the way for Miss Minaj to take centre stage.

Chapter 7

Kiss The Girls

One balmy summer's evening in Los Angeles in 2011, newly minted superstar Nicki Minaj left the popular Hollywood restaurant Katsuya and performed the usual paparazzi shuffle. With her assistant, hype man and oft-rumoured boyfriend Safaree "SB" Samuels at her side, her bodyguard and driver in front of her, she made her way through the throng of loud and pushy photographers scrambling to snap photos of the pint-sized provocateur. It was a dance Nicki was used to by now and she could have done it blindfolded. But as she stepped up to enter her waiting SUV, the rapper heard something that stopped her cold. "Nicki! What do you think it will take for us to finally get a *gay* rapper?" one of the videographers yelled out, with high hopes that the star would gift them with a precious soundbite perfect for the following morning's headlines. She did not disappoint.

"I am a gay rapper! You already got one!" she shouted.

And by most accounts, she is right.

Well, she is the closest the world has experienced to having a mainstream and beloved openly gay rapper – except for one small detail: despite her bewildering outburst at Katsuya, she denies that she is actually gay. But this hasn't stopped the rumour mill churning and Nicki's overwhelming insistence on expressing her love and adoration for her female fans has only served to fuel the gossip further. In 2009, during an interview with VladTV, the male interviewer asked her, "What does it take for a guy to get your attention?" She replied, "Actually, I like for girls to approach me. [They should] just be cute and be themselves, you know how I love you girls. Kisses and hugs to all of my bad bitches. The guys don't have any fun parts that I can squeeze!"

In 2009, SOHH.com asked Nicki about Amber Rose, Kanye West's former girlfriend, reportedly hitting on her in public. The rapper says she was extremely surprised by the gesture. "I was very shocked. It was funny. She said it to me when we met in person so I was like, 'Whoa she's dead serious,' cause she put it on Twitter. I was just laughing like everybody else probably. I had to take it in a little bit." But, Nicki also admitted to being slightly flattered, perpetuating the eyebrow-raising surrounding her possible bi-curiosity. "She's a dope girl. She's real funny. She just took an interest in me. I guess that's a good thing when a bad bitch likes you, you know?"

Nicki made these comments jokingly, but it certainly wasn't the first time the singer has made a statement creating questions over the nature of her sexual orientation. Her breakthrough mix-tape, *Beam Me Up Scotty*, featured a song called 'Still I Rise', on which she raps from the perspective of a hater talking about her: "You know her name Minaj/She a lesbian." On 'Go Hard' she rhymes: "And I only stop for pedestrians/Or a real, real bad lesbian." Such verses indicate her awareness of the rumours that swirl about her sexuality, and certainly the average listener would probably jump to the conclusion that Nicki is gay or bisexual, despite her public announcements to the contrary.

Nicki is always playful, coy and has a knack for punctuating statements with a wink. In an interview in *Complex* magazine, she says to mix "[Johnson's baby oil] and Christian Dior perfume… [and] you can almost imagine me there with you, girls! Later she offered, in a spot-on British accent: 'I don't really like boys at all, I think they are disgusting, smelly and really mean.'"

Some critics have reflected upon whether Nicki's inflammatory comments are actually born out of a sexual desire for women or are simply a means of building a strong female – and lesbian – fanbase by making them feel a part of her "Barbie movement". Nicki says that her affection for women began innocently after witnessing the tremendous effect she had on girls at her shows. They responded with extreme fervour to Nicki's fresh brand of feminine rhyme and searing attitude, and the rapper decided to use the opportunity to instill in her growing legion of fans the confidence that took her years to develop, after what seemed like a lifetime of disappointment and hurt. She wanted to let them know that if a poor black girl from Queens can live her dreams, so can they.

"I started making it my business to say things that would empower women, like, 'Where my bad bitches at?' to let them know, 'I'm here for you,'" Nicki told *Out* magazine. But, to her surprise, that intended empowerment spiralled into something sexual. "When I started going to the shows and it was nothing but girls, it was like, 'Did I go too far with embracing my girls?' Because now they want to kiss and hug me."

During a conversation with media personality Angie Martinez in November 2010, Nicki addressed the fact that girls can't help but approach her in a way that they usually reserve for guys. "Even when girls talk to me, [they do it in the way] that you try to be sexy for a boy. They'll be like, 'So, what's up, Nicki? What's your type, Ma?'" Nicki acknowledges that her fans may have formed this impression of her because she acts so intimately with them, most notoriously through her now trademark move of signing her female fans' breasts. "You know how I act with my Barbz, touching their boobs and all," she continued to tell Martinez. "It's all playful."

Nicki's childhood friend, Tyesha Kollore, told E! about the first time she witnessed Nicki's signature "move": "'What made you do that?' I asked her. She said, 'I don't know. I just got the marker and signed her boob.'" The rapper cannot recall exactly when she started the practice. "I wish I could remember the first boob that I signed," she told *The Fader* magazine. "I don't know why I did it, but now I can't go anywhere and not do it. People come up to me wherever I am – girls, sexy girls – and are like, 'Can you sign my boob?' I mean, [guys] in the club look at me like I'm a pimp, because they [are] fly chicks. I don't know, but I do know it's a great thing."

As well as reaching out to her legion of female fans, was Nicki also using the ambiguity over her sexual preference to pique the interest of those men who find women with lesbian tendencies attractive? In the classic hip-hop double standard, it's perfectly acceptable for a female to be bisexual or even a lesbian, as long as she is pleasuring a male, usually in a threesome. Nicki's guest feature on Usher's song 'Lil Freak', in which he sings not only about having a ménage but how the girls enjoy one another too, furthers this notion.

Usher's lyrics play out what has become known and accepted in pop culture as the heterosexual man's holy grail of fantasies. In the video clip for the song, he instructs Nicki to search the club they are in for at least one other girl in order for them to have a ménage a trois. She then sets off on her mission to find "bad bitches", as she affectionately calls sexy females.

Nicki follows Usher's instructions to the letter. She asks one of the women if she can put her hand down her pants to touch her "kitty kat", which would prove her seriousness. Only then would she allow her access to the true prize: Usher. Always one to interject comedy and wit into her lyrics, Nicki seems to enjoy playing with these notions of hyper-femininity and sexual ambiguity. In the same track she also mentions her habit of signing the breasts of female fans and also warns music mogul Diddy to keep his eye on his rumoured girlfriend, singer Cassie.

Further fuelling the fire, Nicki and Cassie were spotted getting friendly on the set of the video shoot for DJ Khaled's hit song 'All I Do Is Win'. Then they were seen arriving together at New York's Hot 97 Summer Jam in 2010, holding hands and hanging out in between Nicki's several performances with various artists. However, her verse about stealing Diddy's girl was declared in jest; she and Cassie became friends during the short period when Diddy was managing Nicki's career, which would explain their closeness at various events around that time.

However, it wasn't the last time that Nicki's words and actions would link her to a sexy singer. In 2010, rumours swirled about a possible hook-up between her and pop star Rihanna after the two recorded the song 'Fly' for *Pink Friday*. Performing the track together on one of Nicki's tour stops, Rihanna grabbed Nicki's bottom with both hands as they hugged, prompting the rapper to tell the crowd, "Only she can get away with doing that!" When it was time for the island beauties (Rihanna was born in Barbados) to film the video for the song, the rapper was excited but playfully cautious. "I love RiRi!" she told E! "I mean, when she's not grabbing my ass, she's a sweet girl." Once on the set of the video, Rihanna set the rumour mill off once again by tweeting a picture of the two ladies with the caption: "Me and Nikki in our new crib, lol! Gettin busy on set of FLY!!! It's so hard to keep my hands off!"

Quick-wittedly, Nicki responded to the tweet: "Lol. If we're gonna live 2gthr and hook up u gotta learn how 2 spell my name! Lmaooooooo (sic) Gossip Gossip ni#@a just stop it!" Rihanna shot back with a funny and more flirtatious tweet: "b★★ch don't u hear me asking what my OWN name is??? Lol! My bad, I'll make it up to u ★wink★."

Looking closely at the differences in reaction between the two artists to the playful tweets is almost a case study into the difference in attitudes regarding homosexuality in the pop and hip-hop worlds. Nicki seems obligated to explain or clarify each incident whereas Rihanna freely plays with people's perceptions. While Rihanna was tweeting from the set, Nicki tried to get her to clean up the tweets a little, but then their shared silliness won over. "I told her that we should censor that," Nicki told *Blackbook*. "But then she looked at me and we started cracking up. If we could, we would say so much more craziness and just get stuff brewing. We have to foresee what could be taken out of context."

Nicki then took to the airwaves to shoot down the rumours that resulted from the tweets. "I don't know where people got this really insane, hilarious, random rumour that she and I were living together," Nicki told Ryan Seacrest on his radio show, despite the buzz surrounding messages that she and Rihanna had clearly written and sent to each other. "It was like, 'What?' It's like, you can't even be sarcastic any more. It was hilarious, though."

On December 15, 2010, a gossip website posted a picture of Nicki sitting very closely (almost canoodling) with a well-known Midwestern female DJ named Soraya Benjamin. The tabloid site claimed that

Benjamin was the lesbian that "turned Nicki Minaj out". On the day the story was posted, radio DJ "Big Man" Konata, from Ohio station Power 107.5, snagged an interview with Benjamin, who lived in the same area. Konata asked Benjamin if she and Nicki had slept together and in complete refusal to confirm either way, Konata instead plugged Nicki's first album, which had dropped a few weeks earlier. Attempting to re-route his line of questioning, Konata asked how the two rappers had met. "She was at Club Ice," Benjamin said, referring to the popular Columbus, Ohio club, where Nicki had performed two years before. "She was real cool and really approachable. We talked a little bit. We exchanged cards and we was drinking and chilling," Benjamin continued. Still not satisfied, Konata kept pressing for a yes or no answer as to whether she and Nicki had taken their relationship further. Benjamin said: "I am not going to… Nicki is a good person. I play her all the time in the clubs." Benjamin never confirmed or denied the allegations, which has, of course, only served to fan the flames.

All of these very public episodes have left some to criticise Nicki Minaj for her mixed messages. Her back and forth about her sexuality has caused some to label her a "celesbian" or "fauxmosexual", a celebrity who fakes being gay for attention and fame. And according to pop culture journalist Cheryl Aldave, Nicki may be playing a very dangerous game. "If Nicki is feigning her bisexuality, she is playing – and playing with – emotions and perceptions about self-image and self-worth that for many are dangerous indeed," says Aldave. "How many kids have taken their own lives because of the pressures around them to 'straighten up' or who just feel like there's no one around who understands? How many people have been killed for being what Nicki might be pretending to be?"

But during a wave of gay teen suicides around the United States in 2010, Nicki addressed her young gay fans directly, telling MTV: "I would encourage my gay fans to be fighters and to be brave. People face difficulties, no matter who you are. I faced difficulties with a lot of things. I face opposition every day, but I didn't kill myself and now, thank God, I'm here. So I want my life to be a testimony to my fans and my gay fans." Nicki went on to say that the people who hate are the ones that have the problem. "I mean, I could never imagine what they're going through. But, I know that suicide is never the answer and I know that things always get better. So I'm supporting you guys. I love you very, very much and for the people who don't love you, they need help."

Nicki's words and actions since she hit the national stage have confused people, but the rapper seems to be OK with that. While she may sometimes filter herself for the greater good, Nicki says she has no problems with being misunderstood at times. "I don't mind being taken out of context," she continued to *Blackbook*. "It's great to fuck with the media because they fuck with me all the time."

Nicki's attitude is understandable. Both society and media can applaud an artist one moment and attack in the next.

Whitney Houston is a perfect example. She burst onto the musical scene in the mid eighties with her eponymously titled album, which eventually went on to sell a massive 14 million copies, making it one of the biggest debut albums in history. However, despite her success and clear financial independence, Whitney was reportedly sharing an apartment, and with her close female friend and assistant Robyn Crawford. The two of them were inseparable; from interviews to recording sessions, Crawford was present. The rumours began to circulate that the two were in a relationship.

The eighties was a time of extreme growth culturally: great music was made; beautiful and timeless art was created; fashion was more adventurous than ever, but attitudes towards homosexuality were not as open as in the post-millennial society because of the emergence of the HIV/AIDS epidemic and the lack of information and understanding regarding the disease. While homosexuality is still taboo in a small minority of circles (such as hip-hop) today, it is essentially a footnote to the career of a homosexual artist. But during the eighties, having a female proclaim that she liked girls, even jokingly, and not attract some sort of homophobic response, was out of the question.

Houston addressed the rumours about her sexuality in a 1987 *Time* magazine article, which revealed her amazingly progressive attitude for the time: "My mother taught me that when you stand in the truth and someone tells a lie about you, don't fight it. I'm not with any man. I'm not in love. People see Robyn with me, and they draw their own conclusions. Anyway, whose business is it if you're gay or like dogs? What others do shouldn't matter. Let people talk. It doesn't bother me because I know I'm not gay. I don't care."

For Whitney Houston, one of the premiere pop stars of the eighties, to declare that being gay was not abnormal and people should mind their own business, was quite courageous, whatever her intentions may have been. But, whereas Nicki is the target of rumours about her sexuality because she places herself in the firing range with her unfiltered and free-wheeling talk about girls, Houston became a target because of her silence. In the late eighties, it was also rumoured in the press that Houston was having an affair with Kelly McGillis, famous for her starring role in the movie *Top Gun* opposite Tom Cruise. Houston never addressed these rumours, but McGillis, who herself came out in 2009, squashed them: "I think [Whitney Houston] is vastly talented, but I have never met the woman."

During that difficult time, Houston was dealing with a barrage of attacks on both her personal life and career. Not only was her sexual preference up for constant debate, but the African-American community – who had initially helped to make her a superstar on the R&B charts with classics such as 'You Give Good Love' – had turned on her. Whitney's career took a giant leap across musical genres when she crossed over to MTV and the pop world with songs like 'How Will I Know'. But this only served to alienate the African-American community, who denounced her for being "too white", and she was infamously booed at the Soul Train Music Awards in 1989 when her name was announced.

Coincidentally, Whitney met Bobby Brown that same night. Brown was the "King of R&B" at the time; his second album, 1988's *Don't Be Cruel*, would eventually sell upwards of 14 million copies. The two stars went on to marry in 1992, but rumours that Whitney had chosen Bobby as a cure for the biggest ailments in her life – a marriage licence would deaden the lesbian rumours and a hook-up with "The King of R&B" would reinforce her black roots – dogged the couple until their divorce in 2007.

Whitney told *Out* magazine in 2000: "I suppose [the rumour] comes from knowing people... who are [gay]. I don't care who you sleep with. If I'm your friend, I'm your friend. I have friends who are in the community. And I'm sure that in my days of being out, hanging with my friends, having nothing but females around me... But I love everybody. If I was gay, I would be proud to tell you, 'cause I ain't that kind of girl to say, 'Naw, that ain't me.' The thing that hurt me the most was that they tried to pin something on me that I was not. My mother raised me to never, ever be ashamed of what I am."

Other female artists have experienced the same sexuality rumours as Whitney. Queen Latifah, MC Lyte and Da Brat, three female rappers who came before Nicki Minaj, have all suffered at the hands of the press who have insisted on calling them lesbians. Each of them has denied it, however, Latifah, the most successful of the trio, has experienced an interesting career, due partly to her embracing what she has never admitted to.

Born in New Jersey, Dana Owens began her musical career with the hit song 'Ladies First', which served as an anthem for female strength and equality in the late eighties and, since turning her hand to acting in the late nineties, she has made a point of playing strong and resilient women on both the big and small screen. Her portrayal of lesbian Cleo Sims, an extremely masculine (what the gay community deems a "stud") bank robber in the 1996 film *Set It Off*, only increased the talk about her being gay. To Latifah's credit, she did not allow the rumours to keep her from accepting one of the most highly regarded roles in her career.

In 2011, it was widely reported that Latifah had come out in an interview with Jamie Foster Brown, editor-in-chief of *Sister 2 Sister* magazine. "I just like ladies who have class. Period. And if it's 'T and A' you're selling, that's fine, as long as that's what you're selling," she told Brown. "But you don't have to show everything, you know? You can hold some back and just be yourself and let your personality shine and let your individuality show. To me, that's sexier. A confident woman is a sexy woman, in my opinion. And I think guys find that to be the same way."

135

News outlets all over the world interpreted this as Latifah admitting to being a lesbian. But she wasn't. Her quotes were taken wildly out of context by the media, who used photos of Latifah on holiday, embracing her personal trainer Jeanette Jenkins, as "proof" to bolster her supposed admission. But, in a show of self-effacement and humour in the face of the media onslaught, when preparing for the release of her new album in 2008, Latifah toyed with the idea of calling the project *The L Word* to play with public perception (the title worked on two levels, by using her first initial and referencing the hit Showtime network series of the same name, which focused on the lives of a group of lesbians living in Los Angeles). "*L* was gonna stand for love though or LA," she told *Rolling Stone*. "Since people want to play games, I like to jab back sometimes just for fun, but I'm like, 'Nah, that's too much energy wasted.'"

Of course it isn't only female celebrities who have experienced undue speculation into their love lives.

Boy George, beloved for his music and his hugely flamboyant and free-flowing form of dress (coupled with lashings of wild and colourful make-up and a head of long dreadlocks), never admitted to his homosexuality during the heyday of his fame. In fact, he was quoted in a London newspaper in 1984 as saying, when asked about his sexual preference: "I'm not gay, and I'm not a transvestite, no matter what anyone thinks; I'm basically very much a man."

The pressures of celebrity force many of the famous to remain closeted about their sexuality, in spite of the lies they subsequently have to tell. When asked about his sex life, George coyly sidestepped the subject. "Sex? I'd prefer a nice cup of tea," he has frequently been quoted as saying in 1983. It was not until the mid nineties, after the breakup of Culture Club and several mediocre-selling solo albums, that Boy George finally announced to the world that he was a homosexual. In a 2006 documentary, he took it a step further, labelling himself as "militantly gay". In an interview with *The Guardian* in 2011, he said that the gay community, and not even just those who remain closeted, is deciding to conform as a whole. "People aren't so individual any more. There is this sense of why would you want to stand out and make a show of yourself?" He added, "You can find that sort of attitude in the gay community too… that if you are an exhibitionist you are somehow spoiling the big assimilation. Most gay men go out of their way to look normal and fit in."

Of course public and media speculation can appear harmless initially, but if left to fester it can eventually damage an artist's career and essentially wipe away their relevance. Early on in Nicki's career, when she was making appearances on cable access video shows and urban blogs, she was thankful for the attention and, to set herself apart, she would talk about subjects that would capture people's attention. The cute and harmless comments to her "Barbz" did the trick. Her name became a hugely popular Google search term and her YouTube videos received a few million views. But, as Nicki Minaj: The Product, grew in prominence and demand, the mainstream world called and suddenly she was on a mountain, looking down and surveying all that she could gain, and her tune changed in interviews.

Suddenly, Nicki was on the defensive about her sexuality. In 2010, she told *Complex* magazine that she doesn't intend to explain every little thing she raps about: "When I rap, it's just an extension of how I speak, and that's how I talk. If you don't like it, don't listen. I'm also not going to explain something just because I said it in a rap. Take what you want from it. [In the press] I didn't say [I don't like women]. I said I don't have sex with women. If [bisexual is] what they wanna call me, then fine."

In her November conversation with Angie Martinez, Nicki went on to clarify her situation: "I don't have a specific type. I am not gay, Angie. People have taken my words and assumed. With my best friend, I touch her, and kiss her all the time, and touch her forehead, but it's not like that."

After making numerous sexualised comments about women, including one about the possibility of a threesome with Cassie and actress Lauren London (who, coincidentally, has a baby with Nicki's label boss Lil Wayne), Nicki may have realised that speaking so ambiguously about her sexuality wasn't exactly prudent for her burgeoning career. But whether her comments about women were genuine or designed for attention, her staunch support of the gay community is unquestionable.

She told Q magazine: "That's definitely not true [that I am a lesbian]…
I guess some people are thrown off by me embracing gay culture."

Nicki has been very vocal about quantifying her sexuality since
gaining the attention of the media. But she has maintained her silence
on the issue of possible relationships and whom, if anyone, she is dating.
During a visit to *The Wendy Williams Show* in 2010, the notoriously
blunt host asked Nicki if she was "sexually fluid" (meaning was she
sexually attracted to both sexes depending on how she feels). Nicki
replied, "No, Wendy. I don't even like the way that sounds," she joked.
Wendy then asked if she was dating anyone and she replied: "I am
married to Benjamin Franklin."

There's no doubt that Nicki is certainly pulling in the $100 bills
these days, but, at one point, fingers were pointing to her closeness
to another man in her life: Safaree Samuels. Nicki calls Safaree her
assistant, hype man and best friend, and he also serves as Nicki's A&R
coordinator, helping her with all aspects of her music and Brand Nicki
Minaj. "Safaree is not my boyfriend," Nicki told *Rolling Stone*. "He is
one of my best friends from home. I'm gonna fire him though," she
joked. "You shouldn't hire your friends. But, it's good to have someone
around who knows you for you."

And it seems that if anyone knows her, it's Samuels. Both had been
members of a fledgling New York-based hip-hop group called the
Hoodstarz. Along with two other male members, Nicki and Samuels
looked liked the typical, bare-knuckle rap collective, acting and rapping
about their life at the time and what they aspired to be in the future. On
a group freestyle, Nicki, still using her real last name, raps about wearing
Prada and being "too pretty/skilled/but still gritty". Her tone and flow
are vastly different; in fact, she sounds very similar to nineties rap star
Foxy Brown and worlds away from the 'Super Bass' sing-a-along that
was to come.

In pictures with the group, Nicki is front and centre, filling the
requisite role of the lone female in an all-male cipher (Lil' Kim having
perfected this position in Junior M.A.F.I.A.). Essentially, she looked like
a girl making her way in a group that she knew was only temporary.
Holding a glass of champagne and surrounded by the three other

members, including Samuels who is grasping a champagne bottle, Nicki appears upset and disinterested. In another photo, she looks like LL Cool J's classic 1990 song 'Around The Way Girl' come to life: big, gold-plated earrings, long nails, hair extensions and lots of attitude. In both photos, her facial expressions seem to indicate her awareness that the Hoodstarz is merely a means to an end on the road to superstardom.

Sure enough, Nicki left the group and from there began her stint with Fendi and Dirty Money Records. Once her career began taking off she recalled how much she had loved Samuels' energy onstage; she really admired his lack of fear and willingness to look clownish for the sake of motivating the crowd. With this in mind, Nicki asked him to be her hype man. Soon he was accompanying the burgeoning rap superstar wherever she went.

He was by her side as she toured her mix-tapes up and down the country, and when she hit the road with Lil Wayne and the Young Money crew he was there. He is listed as a co-writer and vocal contributor on the hit song 'Did It On 'Em' from Nicki's debut album. When she accepted her BET and MTV Video Music Awards in 2010 and 2011, he walked with her to the stage, holding her hand, and remained in earshot as she thanked him for being her "best friend", and on the many occasions that she has walked the red carpets at award shows and events, he is usually near, if not by, her side. With his own Louis Vuitton backpack or duffle bag in tow, he may also carry Nicki's bags as they walk through the airport. He sat next to her as they co-hosted Nicki's U-Stream shows (U Stream is a social media site that allows participants to broadcast themselves live) and joked and interacted playfully with the watching fans.

But on the afternoon of July 11, 2011 in Dallas, Texas, the two were not so good-humoured.

In the southern town for a stop on the Britney Spears Femme Fatale tour, Nicki and Samuels were lounging by the pool and a disagreement ensued. According to the Dallas Police Department report, the argument escalated and Safaree left the pool area. Nicki gathered her things and left as well, returning to the hotel room the two were sharing. When she arrived, Samuels was packing his suitcase. Worried that he was taking something that belonged to her, she was looking in the case as he closed and lifted it. The suitcase made contact with her chin and the inside of her bottom lip hit her teeth, causing a bloody gash. The police were called. Samuels left the scene. On the 911 call, Nicki is audible in the background saying: "Look what he did to my face." She decided not to press charges or have any pictures of her face taken. But the entertainment blogs went crazy.

A few days later, Nicki tweeted a response: "The fact that you believe a man either slapped or punched me in the face & didn't leave on a stretcher with his balls hangin' off. #getaF%kinLife." The police report states that Nicki told the officers that she and Samuels were just friends and were never intimate.

Whatever happened that day, the two remain stealthily loyal to each other. In November 2011, the rapper found herself engaged in the most unlikely of Twitter battles. An overzealous and misinformed fan of singer Cher tweeted her and asked if she knew that "bitch" Nicki Minaj "dissed" her with the line from Nicki's song 'Did It On 'Em': "If you could turn back time, Cher/You used to be here/Now you're gone, Nair". Cher tweeted an immediate response: "I've seen lots of people come and go. No biggie!" Samuels, knowing that the line had not been meant in a disrespectful way and was merely using the title of Cher's song 'If I Could Turn Back Time' metaphorically, responded in his friend's defence: "Yo! @Cher Listen to the words before you say some dumb shit on Twitter! Do you know what a rap metaphor (sic) is? TM (Team Minaj) is a cult you don't want it with!" Realising that she was wrong, the 65-year-old singer immediately tweeted an apology. "You're right! I'm wrong! U R Right! Someone said I was dissed… I've been dissed b4, but instead of finding out… I just got defensive! I should know better! Dumb. What does that say about me? Insecure? Want 2b understood? What?"

On another occasion, Nicki called a maid service to her Los Angeles condo one afternoon. While the maid was supposed to be cleaning, she apparently went into the trash and retrieved a photo of the rapper, asking Nicki to sign it. Nicki was livid, seeing the maid's actions as unprofessional. She quickly fired her, asked her to leave, and called the service for another cleaning person to replace the one she let go. As a result the whole issue degenerated into claims and counter claims, much to the delight of scandal hungry celeb web sites.

Months later, Samuels took to Twitter once again, this time to broadcast much happier news: "Blurry vision got you seeing double," he tweeted, along a pic of matching Bentley Continental GTs that he and Nicki had just bought: hers pink and his red. "Shout out to my new Bent... Matte Red Only 1 in the USA Continental GT. Even though I hate it, they force me 2get da new Bent," he boasted via the social media site. After people raised questions online about his financial status (the car is worth $200,000), he replied on Facebook: "I got ova $600,000 in insured jewels, so I think I can afford to buy a Bentley. I shoulda bought a [Honda] Civic. LOL All good."

Despite rumours to the contrary, Nicki has denied being in an intimate relationship with Samuels, but she has admitted to being his business partner. SB knows Nicki as an artist and she trusts his direction. "He is the reason for 'Did it On 'Em' being on my album," she told The Breakfast Club. "He knows lyrically what I am capable of and I keep a small circle, even in the studio. So that's a point, I have people that I can trust right by my side." Nicki says that not only is he her A&R representative, helping her to secure music, producers and guest features from artists, but he co-helms the entire operation. "We run our own ship," she continued. "We have a couple of companies together. I don't know what people want me to say," she said in frustration over the continuing gossip about the nature of their relationship.

Their bond is reminiscent of another music star and the man present in every aspect of her life: Janet Jackson and her ex-husband René Elizondo, Jr.

Janet Jackson was born into celebrity. By the time she was a toddler, her brothers were signed to Motown and headed to worldwide success. By the time Janet turned 18, she was ready to venture out on her own. She had already experienced tremendous success in her teenage years as a television actress (starring in *Good Times*, *Diff'rent Strokes* and *Fame*), but she wanted to explore life beyond the beautiful, but sheltered grounds, of Hayvenhurst – the Jackson family compound where she grew up.

So, in 1984 she eloped with R&B singer James DeBarge (of the eighties family group DeBarge). The marriage lasted less than a year before it was annulled in mid 1985.

Two years later, during the height of Janet's success with her 1986 album *Control*, she met Elizondo, a dancer, on the set of one of her videos. The two fell in love and remained together for 13 years. However, Janet managed to keep the fact that they had been married for eight of those years a secret, right up to when Elizondo filed for divorce in 2000. Elizondo claims to have been a frequent, uncredited contributor to Jackson's work for many years of her career (her 1998 album *Velvet Rope* was the first and only album on which he received songwriting credits). They eventually settled three years later in 2003.

Nick Minaj and Safaree may not be dating, but their creative partnership and friendship appears weighty in the same vein as Jackson and Elizondo had.

During her long career, Jackson has also faced questions about her sexuality. Beginning with the 1993 multi-platinum album, *Janet*, she started exploring sexuality in her music and by 1998's *Velvet Rope*, she was singing about homosexuality and having the courage to live in truth: "Boy meets girl/Boy loses girl/Boy gets cute girl back/Girl meets boy/Girl loses boy/Girl gets cute girl back/Free to be/Who you really are/One rule, no rules/One love, Free Xone," she sings in the track 'Free Xone'.

Janet has admitted to hanging out in gay clubs and being questionably affectionate with females in her entourage, but has denied being bisexual. "No, I am not bisexual," she told *Ebony* magazine. "I have been linked with dancers in our group because we are so close. I grew up in a big family. I love being affectionate. I love intimacy and I am not afraid to show it. We fall asleep in each other's arms. We hug, we kiss, but there is nothing beyond that."

When asked why she and other women in the public eye are plagued with accusations of bisexuality, she intimates that some people just can't believe that women can just be powerful without anything else underlying. "Maybe because it's just that we're strong women," she said. "I don't know. Maybe they want to put something else behind it because of the strength. Like, you can't be a woman and be strong, and there has to be something else to it." And, similar to Whitney Houston in the eighties, Janet has stood up for acceptance. "I don't mind people thinking that I'm gay or calling me gay," she told *Ebony*. "People are going to believe whatever they want."

Nicki does not seem to mind that some people think she's gay or bisexual; she makes bold, albeit comedic, statements like "I'm a gay rapper" and plays up to the stereotype. Despite speaking with *Black Men* magazine and categorically denying being a lesbian ("I don't date and I don't have sex with women"), she has also proven that she will not allow societal rules to suppress who she is. "Everyone is not black and white," she said to *Out* magazine. "There are so many shades in the middle, and you've got to let people feel comfortable with saying what they want to say when they want to say it. I don't want to feel like I've got the gun pointed at my head and you're about to pull the trigger if I don't say what you want to hear. I just want to be me and do me." In stark contrast to the other female rappers preceding her, Nicki *has* dared to use the word lesbian without trepidation. She is daring to be an individual and confront sexual stereotypes. "People who like me – they'll listen to my music, and they'll know who I am," she told *Out* magazine. "I just don't like that people want you to say what you are, who you are. I just am. I do what the fuck I want to do."

Whether Minaj is a so-called "fauxmosexual" or not, her consistent support of her gay fans and inclusion of them into her Barbie movement has shifted hip-hop into another direction. Hip-hop as a genre and culture has been largely non-accepting of homosexuality, yet Nicki is helping to bridge the gap: "Homosexuality in hip-hop is very taboo," says videographer Jabari Johnson. "But, she rides for [the community] so hard." Her self-expression and freedom may be the attraction. "We did a few shows where even the guys had on pink wigs," said DJ Kuts. "Nicki has a big gay following because she is herself. They love that about her."

And Nicki hopes that she can be a vessel for curing the genre of its prejudices. "Normally, Wayne probably wouldn't have gay guys coming to see his shows much, but they're definitely a big part of my movement, and I hope they'd still come out and see me… I think that will be really, really interesting, just to start bridging that gap. We'll see," she said in 2010 before the release of her debut album. And when Nicki Minaj, the biggest force in the genre in well over a decade, sat on the couch on *106 & Park* and said, "Well, my Ken Barbz wear the same things my Barbz wear," it was monumental. In that moment, she allowed thousands of gay teens watching the country's number one music video show to feel understood and embraced. Her support and simple words on the show did more for the health of America's youth than any other rapper has managed, or even cared, to do.

Chapter 8

A Brave New World

Nicki Minaj now exists in a bizarre universe, a world which is the exact opposite of the one she was born into. Just a few years ago she was a simple outer-borough girl who had just clocked-off from minimum wage and was going to the studio to write and record the material that eventually surfaced as her first mix-tape, *Playtime Is Over*. No one knew what a declaration this then MC minion was making. Wrapped (or trapped) in a doll box on the cover, many observers took one glance at the cover art and, with a collective eye roll, thought, "Wasn't Lil' Kim the Black Barbie?" Yet some interpreted the image of Nicki's hands pressed against the packaging as a doll trying to escape from the box.

She was.

South Jamaica, Queens was fine for those who wanted to remain there, but Nicki had dreams: stadium-sized ones. Her future did not include anything that was around the way. She envisioned a life full of opportunity, money and acclaim. "I've always wanted fame," she told *Blackbook*. Sure enough, Nicki achieved what she set out to do, leaving her life in Queens far behind.

But, on July 4, 2011, something happened that would bring her right back to the streets of her hometown. While America was celebrating

Independence Day, Nicki was in Canada, on tour with Britney Spears. She was celebrating as well – not Independence Day, but Safaree Samuels' birthday. Little did she know that around the same time she was wishing her friend a happy birthday, her 27-year-old cousin, Nicholas Telemaque, was murdered in Brooklyn, New York. Later she took to Twitter to share her grief with her followers: "Lived in Brooklyn his whole life. My precious cousin. My baby. Killed last nite," she tweeted, along with a photo of Telemaque, who was leaving a club only blocks from his home in the New York City borough when he was shot multiple times in his upper torso. Nicki tweeted again: "My cousin Nicholas. Also goes by Juse. Murdered. Last nite. Near his home. Brooklyn, NY," and she posted another picture.

A few days after Telemaque's death, the song 'We Miss You' hit the internet. In it Nicki raps: "Why'd you have to leave in July?/On a peaceful and serene summer night?/You said that you would leave these streets, and I know you didn't mean in a body bag/But now we see you were not bulletproof." The lyrics were incredibly poignant and revealed much about the situation, which had the Barbz Nation believing their leader had retreated to the studio to express her sorrow through her art. But this was not the case; strangely enough, the song had been recorded a year prior to her cousin's death. Again, Nicki took to Twitter to address it. "Tho the lyrics of 'We Miss You' eerily depict the circumstances surrounding my cousin's death, I wrote & recorded that song on 5/24/2010. It was sent to Mariah Carey & Keyshia Cole over a year ago for a possible feature. It didn't make *Pink Friday* due to clearance issues. It's an unauthorised leak." In fact, subsequent lines in the song indicate that it was, in fact, about a former lover ("I'm mad 'cause you were the best that I ever had"), but the timing and subject matter were eerie all the same.

Growing up in New York, Nicki had been exposed to gun violence and its effects before. On November 25, 2006, three men were leaving a strip club in Queens in the early morning and an undercover cop approached the car with the men on the suspicion that they were carrying a firearm. The car was already started and, rather than stop, the driver, Sean Bell, continued. As a result, the police on the scene fired over 50 shots into the car, killing Bell. It was a day before his wedding. "Two of the guys that were shot with Sean Bell were my friends," Nicki told *The Heat* on Sirius FM. "Those are people that I see and talk to." Nicki felt that they were fired upon unjustly and she had similar feelings regarding the Trayvon Martin case, in which an unarmed 17-year-old African-American male was shot and killed by a 28-year-old white Hispanic man named George Zimmerman, who alleges that he was the community watch co-ordinator of the neighbourhood Martin had been walking through on his way home. Zimmerman said that Martin, who was donning a hoodie, looked suspicious. "[Trayvon] was not doing anything wrong," Nicki continued to Sirius. "I want justice to be served. President Obama rocked me when he said 'If I had a son, he would look like Trayvon.' It's the truth. I hope we talk about it enough to get something done."

The tragedy of her cousin's death hit closer to home and took a toll on Nicki; however, she remained on the tour and received support from her tourmate Spears, who also took to Twitter: "Please keep @NickiMinaj & her family in your prayers....keep up the amazing love and support you guys have for her". (On her 2012 sophomore album, *Pink Friday: Roman Reloaded*, Nicki mentions her cousin's death on the track 'Champion'.)

With the exception of the sad death of her younger cousin, 2011 was a stellar year for Nicki. By autumn, *Pink Friday* was certified double platinum with over two million copies sold, she had earned a Grammy nomination for Best New Artist, her single 'Super Bass' was certified triple platinum, she had recorded two tracks for Madonna's album *MDNA* and the Material Girl had asked Nicki to join her onstage for the following year's Super Bowl halftime show. However, despite all of those accomplishments, her boss Lil Wayne believed she was capable of more and the world had yet to see her full potential. "I'm not satisfied with anything she's done," Wayne told *Vibe*. "I believe she can do a whole lot more, and I believe she will do a whole lot more. It's not shocking, and it's not surprising. It's quite fitting. But other than that, it's nowhere near the end."

Pharrell Williams, rapper, singer and record producer, believes the only way for Nicki to reach the proverbial next level is for her to silence all of her outside influences and dig deep within. "She's done everything and she's everywhere in a time frame that breaks every record," he told *Complex*.

Pharrell is certainly a man that knows the music scene and has, unlike a lot of his peers, seen it from multiple angles. He started out as a beat maker, under the tutelage of producer Teddy Riley, then after producing the mega-hit 'Superthug' for N.O.R.E., he and his partner, Chad Hugo, now established as the Neptunes, were in high demand. Hits for Jay-Z, Usher, Kelis and Diddy led to the duo working with Britney Spears, resulting in one of her signature songs 'I'm A Slave 4 U'. Williams, himself a successful solo artist, is a master of pop music: not only can he craft hit songs, he can spot a star. His work with R&B singer Kelis made her an international figure. And he believes, as an artist, that Nicki stands alone on the scene, thus, the sole person that can challenge her is Nicki. "The only thing left is… [for her to focus on her] inner," he continued. "We know when she flexes there's nobody who can stand next to her. But talking to yourself is the next challenge."

On the eve of the release of her second album, *Roman Reloaded*, Nicki admitted that she had no time for inner reflection, because of her busy schedule. But her understanding of self-analysis may be a little different from the norm; simply through her insatiable grind, and her expectations of those around her to commit to the same ("If I could leave one thing with the Barbz it would be for them to love themselves unconditionally and have drive," she said on *106 & Park*. "I hate lazy people. I can't take it. I don't understand that language."), she *is* displaying a form of self-reflection. Every day she is determined to be better than the day before. When she was harassed by bloggers and some fans for supposedly lip-syncing during her first BET Awards performance in 2010, she promised herself that, while she insists there was no miming in her performance, she would undoubtedly triumph during her next major televised performance a few months later: the MTV Video Music Awards.

During the pre-show, she and Black Eyed Peas frontman will.i.am performed their song 'Check It Out', from *Pink Friday*. It was a spectacle: will.i.am was, controversially, a spaceman in a "blackface" outfit and Nicki emerged from her own ship, most likely from Mars, in a purple and pink, second-skin astro-suit, to lead a troop of Barbie Martians through a focused, agile and steady performance. When the time came for one of her trademark, rapid-fire rap breakdowns, she anchored herself, placed clenched hands on her hips and reminded the fans why they had bought into her: her rhyming skills were unrivalled.

With her stellar success, Nicki had entered a brave new world. Some criticised her for embracing the pop elements that she'd always intended on pursuing. But in this new YouTube-driven society, where music can go viral in a millisecond, an artist working for long-term influence *and* a legacy of influence knows that to stay still, and worse, the same, is to guarantee sudden death. Just ask Lil' Kim and Foxy Brown. They both rode the wave of sex-driven hit records until it crashed. Listening to Foxy Brown spout "He fooled you girl/Pussy is power, let me school you girl/Don't get up off it 'till he move you girl/And let no playin' nigga rule your world and screw you girl/I got 'em hatin' me, I throws the pussy down, keep 'em chasin' me," on her 1999 single 'I Can't', is a reminder of a time when the sole purpose of the female rapper was to serve as eye-candy for men and evangelise about the wondrous power between their legs.

Nicki has her fair share of soft porn-worthy rhymes, but she decided while making her first album that she would refrain from using the only model that was taught to female rappers. She exchanged the playbook. A female rapper that idolised Cyndi Lauper from childhood surely couldn't be expected to only wear booty shorts and only rap about sex.

"I went above and beyond to prove that I could not talk about sex and not talk about genitalia and still have a successful album," Nicki told *Vibe*. "And I proved that. And now my time for proving things to my critics is over. I don't really need to prove anything to anyone else any more."

But her critics didn't stay quiet for too long. When Nicki was invited to perform her single 'Roman Reloaded' at the 2012 Grammy Awards, she was about to stir up the hornet's nest once again.

It is a major accomplishment to be invited to present a solo performance at the annual presentation ceremony, which recognises outstanding achievements in the music industry and is attended by every mover and shaker in town. Not only does it signify that an artist is relevant in their genre, but it also shows they matter to pop culture overall. Nicki used her major coup to showcase four minutes of Roman Zolanski madness, in a reintroduction to the alter-ego that first emerged on Trey Songz's 'Bottoms Up' and then again on her *Pink Friday* track 'Roman's Revenge'. Nicki had initially intended to perform a different track, but it was the Grammy officials who changed her mind. "I painted this picture for them," she told *The Breakfast Club*. "Then they heard the song and went crazy."

Nicki's Grammy spectacle began with her entrance. "When I was at the Grammys last year, it was like I did not even exist," Nicki said during an interview with the Recording Academy in January 2012. Well, there was no chance of Nicki thinking *anyone* was ignoring her at the 54th Annual Grammy Awards. At 5.24 p.m. on February 13, Minaj had mouths agape when she stepped onto the red carpet dressed as a nun, outfitted in a hooded, floor length, bead-embellished, crimson-coloured robe designed by Atelier Versace; but it was her date that arched everyone's eyebrows to high heaven: a man dressed as Pope John's doppelgänger.

Nicki's Catholic couture ignited wildfire, with chaotic calls of "Nicki, over here!" from the paparazzi amid a blitzkrieg of flashes from their cameras.

Later in the night, she debuted the single 'Roman Holiday' in a performance entitled "The Exorcism Of Roman", which was an extension of her red carpet statement. When the lights came up, Nicki was sitting in a confessional facing a priest, before she launched into the first verse from her previous hit 'Roman's Revenge'. But then she switched mid-song to a creepy version of *West Side Story*'s 'I Feel Pretty'. The performance cut to a video of a priest arriving at a home and him asking, "Where is the child?" The woman answering the door pointed upstairs and he headed up to where we saw a fresh-faced, but psychotic looking, "Nicki" putting lipstick on awkwardly. When the priest opened the door, she jumped up to the corner of the ceiling and the priest asked, "Who are you my child?" In response she screamed, "Romannnnn!" The show then cut back to the stage where a levitating Nicki and dancing priests performed the song.

Unsurprisingly the Catholic community was outraged by the performance, which starred Nicki's "gay boy" alter ego: "Nicki Minaj, fresh off looking like a fool with Madonna at the Super Bowl, showed up last night on the red carpet at the Grammys with a guy dressed like the pope," said Bill Donohue, President of the Catholic League. "This was just a prelude of what was to come. Whether Minaj is possessed is surely an open question, but what is not in doubt is the irresponsibility of the Recording Academy," he continued. "Never would they allow an artist to insult Judaism or Islam."

Donahue had also unleashed his witty critique on Lady Gaga in 2011, whose video for the song 'Judas' had Gaga portraying a dancing Mary Magdalene in a sea of Catholic imagery. "In her 'Judas' video, Lady Gaga plays fast and loose with Catholic iconography, and generates several untoward statements, but she typically dances on the line without going over it. Perhaps that is because the video is a mess. Incoherent, it leaves the viewer more perplexed than moved. The faux-baptismal scene is a curious inclusion, as is her apparent fondness for the Jesus character. But if anyone thinks the Catholic League is going to go ballistic over Lady Gaga's latest contribution, they haven't a clue about what really constitutes anti-Catholicism."

Gaga's former creative director Laurieann Gibson had been working with Nicki since her MTV performance and she also produced Nicki's Grammy performance. A few months later, when promoting *Pink Friday: Roman Reloaded*, Nicki visited Power 105.1's morning show *The Breakfast Club* to discuss her Grammy performance. "Laurieann gets me," she said about Gibson, who starred on Diddy's MTV reality show *Making The Band*. "She is the only one that gets me. I tell her my idea and then it's done." After receiving her instructions from Nicki, Gibson, an industry veteran of 25 years (the 2003 movie *Honey*, starring Jessica Alba, was based on her life), did what she always does: she got to work.

"It all started with Nicki wanting Roman to be exorcised," Gibson told globalgrind.com. "I had to also consider that Nicki was working with [director] Hype Williams on a video to accompany the performance, which was basically based on the 1973 classic *The Exorcist*. I never watched *The Exorcist* as a child because it scared the boots off of me, so I looked to the House of Borghese and the Vatican for inspiration. The rich colours and that architectural world provided so much theatrical inspiration that I could use to bring the idea to life."

Her production for the Grammys was a lightning rod for heated talk around the water cooler and beyond. Gibson, a religious woman, had publically shared her faith with colleagues and dancers she was mentoring on Diddy's show and her own two reality shows, the Ryan Seacrest-produced *The Dance Scene* on E! and *Born To Dance* on BET. Her respect for God had almost caused her to walk away from Lady Gaga long before they eventually went their separate ways in 2011. While coming up with the concept for Gaga's video for her song 'Judas', Gibson and Gaga had disagreed on how far to take the religious imagery. "It went through several changes and late-night debates because at one point, there were two completely different views and I was like, 'Listen, I don't want lightning to strike me! I believe in the gospel and I'm not going there,'" Gibson said. The two came to an agreement where both were happy with the final cut. "I do believe God inspired and worked on everyone's heart, but yes, I would have been like, 'Goodbye, I ain't doing it. No way.'"

Gibson and Nicki avoided such a situation, both agreeing to leave out of the Grammy performance the most blatant images that would cause distress and furore. "I personally chose to stay away from any religious moves," Gibson told globalgrind.com. "There were no crosses. There were no religious symbols. We made sure we were very respectable. The bishop was a symbolic figurehead. He was not intended to be viewed in a negative light, but in a position of authority."

Looking back, of course, Nicki and Gaga were not the first female pop stars to upset the Catholic Church. Artists who intend to stimulate cultural conversation or stir the pot a little typically do this by commenting on sex, religion and race through their music.

Madonna's infamous video for her 1989 hit 'Like A Prayer', directed by Mary Lambert, is perhaps the most famous inflammatory pop video ever made. We find the Boy Toy running into church for safety after witnessing a murder and Madonna dreams of sleeping with a black saint and dances in front of burning crosses. For that, she won a protest from the Vatican (a testament to Madonna's juice as an icon – no Catholic League representatives here!) as well as other religious and family groups, who targeted Pepsi, since the singer was a spokesperson for the company. Pepsi, in turn, cancelled its campaign with her, although it allowed her to keep her advance money.

While Nicki had also attracted criticism from members of the Catholic Church for her Grammy performance, the secular crowd found the stage show either wholly entertaining or a complete disaster. "At the Grammys, she gave the most shocking performance, part exorcism and part Broadway spectacle," wrote *The New York Times*. TMZ called it a "weird, exorcist performance [and] it was terrible and embarrassing".

When making an appearance on *Live! With Kelly* Nicki explained her take on the performance. "I created Martha and Roman over two years ago and I never had a format to present them to the world," she told Kelly Ripa. "Roman had been ridiculed, and torn down and pulled down. I wrote the song and envisioned it being in a monastery because Roman gets shipped away by his mother, Martha, who thinks there is something wrong with him. In fact, there is nothing wrong with him or wrong with him being different or eccentric, and that's what I wanted to show. I wanted to show how ridiculous people look when they try to change someone just because they are creative and different."

During her visit to Power 105.1's *The Breakfast Club*, when prodded to speak about the critics who flogged her Grammy performance, Nicki was far from embarrassed; in fact, the confusion was an added bonus in her eyes. "I'm glad they did not understand it," she told the hosts. "I don't want to always be understood. Even with my lyrics, I don't like it when people understand all of my lyrics. I purposely say things in a crazy way [because] I want my fans to go and dissect the lyrics. You have to talk in code sometimes and I don't want people being able to figure out my next move. But, I loved my Grammy performance. I loved the production. I loved my Oscar de la Renta dress. I loved the Versace custom-made robe flown in from Milan. It's a theatrical piece. It was my best performance ever."

But although Nicki had proved the talking point of the 54th Grammy Awards show, the rapper, having been nominated in three categories – Best New Artist, Best Rap Album (*Pink Friday*) and Best Rap Performance (on 'Moment 4 Life' with Drake) – went home empty handed. "At the end of the day everyone wants to be recognised and feel like you recognise that this is hard work. The Grammys are what you work for," Minaj told the Recording Academy weeks before her losses at the awards ceremony.

Like all recording artists, she acknowledged the significance of winning an award voted on by your peers, music execs and professionals in the industry and the benefits a Grammy win can bring to a musician's career, from a boost in CD sales to increased performance rates. However, her supposed defeat may not have been as big a shock as some suggested. During the same interview, Minaj predicted her own upset. "I really don't think I am going to win anything," she said. "But, I know eventually in my career that I will have Grammys. This year is about feeling grateful and feeling like my fans and I have come a long way. Nothing else matters but them getting to see a girl from the hood take these steps and still taking these steps."

So, Nicki's day at the Grammys is still to come, and her fame has come at somewhat of a cost to her, as she is still facing her daily critics. "When I achieved fame, I started realising that it wasn't as important as being great at what you do, or being critically acclaimed," she told *Blackbook*. But although her new status as the reigning femcee in hip-hop and a rising pop star is accompanied by an assault of criticism, she is fine with that. "Still, I never wish I wasn't famous." She is working tirelessly to redefine what it means to be a female rapper. And she knows that not everyone will "get" the type of artist she has evolved into. "I am an experimental artist," she told *The Breakfast Club*. "Everything that I do is not going to go number one or be received well. I take chances."

Nicki's risks were clearly misunderstood by those who heard her recording her debut album. Lil Wayne, she says, was supportive of her venturing from the porno phrasing expected from female rappers, but others who heard her multiple-personality flows weren't so enthusiastic. "When I started making those weird voices, a lot of people told me how wack it was," Nicki told *Blackbook*. "'What the fuck are you doing?' they'd say. 'Why do you sound like that? That doesn't sound sexy to me.' And then I started saying, 'Oh, that's not sexy to you? Good. I'm going to do it more. Maybe I don't want to be sexy to you today.'"

An individual commenting on one of the countless cover stories Nicki has amassed admits that their opinion of her has evolved at the same time as the naturally guarded rapper started peeling back the layers of her life and opening up: "I am not a fan of all her music, but I gotta admit some of the tracks she does [are] SICK. She is very talented at what she does. She is so interesting and it's hard to ignore," the reader's comment stated on complex.com. "But, the 'Barbie' movement, bubblegum sounding raps, multiple alter egos, and disrespect to [Lil'] Kim threw me off a HUGE bit. These are the things I HIGHLY disliked about her and didn't respect. But, I always appreciated her creativity, beauty, strength and ambitions. I LATER discovered her talent. She is DEFINITELY a misunderstood, love and hate type of artist. Do you girl."

Whether positive or negative, Nicki says she learned a long time ago to avoid the blogosphere. "I do not go on blogs. That's the mistake a new artist can make," she told *The Breakfast Club*. Nicki has been blog and tabloid-worthy for years, even before her album dropped. As the new girl on the block, demanding attention with her skill, beauty and eccentric dress, everything about her was fair game to either praise or pick apart. "The [blogs] will drive you crazy; I did that in the beginning and it ruined me for a minute."

In the end, Nicki knows that the majority of her critics could not handle what it takes to achieve her level of success. "There are a million people in the world, that if they got a taste of this for a month, they would trade it all," she said to MTV.

Those people also include the growing clique of female rappers who now take shots at her, despite her miraculous resuscitation of female rap. On the song 'Still I Rise' from her *Beam Me Up Scotty* mix-tape, Nicki raps about how her (hoped for) success will provide inspiration for other femcees: "Anyway, real bitches listen when I'm speaking/ Cause if Nicki win, then all of y'all gettin' meetings."

Nicki knew then that if all the hype panned out, she would be in a position to create opportunities for other women in the testosterone-dominated rap world. However, in an interview with *Vibe* magazine in the April/May 2012 issue, her attitude was slightly different. The writer asked Nicki: "Does it give you a sense of accomplishment that you opened the door a bit for women in the future?" Sounding a bit irritated, Nicki responded: "I have no idea. That's not something I want to discuss. There's really no right or wrong answer for that. I don't know. I am just doing Nicki Minaj. Anyone that gets in the business, you would have to ask them if I opened the door for them."

Speaking again on the same topic in a *Complex* magazine cover story, released shortly after, Nicki said: "In order for my theory [from 'Still I Rise'] to be proven right, I have to open doors for women. The up and coming females wanted to get in – when you guys are coming out and dissing me, and all that negativity... they saw me as a threat instead of seeing me as 'she's going to open the door for us.' I never came into what I'm doing dissing anyone. I gave everyone their props and it's unfortunate that people felt intimidated and attacked me. Then it became a ripple effect. But, now it's all love. My music is a way for me to have fun. Sometimes I'll say things and laugh. But, it's all love. I'm in a great place and I just wish everybody the best."

Beyond the critics, disbelief and especially the beefs, Nicki's focus is singular: she is focussed on establishing her empire. She is not concerned with who the best female rapper is, rather she is tackling a much bigger issue. "Why is there no female rapper turned mogul?" she asked on the MTV special *Nicki Minaj: My Time Now*. "I mean *mogul*. Having an empire that lives on beyond your rap career," she continued. Lil Wayne may have been her mentor, but Jay-Z is her muse. "I've watched what Jay-Z did and I feel that if he can do it, I can do it," she told *The Breakfast Club*.

Nicki has publicly praised Jay-Z for his superhuman triumphs in business. The Brooklyn-born rapper's empire includes the record label and management company Roc Nation, clothing line Rocawear (he sold the line for $250 million and still maintains operational control), the basketball team the New Jersey Nets (he is a part owner), the 40/40 Club and Spotted Pig restaurant in New York, and he co-owns both Translation (a marketing firm) and the popular skincare company Carol's Daughter. He's enjoyed working relationships with Microsoft (the company put up $1 million to promote his 2010 memoir, *Decoded*), Budweiser, Hewlett-Packard and Coca-Cola, and in addition to owning other companies, he has served as the CEO of Def Jam Recordings and, in return for his tenure as President Carter, he will receive full ownership rights to his recordings in 2014. And there's more: he has sold 50 million albums, raked in 14 Grammys and has had more number one albums on the *Billboard* 200 than any other artist except the Beatles.

The thought of building even a sliver of Jay-Z's enterprising muscle would likely short-circuit most people's brains, but not Nicki Minaj. In the fall of 2011, Nicki performed her triple platinum hit 'Super Bass' at the Victoria's Secret fashion show and afterwards ran into Jay-Z backstage. Of course, this was not their first time meeting – she had already outshone him on the monumental 2010 song 'Monster' – but it was still a moment of respect for Nicki. And she voiced it in her own way. "Yeah, I'm coming for you," she said to Blue Ivy's dad. "I'm coming for your spot, Mr Mogul."

And she meant every word.

Chapter 9

Giving Bitches The Business

The girl who'd once considered a career as a bus driver and had once worked as an office manager in a hole-in-the-wall room, has a new hustle that hovers above mostly everything any female rapper has achieved before her. Beside its charges of sexism and misogyny, ironically, the business of hip-hop has arguably produced more female corporate executives than any other musical genre. But, sadly, its female rappers have not experienced the same rise to the top. Those that have flown high were most likely found parachuting on the backs of the men co-signing them, and history has shown that once those relationships sour, the femcee's career follows suit. But, in order to answer Nicki's question about why there has never been a female rapper-turned-mogul, we have to go back to hip-hop's very first commercial outing.

The year 1979 in the US was a funky one – both financially and musically. Inflation was at 13.3%, gas prices were high, with supply low, and California was the first state to begin rationing gas. However, as is common to most depressive times, the party scenes around the country were thriving. And disco was the driving force. Cheryl Lynn's 'Got To Be Real' topped the charts and Michael Jackson's 'Don't Stop 'Til You Get Enough' was moving the crowds.

No other city in the world had nightlife like New York during that period. On one particular night, while partying at the popular uptown club Harlem World, former singer Sylvia Robinson, accompanied by her son Joey, was entranced by rapper Lovebug Starski, who was rhyming over the breakbeat of a popular disco song. Robinson and her husband, Joe, owned All Platinum Records, but the label was sinking under the weight of several lawsuits and severe debt. Listening to Starski and taking a quick glance across a room full of people swaying to the mix of R&B and improvised breakbeats, Robinson had an idea. She leaned over and asked her son: "Wouldn't it be great to make a rap record?" Not wasting any time, she went home to New Jersey to share her crazy idea with her husband. After the two secured some initial funding, Sugar Hill Records (taking its name from the once affluent and culturally rich Sugar Hill neighbourhood in Harlem) was born.

Sylvia had already experienced her own taste of fame when she had a hit with the sexy and erotic single 'Pillow Talk' in 1973. With its moans and subtle pants (it's considered a precursor to the late Donna Summer's more orgasmic groans on her hit 'Love To Love You Baby'), it sold two million copies and Robinson went on to have four solo albums. But, it wasn't until after she'd signed three rappers from New Jersey, christened them the Sugarhill Gang and had them rap over Chic's disco hit 'Good Times' that she would accomplish the feat that would come to define her career. The 1979 single 'Rapper's Delight' was the first ever rap song on wax, introduced the revolutionary practice of "sampling" music tracks and launched the rap genre into the public music arena.

Fast-forward 15 years. Bill Clinton was president and, although the country was experiencing an economic boom, his presidency began unravelling as allegations of sexual harassment during his governorship in Arkansas were made in a civil court. Kurt Cobain, lead singer and musician in the grunge-rock group Nirvana, had shocked the world by committing suicide with a single gunshot to the head. R&B group Boyz II Men ruled the radio with their ubiquitous ballads 'I'll Make Love To You' and 'On Bended Knee'. America was singing along with Swedish group Ace of Base's mega-hit 'The Sign' while Janet Jackson was cooing and seducing with her hit 'Anytime, Anyplace'. Hip-hop

An Early Snack: Nicki performs on *Good Morning America* in New York's Central Park in 2011. JOE STEVENS/RETNA LTD/CORBIS

Poised and coolly coiffed, Nicki attends the Carolina Herrera 2012 Spring Show at Lincoln Center in New York City. WALIK GOSHORN/RETNA LTD/CORBIS

Nicki salutes her fans during a stop on the 'I'm Still Music II' Tour at the Staples Center, in Los Angeles. STARTRAKS PHOTO/REX FEATURES

Nicki leaves the 2011 Grammy Nominations Concert Live! in Los Angeles with her hype man and business partner Safaree Samuels, in her pink Bentley. BROADIMAGE/REX FEATURES

Super Win: Nicki embraces the award for Best Hip-Hop Video for 'Super Bass' at the MTV Video Music Awards 2011 in Los Angeles, California.
EPA/PAUL BUCK/CORBIS

(L-R) DJ David Guetta and rapper Flo Rida support the tiny femcee on the set of *America's Got Talent* in Los Angeles in 2011.
SOZUFE ADELERI/RETNA LTD/CORBIS

A Heavenly Date: Nicki arrives to the 2012 Grammys with a Pope-look alike and outfitted in a crimson, custom-made Versace nun's habit.
FRANK TRAPPER/CORBIS

Look At Me! Nicki takes the attention from the models on the catwalk at the 2011 Victoria's Secret Fashion Show in New York.
BILLY FARRELL AGENCY/REX FEATURES

Naughty and nice all at once, Nicki attends the MAC Viva Glam Party at Stage 37 in New York City. LAN/CORBIS

Nicki performs with Madonna at the Bridgestone Halftime Show during the 2012 Super Bowl XLVI in Indianapolis. JOHN A. ANGELILLO/CORBIS

Nicki promotes her *Pink Friday: Roman Reloaded* at FYE in Philadelphia. SCOTT WEINER/RETNA LTD/CORBIS

Harlem Nights: Nicki and Scaff Beezy (Safaree Samuels) ham it up at the 117th Street Best Buy in uptown Manhattan.
NANCY KASZERMAN/ZUMAPRESS.COM/CORBIS

Pink Flower Bomb: Looking gorgeous, Nicki is joined by Birdman on BET's *106 & Park* during an appearance in 2012.
HARRY PLUVIOSE/RETNA LTD/CORBIS

Harajuku Goes Home: Nicki arrives at Narita International Airport kicking off her promotional tour of Japan in 2012. MASATOSHI OKAUCHI/REX FEATURES

A neon covered Nicki brightens up a rainy London in 2012.
BERETTA/SIMS/REX FEATURES

The Starship Has Landed: Nicki hits the big time with her performance of the hit song 'Starships' on America's biggest show, *American Idol*, in 2012.
PICTUREGROUP/REX FEATURES

Nicki shocks the crowd in New York's Times Square with a surprise performance for the launch of the Nokia Lumia 900 smartphone in 2012.
STARTRAKS PHOTO/REX FEATURES

produced three juggernaut artists that year: Nas, the Notorious B.I.G. and Outkast. The genre was on its way to becoming the multi-billion dollar global force and cultural catalyst it is today.

Sylvia Rhone, a Harlem native and Wharton business school graduate, had watched as hip-hop had grown from its infancy in the Bronx and by 1994, she was in the thick of it all and on top of the world.

Rhone had started out as a secretary at a fledgling music label and by the mid eighties she had risen to senior vice president and general manager of Atlantic Records. She has become a pre-eminent force in the music industry, shaping the careers of R&B and hip-hop acts such as Brandy, En Vogue, Yo-Yo, the D.O.C. and MC Lyte. "Sylvia Rhone gave me my start in this business," Lyte told Jamie Foster Brown of *Sister 2 Sister* magazine. "And because of her, I still work."

In the summer of 1994, while everyone around the country was jamming to Da Brat's 'Funkdafied', Rhone was busy becoming the CEO and chairman of Elektra Entertainment – the first woman and African-American in history to achieve such a coveted position in the music industry. In 2004, she was appointed president of Universal Motown Records, an umbrella company covering multiple labels including the Cash Money/Young Money imprints, the musical homes of Lil Wayne, Drake and Nicki Minaj. She left her post at Universal Motown in 2011, but her legacy as one of the most powerful women to have ever worked in the music industry is largely unmatched.

In 1996, Rhone signed rapper Missy Elliott to her first contract at Elektra, which included Elliott receiving her own label, The Goldmind, Inc., through which she could release her own records and sign other acts. Missy had become a true hit factory: she turned out her own chart-topping singles and others for her own artists, all under her own company roof. In regard to her quest to be the female Jay-Z of the business, Nicki Minaj said to Power 105.1: "I came into the game writing my own rhymes and saying this is who I am. Because I'm a girl, does not make me unqualified." Missy Elliott shared the same philosophy and became the most successful solo female rapper up to that point, not only selling millions of records, but making millions through clever corporate moves.

The year 1998 saw the ladies ruling the charts. Brandy and Monica burned through the entire summer at the number one spot on *Billboard*'s Hot 100 with their girl-fight groove 'The Boy Is Mine' and the year was also hot for Missy Elliott. Still flying high off the success of her debut solo album, *Supa Dupa Fly*, she had become a go-to/one-stop-shop for artists vying for platinum records.

Madison Avenue took notice. Coca-Cola, one of the most recognisable, profitable and powerful brands in the world, reached out to Elliott to be a spokesperson for Sprite, and that year Elliott appeared in a commercial with basketball stars Kobe Bryant and Tim Duncan. Impressed with Elliott, the corporate juggernaut tapped her up again five years later to not only represent one of its products, but to launch its newest brand, Vanilla Coke. Also in 2003, Missy and Madonna hooked up for a Gap television ad and an accompanying remix/mashup of Madonna's songs 'Into The Groove' and 'Hollywood'. Missy relished the opportunity to work with Madonna, a woman she had looked up to since she was a kid in Virginia. "Madonna is basically the icon to everybody in this business," Missy said on her reality show *The Road To Stardom*, "I have learned so much from her."

The following year Missy was chosen by MAC to represent its MAC Viva Glam V lipstick, with 100 per cent of the proceeds going to the MAC AIDS fund (a cause also close to Madonna's heart).

That same year, Missy made history while also strengthening her corporate clout. After being a long-time fan of Adidas and with the company's historic connection to hip-hop, Elliott was chosen by the company to start her own line, entitled Respect M.E. With this, Elliott became the only woman and second artist in hip-hop to have a line with the shoe company (Run-D.M.C. being the first). "You have to be different," Elliott stated during a video for Adidas Originals, which feature individuals almost peerless in their respective trades. "[And] you have to be a person that takes risks."

Because of her own willingness to take chances, other major brands jumped on board, including Jeep Commander, Doritos and *another* soft drink: Diet Pepsi. Through fragrance giant Parlux, she now retails her own perfume, known simply as "Queen". With endorsements, publishing, songwriting royalties and her film and television credits, Elliott has reportedly amassed a fortune of $225 million.

If Nicki is looking towards a maven as mogul for inspiration, Missy Elliot is definitely the "multi-slashed" blueprint. So far, she has proven to be the most successful female rapper in history. However, Nicki can also look to Dana Elaine Owens, better known around the globe as Queen Latifah.

Born in Newark, New Jersey, Latifah launched her music career as a teenager with anthemic and funky raps in the late Eighties and early Nineties. Her first album, 1989's *All Hail The Queen*, established her as one of the most respected female rappers of all time. Barely into her career, at 20 years old, she co-founded Flavor Unit, a management and production company, with childhood friend Shakim Compere. Together, over the past two decades they have managed top-tier talent such as Academy Award-nominee Terrence Howard and Grammy award-winning rapper and actress Eve. Compere says he and Latifah's journey has been a long one and that rappers today are spoiled. "A lot of these rappers don't know how good they have it," he said to *The New York Times*. "We would play Madison Square Garden and then do a rodeo. There were these two brothers in North Carolina, gangsters, who had us playing in a softball field." He and Latifah transformed their far-ranging opportunities into a career neither one of them could have fathomed as children. "[I realised] how important life is, how short time is, how important it is to follow your dreams and your goals," Latifah told beliefnet.com. "[Your dreams] are part of who you are and you take away from it by not doing it."

Well, she certainly followed her own advice. She branched off from music into film; and now has over 35 films to her credit (starring alongside superstars like Denzel Washington, Angelina Jolie and Steve Martin), including the Rob Marshall-directed musical *Chicago*, for which she garnered an Academy Award nomination. She also led the cast in the *Barbershop* franchise spin-off *Beauty Shop* (which was Flavor Unit produced), for a reported $10 million pay cheque. She became a television star as the anchor cast member of the Fox network comedy *Living Single*, which depicted five friends living and loving in New York

City. The show, along with *Martin* and *In Living Color*, helped establish the then fledging Fox network as a major player in Hollywood and the show also served as a framework for what would make the sitcom *Friends* a runaway success on NBC. Latifah also helmed her own syndicated talk show, *The Queen Latifah Show*, for three seasons. As if that were not enough for a life achievement award, through Flavor Unit she also produced small-screen movies such as 2007's *Life Support* (in which she starred and won a Golden Globe for her performance) and VH-1's hit scripted series *Single Ladies*. For the silver screen, she and Compere also produced *Just Wright* (a romantic comedy starring rapper Common and Latifah) and *The Cookout*.

Latifah says that because she never saw herself as the absolute best in any arena, including rapping, she thought it wise to diversify her career. "[I do] whatever I feel in my heart," she said to beliefnet.com, "whenever I feel I can. I never pictured myself as just a rapper, I always wanted to act and do whatever else I could do." This was an uncannily similar mandate to Nicki Minaj's reflections on the eve of the release of *Pink Friday*, when she told this author: "[I cannot] be suffocated by the hip-hop culture. I am somewhere in the grey area. Hip-hop and me, we have to make a compromise. Hip-hop is going to have to accept me for who I am." Just as Latifah, Nicki knew early on that she was more than a rapper and, most importantly, she was going to *be* more than a rapper. She told beliefnet.com: "I always felt like I could do a lot of different things. So when it came to making music, I love making music, but I didn't feel like I was the best out there. I felt like [unless] I could call myself the best rapper on the planet, then there was no way I was going to put all my eggs in one basket. I just wasn't raised like that. That's my momma saying, 'Don't put all your eggs in one basket at one time.' I felt there were males and females that might be better than me, and so I always kept my eyes open and my mind open for some other opportunity and creating another opportunity. So, that's what we always did. I think other people had the opportunity to do that; it's just that some people need someone else to go to first and some people are the ones to take a chance and go for it. I'm kind of the one to go for it, I'm that type."

One of the largest eggs in Latifah's basket is her contract with cosmetic juggernaut Cover Girl, the make-up line she has represented since 2001. Not only does she have an exclusive deal with the main brand, she has also launched the Queen Collection offshoot, which was her idea and is designed to help women of colour find the right shade of make-up for their skin tone. As with all of her business ventures, Latifah was hands on and was involved with the majority of the decision-making steps. "I learned early," she told *The New York Times*, "that I had to work harder than the white kids and harder than the boys." All of her hard work has led to her becoming one of the few female hip-hop moguls, amassing a reported fortune of over $50 million.

Growing up, Nicki Minaj also witnessed another female singer using her music career as a launchpad to becoming a multi-million dollar brand: Jennifer Lopez. Although not a hip-hop artist, Lopez's career in music is closely related to the culture: she was a dancer on the hip-hop drenched comedy sketch show *In Living Color*, she infamously dated Diddy and many of her songs and remixes feature hip-hop beats and rappers as guest artists. After the release of her debut album, 1999's *On The 6*, Jennifer Lopez was suddenly everywhere. And with the release of her second album, 2001's *J.Lo*, which topped the US chart, she made history due to having the number one movie (*The Wedding Planner*) in the same week. Very soon thereafter, the very stylish singer/actress also added "perfumer" to her resumé, and her bestselling fragrances have led to her often being credited with resuscitating the celebrity fragrance industry.

J.Lo, as she became known, also turned her hand to fashion designing, releasing her line J.Lo by Jennifer Lopez and, in 2012, she went on to create male and female clothing lines along with ex-husband Marc Anthony for Kohl's department stores. She is now a huge TV star, joining Steven Tyler of rock behemoth Aerosmith and world-famous record producer Randy Jackson as one of the judges on the television franchise *American Idol*.

The week before the release of *Roman Reloaded*, Nicki performed her dance song 'Starships' on the show with an over-the-top spectacle based in her island roots and ready-made for Carnival. After her performance, she joked with Jennifer Lopez about coming back to the show as a guest judge, "J.Lo, can you scoot over?" Without missing a beat, J.Lo shot back, "I don't know if there is enough room up for *both* of *us*, baby," referring to both stars' much discussed booties. It was a staggering moment in time for Nicki: she was performing the new single (already in the *Billboard* Hot 100 Top 10) on the number one show in America and enjoying playful banter with a mega-star, also from New York, whose ambition and success had surely inspired her as an artist. It was truly a full-circle moment for the former Queens girl.

And it wasn't long before she was challenging those women who had reached the upper branches of the tree.

In 2011, Nicki Minaj became the first female to make *Forbes* magazine's closely watched annual "Hip-Hop Cash Kings List". Coming in at number 15 – ahead of 50 Cent, Rick Ross and Swizz Beatz – the magazine reports that she made roughly $6.5 million in that year. Elsewhere, there are reports that her overall worth is an estimated $14 million. Nicki's intentions are clear. With the same young and optimistic guise of Madonna declaring in 1983 to Dick Clark on *American Bandstand* that she "wants to rule the world", Nicki proclaimed that she wanted to rise to hip-hop's biggest star, Jay-Z's, level. Her second album, *Pink Friday: Roman Reloaded*, even featured an entire song devoted to her new obsession. The title 'In The HOV Lane' is a pun of sorts: in one sense the rapper, boasting of her accomplishments, races past her competition, her colourful hair blowing in the wind, in the high-occupancy vehicle (HOV) lane, in which you can speed past cars stuck in traffic in the other lanes. But it's also a way to compare herself to Jay (one of his many autonyms is Jay-Hova, with HOV being an abbreviated version).

The song is essentially an ode to where she is in her life at this point; a one-sided interview in which Nicki allows the audience a glimpse into her progressively over-the-top existence. "Big ass chain/I'm heavy... And it didn't cost me a penny/They pay me to rock it," she raps at the onset of the song, bragging about the big piece of jewellery around her neck that was given to her because the company profits from matching her celebrity with its product. Then, she heads straight into her key appearances in 2012 that were amazing fêtes: "Super Bowl, Grammys/

Where the hell is the jammy?/All these bitches my sons/I'mma get em' a nanny/Argentina for Pepsi/Orlando All Star," in reference to her many achievements up to that point, including a 2012 performance at an NBA All-Star game.

Nicki also pays lip service to her multi-million dollar deal with Pepsi to peddle a new natural soda brand called "Pop". The commercial, starring Nicki, was filmed in Argentina and the clip was the first step in introducing her as the spokesperson for the new brand. "She will be the face of the brand," said the deal's broker, Derek Jackson of the GLU Agency, to *Forbes*. (Incidentally, Pepsi's last foray with a rapper did not fare so well. The deal with rapper Ludacris in 2002 failed miserably after Fox News pundit Bill O'Reilly accused Pepsi of being "immoral" for hiring a rapper who glorified intoxication, selling drugs and the degradation of women. The TV host called Ludacris a "rap thug" and the soft drinks company dropped him. Hip-hop impresario Russell Simmons protested the firing, which ultimately led to Pepsi paying out $3 million to Ludacris' foundation, which helps middle and high school students pursue careers in the arts.)

In the same vein as Queen Latifah, Nicki looked to put her eggs in several different baskets from the moment she was able to. "I never thought about music as just being the end-all, be-all. I always looked at it like a business, something that I could create an empire out of," Nicki told *Allure* magazine.

During several appearances in the fall of 2011, Nicki was snapped wearing playful, semi-gaudy jewellery shaped as food. The pieces she wore caused quite a stir: there was the purple pretzel at designer Betsey Johnson's show, the ice cream cone necklace at the VMAs, and the pink chicken-wing necklace she wore to perform on *Good Morning America*, to designer Prabal Gurung's show and to the iHeartRadio Music Festival. Some thought that, with the wing piece, Nicki was attempting to make a socio-economic statement (in the US, there is a pervading stereotype that African-Americans love fried chicken), while others simply saw the loud jewellery as part of her Willy Wonka style. In fact, she had signed a deal to represent Onch Movement, the makers behind the culinary chic pieces.

When Nicki appeared at an event hosted by New York DJ Angie Martinez in November 2010, an audience member asked the head Barbie whether toymaker Mattel was planning on making a Barbie doll in her likeness. Nicki laughed before saying: "You know [Mattel] will never reach out to me. They are going to hear that first mix-tape and say, "Yeah... um... we'll call you guys back." Again, Nicki felt conflict over her former career as "Underground Nicki", concerned that her earlier decisions would prevent her from taking on certain opportunities. The song 'Dear Old Nicki' from *Pink Friday* best addressed that inner conflict, and attempted to explain the changes she made in her career.

Fortunately for Nicki, the words, actions and work she now finds regrettable have not stood in her way. In fact, Mattel, realising the growing power of Brand Nicki Minaj, did contact her and in December 2011, the company issued a one-of-a-kind Nicki Minaj Barbie, which it made available for auction on charitybuzz.com. "Barbie is obviously a pop culture icon. She's been in the spotlight for over 50 years, and strikes that chord with girls of all ages in terms of being representative of the times," said Stefani Yocky, a spokeswoman for Barbie. "And Nicki is a big part of pop culture and also huge within the fashion industry, as well as a big Barbie fan. It's really exciting for us that she's been so generous to allow us to create this one-of-a-kind doll to support such an important cause."

Nicki was shocked. "I never thought Mattel would even pay attention to me," she told *Billboard*. "For me this is a very major moment, because it just shows that you can come from nothing and still be a force in the main world, a businesswoman, and hopefully a mogul one day. It shows that my Barbz are special, and everyone loves them as much as I love them, so I want to thank them most importantly." The bidding for the hip-hop Barbie began at $1,000, eventually rising to $15,000, with all proceeds benefiting Project Angel Food, a charity that helps men, women and children battling with HIV/AIDS.

Beyond the Barbie coup, one of Nicki's first endorsement deals was with the popular nail polish brand OPI Nail Lacquer. In January 2012, six limited edition colours – from candyland brights to downtown metallics – were released, each of their names referencing a song from

Pink Friday, including Metallic 4 Life, Fly, Save Me, Did It On 'Em and Super Bass Shatter. "Now you can have Nicki Minaj at your fingertips, literally," she said via her website, mypinkfriday.com, "I [have] teamed up with OPI bringing lots of cute & fun colours for the Barbz mittens." OPI is regarded as a global leader in nail care and the company is beloved for its bold and forward use of colour and design, which meant Nicki was a seamless fit. "Nicki has taken the hip-hop world by storm, but her music is only part of the equation," said Suzi Weiss-Fischmann, OPI's executive vice president and artistic director. "She's also become a fashion inspiration, noted for her daring costumes and hair colour both on and off the stage. [Plus] I have a 16-year-old daughter who's a huge Nicki Minaj fan, and that tells me that she has lots of appeal beyond her core base."

Nicki was also chosen to represent another brand that is synonymous with being bold and courageous: MAC Viva Glam, which has collaborated with many high-profile celebrities, including, of course, female rappers Missy Elliott, Lil' Kim and Eve, and singers Lady Gaga, Cyndi Lauper, Boy George, Mary J. Blige and Fergie of the Black Eyed Peas, among others. Nicki was asked to represent a lipstick alongside pop superstar Ricky Martin, who was selected as the face of MAC's first unisex lip conditioner. Both were chosen because of their links to the company's HIV/AIDS campaigning: while Martin, although born in Puerto Rico, is the perfect representative for Latin America, where, since 2009, more than two million people are living with the virus, the MAC AIDS Fund is also dedicated to helping to eradicate HIV/AIDS in Nicki's native Caribbean (which is the second most-affected region in the world for those between the ages of 15 and 24 suffering with the disease).

MAC's executive team also believed that Nicki's pop culture phenom status, coupled with her extensive reach among young women around the world, would make her a perfect choice for the campaign's effort to increase education and spark change. "[Nicki's] become one of the leading voices for young people and really has captured the imagination of the day," said John Dempsey, group president of Estée Lauder Companies, in a public statement. "We also believe she can sell the lipstick. I'm sure of it because we had a little experiment. When Nicki came to us before she launched her first album, *Pink Friday*, she was a big fan of a pink shade of our lipstick, and we actually created a variant of the shade for her album launch, which we put online only. We thought we would sell 2,500 pieces over four Fridays. We sold 40,000. Before she really broke through to the general public online... through her communication to her Barbz, she really made an impact. She was the most well loved online success the company has ever had. If you watched the Grammys, she wore the Viva Glam lipstick during her performance. I think she definitely made a statement (at the Grammys). It got people's attention, and that's what MAC's all about."

Growing up in New York City, Nicki would walk the streets of Manhattan and stand amazed at the vibrant and ultra-cool Viva Glam billboards, with their array of stars from music and screen, and she hoped she would also be involved one day. Her day came. "When I was chosen by MAC to be the next Viva Glam spokesperson, I wanted to hug everyone who worked at the company for giving me the opportunity. I have always wanted to be a Viva Glam girl," she said on the set of the shoot, helmed by famed photographer Dave LaChapelle. Nicki admitted that her initial excitement at being asked to join the project was down to the "fabulous factor" of it all, but it quickly developed into a personal passion after she met with the MAC team. "I did not know that there was a bigger story at first and that every cent goes to the MAC AIDS Fund, helping men, women, and children all over the world [fight] HIV/AIDS," she said on *Live! With Kelly*. "It's incredible to be a part of something so intense and major and helpful to the community."

The rapper also learned that the disease hit much closer to home. "AIDS is the biggest killer of black women between the ages of 18-30. I don't want people to think that this is a gay disease; this is something killing everyone, no matter your preference, religion or race," she said to Robin Roberts, host of *Good Morning America*. "I had an uncle that passed away from AIDS. He was living in Trinidad. It's duly important for me. It's my family and in addition that's my country. When MAC reached out to me we spoke a lot about us going to the Caribbean and raising awareness there. It's important that people on the islands know that it is not something that should only be addressed in America. This is something that everyone has to get on top of. I have such a young fanbase. I want them to start protecting themselves now. I want them to abstain first of all, that's the best decision... I love them so much and I don't want them to ruin their lives."

Nicki's affiliation with such iconic brands, according to reports, may also stem from the fact that she is known to contribute some of her own money to the budget of her videos to attain the very best quality. By working with huge brands such as MAC, they can help to cover the costs of making videos and producing concerts. And Dempsey, ecstatic over working with Nicki, is looking to further their relationship. "We'll work with her in many different ways," he told *Billboard*. "Pop stars are sort of what the movie stars were before, in the golden era of Hollywood. They're doing the videos people are talking about, they're the people that everybody's watching."

Just as Jennifer Lopez had tremendous success with her line of fragrances – with Britney Spears, Beyoncé, Jessica Simpson, Rihanna and Katy Perry since joining her club – Nicki is also trying her hand in the world of perfume. Partnering with Give Back Brands (whose first fragrance licensing agreement with teen heart-throb Justin Bieber's scent for ladies, called "Someday", proved to be the most successful female fragrance launch of 2011), Nicki is scheduled to debut her scent in autumn 2012. Just as in all other areas in her career, Nicki will have creative input in every aspect of the perfume, from development to advertising.

"I am so excited about my fragrance debut, and am proud to partner with Give Back Brands for such a personal project," said Nicki in an issued statement. "I have always been a huge fan of great fragrances; this is yet another extension of my creative expression and I can't wait to share it with the world. I designed this scent and bottle with my Barbz in mind; I know they will love it!"

The company is similarly excited to join forces with brand Nicki. "Nicki Minaj has proven relevance as an artist, as well as a captivating talent in the facets of beauty, style and fashion. Her appeal is rising at an incredible rate; her unique creative expression lends her brand name to a broad range of possibilities without boundaries. We are extremely proud to partner with Nicki Minaj on this initiative," said its executive vice president of Global Marketing, Noreen Dodge. The co-founder of the company, Robert Hollander, is certain her release will be as successful as Bieber's. "[We] achieved remarkable success with Justin Bieber's fragrance 'Someday'. And now we are thrilled to collaborate with Nicki on her first scent. We anticipate her signature fragrance will generate tremendous appeal and excitement among consumers and retailers. Nicki adds another unique dimension to our portfolio strategy of powerful celebrity brands," he said.

Nicki's endorsement track continues to expand. And taking another note from the Missy Elliott handbook, the hip-pop star inked an endorsement deal with sneaker behemoth Adidas. In April 2012, she shot parts of a campaign modelling pieces from the Jeremy Scott X Adidas 2012 autumn/winter line. Scott, an avant-garde fashion world darling, is a personal favourite of stylish celebs, including Kanye West, Rihanna, Madonna, Gwen Stefani and Lady Gaga. *The Fader* praised his previous collections for Adidas: "It's a glittery-gold selection of irresistibly cut (wearable) harem pants, sequins, sporty fringed tanks and coveted winged high-tops, while his next installment abandoned that black-gold-and-silver, Studio 54 palette for an explosion of colours and elongation of the tribal street wear trend pioneered by M.I.A. and Cassette Playa." It suited Nicki down to the ground.

In addition to the jewellery, cosmetics, soda and fashion deals Nicki has scored, she has added big-screen actress to her growing list of accomplishments. In 2011 the former drama student signed a deal to join the cast of the animated flick *Ice Age 4: Continental Drift*. "My agency sent me out on an audition for some people who wanted to hear me," Nicki told MTV. "They knew I liked animation, they knew I liked to do voices, and so they said they were doing that so I thought, 'This is amazing.'" Reportedly, Nicki was rejected for the original role she auditioned for, but she impressed the producers so much they had a role written specifically for her. Nicki joins an all-star cast that includes comedienne and talk show host Joy Behar, actor and comedian J.B.

Smoove, Queen Latifah, Jennifer Lopez, Wanda Sykes and the rapper Drake.

In less than five years, Nicki Minaj has catapulted herself from a Queens girl selling her own mix-tapes from her used white BMW, a car that she bought with money from odd jobs and proudly navigated around the city while chasing her dream, to being well on the way to finally grasping it. Is Nicki finally in the mogul HOV lane with Jay-Z himself? She summed it up best on her verse on Madonna's 'I Don't Give A': "Yo, I ain't a business woman, I'm a business, woman! And I'm known for giving bitches the business, woman."

Chapter 10

When In Rome

"I know what people need," a confident Nicki Minaj told MTV while speaking of her highly anticipated second album, *Pink Friday: Roman Reloaded*. "It's gonna be an important album for hip-hop culture and pop culture." Sounding more hopeful than arrogant, the number one female rapper in the world believed that her album had everything both her hip-hop and pop fans were thirsting for. After all, it had been a little over a year since Nicki had released her first album, *Pink Friday*, and she knew that her Barbz and Ken Barbz needed nourishment.

Roman Reloaded was originally set for a Valentine's Day 2012 release. Nicki's fans *and* critics were waiting to see what the most electrifying figure in hip-hop in over a decade had cooked up. Nicki released the track 'Roman In Moscow' in December 2011 and the blogs were abuzz that the edgier Nicki had finally returned. Her Indian summer smash 'Super Bass' had been high on cutesy Harajuku Barbie and low on the octane-fuelled antics of Roman Zolanski, and the new single brought the lunatic back: "I'm big Willie, no bike gear/I told you bitches last year, I'm a rap bitch nightmare/That's why I call you Buzz Lightyear/'Cause by the time you start buzzin' bitch, you gonna have white hair," Roman warned, his forceful delivery reminiscent of Nicki's landmark track 'Roman's Revenge' with Eminem. In defence mode, she raps in full battle posture, as if mindful of the criticism directed at her that she had "gone pop".

The process involved in making the song provides a little insight into the mind of Minaj, and serves as proof that when she told this author that she views herself as a perfectionist, she was hardly blowing smoke. The track's producer, StreetRunner, told MTV that getting the song right for the fickle rapper was hard work. "Once we heard from Nicki's camp that they were really interested, we had to go back in on it and tailor it a little more for her. It took a good eight tries to get it into pocket, but once we got it, we knew it." Nicki's lyrics once again display her hardcore, but humorous side, and through only two verses, with no hook, she lets the victim of her venom know that that is all she needs to complete her mission: "Yeah ain't no motherfuckin' prayers bitch, ain't no motherfuckin' hook, ain't no motherfuckin' third motherfuckin' verse/Roman's back, bitch/I fucked up your life last year this time, remember dat?"

In an interview with MTV, she hinted at the fact that the song would not play a significant role in the album. "'Roman In Moscow' is like a teaser to *Roman Reloaded*. It's like a trailer to the movie, it's like setting the stage and I just wanted to touch the surface. It's the wackest thing on *Pink Friday: Roman Reloaded*." By saying that the track was the worst piece on the album, was Nicki in fact stating that it was the worst of the best?

Unfortunately for StreetRunner, who was nominated for a Grammy for his work on Lil Wayne's *Tha Carter IV*, this didn't prove to be the case, and Nicki meant exactly what she said. The song, although released on iTunes, eventually failed to make the final cut for the album. Nicki tweeted to her fans: "I didn't like [it] sorry Barbz." But later in an interview with *The Breakfast Club* she said: "I feel bad. I did not know my fans cared about that stupid song."

However, the second release from the album literally was stupid, at least in title. 'Stupid Hoe' hit the airwaves and caused a stir because not only was Nicki verbally assaulting someone again, but the video features the rapper dancing suggestively, repeating 'You a stupid hoe' at a machine-gun-fire pace. The lyrical content is puerile, but that is the intention: it's a throwback to the silly, typically uncultivated raps of yester-year, such as the U.T.F.O.-led Roxanne franchise of the eighties, which spawned the battles between the Real Roxanne and Roxanne Shanté. But juxtaposed with the sophistication of Hype Williams' frenetic and minimal direction, the video is a pop culture feast.

The opening scene with Nicki double-dutching is perfect; Nicki's impish words are intentionally child-like. Directed at her "haters" and, at one point, Lil' Kim, she's implying how silly it is for "them" to think they could even touch her, and even sillier of her to address it, but since she is, she then proceeds to present some of the female artists that she *doesn't* think are "silly hoes" and whose work she admires. She achieves this by recreating tableaus from some of their most recognisable works.

In the opening scenes of the video, Nicki pulls her leg to the back of her head in homage to Grace Jones' 1985 *Island Life* album cover. The image was famously crafted by French photographer Jean-Paul Goude using his cut and paint technique and originally appeared in *New York* magazine in 1978. Dressed in leopard print and writhing around in a cage, Nicki then goes on to reference Shakira's video for her 2009 track 'She Wolf', highlighting the Latin songstress' powerful sexuality. But when Williams' camera zooms impossibly close to Nicki's face, she suddenly has gigantic eyelashes, her heavily made-up face resembling that of Lil' Kim, and she is now holding on to the bars as if she were imprisoned. That she is wearing leopard print (as Kim does in her infamous *Hard Core* album promo poster) only increases the suspicion that the song is directed at the former Queen.

Mike Barthel, of *The Village Voice*, believes Nicki has a talent for conveying an entire conversation without uttering many words. "As good a lyricist as Nicki is, she's also frighteningly good at communicating through tone, through timbre, through visuals, and through style. Like a great Jimmy Page guitar solo, even if there aren't words, you get the point," he wrote. And we definitely got the point when it came to 'Stupid Hoe'.

Furthering the "visual conversation" in the video, Nicki constructs distorted – yet routinely gorgeous – facial expressions, so much so that it has become a sport for her. However, in straight contradiction, she despises the camera while also loving the power she channels through it. "I hate cameras," she told *Complex*. "And I hate camera phones. The camera's my worst enemy and my best friend. It's the way I convey my emotions to the world without saying a word, so I use it."

Nicki does manage to get in several direct shots at Kim, saying that Kim made the wrong decision in attacking her and, with slight conceit, adding that, had she reached out to her, Nicki could have resurrected the rap legend's career: "Bitch talkin' she the queen when she looking like a lab rat... Stupid hoe should have befriended me/Then she could have probably came back," she taunts.

Later in the video, Nicki makes a return to those artists who have inspired her. In another scene, she appears as an outrageously doe-eyed child, referencing Lady Gaga's signature hit 'Bad Romance' from her 2009 album *The Fame Monster* (in the video for the track, Gaga appears with digitally enlarged eyes in one scene), as well as the popular Bratz Dolls, with their almost alien-like, different-coloured eyes. And in a triple play, the child may be one of Nicki's other alter egos: "Loriee Zolanski", Roman's little sister. She is chanting some un-childlike words in this song, because, according to Nicki, Roman is teaching her some bad words.

Producer Williams also gives a quick nod to his own catalogue of work by referencing Beyoncé's 'Check On It', the explosively pink affair of a video that he directed back in 2005. Finally, Nicki appearing on an oversized chair is a nod to British singer Jessie J's video for her anti-materialism anthem, 'Price Tag'. Nicki signs off at the conclusion of the video with "I am the female Weezy," meaning she is the feminine incarnation of Lil Wayne (Weezy is his alter ego).

Accustomed to breaking records already, Nicki managed it once again with the 'Stupid Hoe' video. It garnered the most views in a 24-hour period in music video website VEVO's history, with 4.8 million views. It was also banned by BET. However, the network did not specify why. Curiously, Nicki's friend and sometime collaborator Rihanna had also come under fire from the same network for depicting rape and murder in the video for her 2011 single 'Man Down' from the 2010 album *Loud*. In the clip, the Bajan singer is sexually assaulted and kills her assailant. But curiously, instead of banning Rihanna's more explicit video, the network decided to host a domestic violence forum on its flagship programme *106 & Park*. Despite the ban, Nicki refused to censor her video, tweeting to her millions of fans: "Can't premiere on a network because it's important that my art is not tampered with, or compromised prior to you viewing it for the 1st time."

As more teasers for the album were released, they confused some and irritated others. Idolater.com wrote: "Minaj's titular alter ego gets his due on foul-mouthed 'Roman In Moscow', which gives us everything we could possibly want from the female Weezy and more." On the other hand, barkandbite.com found the Lil' Kim diss unnecessary: "There's no real beef behind it. When 'Roman's Revenge' came out, tongues were wagging because everyone knew that Nicki was lobbing grenades at Lil' Kim. But Nicki's been dragging Lil' Kim in nearly every verse since then. She even put the chick on blast on a Britney Spears record. At this point, making fun of Kim for having a stalled career is like making fun of Michael Jackson for being white. Time to find a new horse to beat."

Writer and blogger Thembi Ford compared watching the 'Stupid Hoe' video to the torture practice of water boarding: "…It is just straight up confusing and makes me think that she may have jumped her own shark. Not only does the song itself sound like a more-vulgar version of her Big Sean collaboration 'Dance (A$$)' – and I mean just like it – but watching the video kind of feels like torture – I mean the *Clockwork Orange*, Guantanamo Bay kind."

But across the pond in the UK, 'Stupid Hoe' jumped 74 spots in its second week of release, despite it being only a promo single. Amid these mixed reactions to the previews of *Roman Reloaded*, Nicki announced that the album was being pushed back from its original release date of Valentine's Day 2012 to April 3. The Head Barbie quickly issued a calming tweet to all of the vexed Barbz and Ken Barbz telling them not to worry and that she had plenty of surprises in store for them.

And she kept her promise.

The year 2011 had been a blockbuster year for Nicki and she continued this momentum into the following year, kicking off 2012 with a torrent of music and appearances. First, she performed on the quintessential New Year's Eve show, *Dick Clark's New Years Rockin' Eve*, delivering her hits 'Super Bass', 'Turn Me On' (her double platinum single with David Guetta) and 'Roman Reloaded'.

And by the beginning of February, the Minaj machine was in full swing. In addition to gracing the covers of magazines, including *Vibe*, *Wonderland*, *Paper* and *New York*, she performed as reported with Madonna and M.I.A. at the Super Bowl. She told Ryan Seacrest how elated she was over the show. "This performance was it and this is the first performance that I'm proud of in my entire career," she said. A week later she debuted the single 'Roman Holiday' during her now infamous set at the Grammys (she told Seacrest that it was the "most comfortable" she had ever been onstage). The following week she performed at the NBA All-Star game, where she sang 'Turn Me On' and the inspirational hit 'Moment 4 Life'. She then appeared in the March *Vogue* issue (as an *Avatar*-like Marilyn Monroe) and during the month of March she and partner Safaree Samuels jetted to Japan, where they received remarkable love from the original Harajuku girls and her multitude of fans in the Far East country.

Her Japanese tour not only gave her fans there an up-close-and-personal look at their favourite rap star, but it also gave her American audience some insight into her relationship with Samuels. Talking about the trip on Power 105.1, she peeled back the layers a bit and revealed more about the role he plays in her life.

"Even when I was in Tokyo, they were like, 'Who is SB?' People are intrigued," Nicki said of her relationship with Samuels. "He has a great ear for hood beats and sometimes I am off in 'La La Land' and just want to listen to my dance records, he's like, 'You gotta do this [as well]'. He knows lyrically what I am capable of. He tells me the truth. Sometimes he tells me his truth and it's not the world's truth. He said he hated 'Super Bass'. But, you can see why he hates 'Super Bass', he's a coon," she jested, about his tendency to act foolish at times when he dances and makes jokes. She explains that in order for her to ensure that all of her varied tastes are catered for, she needs Samuels to assist her in doing so. "I always have good cop/bad cop on my shoulder," Nicki continued.

"It keeps me to the point where I can do an album like *Roman Reloaded* and put on the rap stuff and the dance stuff and my girly records. That's the role he plays."

On the day of the release of the album, Nicki visited *106 & Park* and backstage Safaree, who served as the co-executive producer of *Roman Reloaded* as well as the A&R coordinator, spoke of how outrageously supportive Nicki's fans are. His words also gave a little insight into what he thinks about the huge variation in the fans Nicki draws in: "Today we pulled up and saw a dude with a pink wig on and a cheetah bodysuit," he told BET.com. "It's support! He's supporting the brand all day. Whether you're a dude, bisexual or straight, it's all love."

The anticipation for the album was high and, like most releases of its type, it was leaked a week before the original date. The blogosphere went into overdrive and began to review the music, with a mix of the positive and negative.

A few days after the official release of *Roman Reloaded*, Nicki shocked thousands of fans and unknowing New Yorkers by turning up as the surprise guest for the launch of the Nokia Lumia 900 smartphone in the middle of Times Square, the virtual crossroads of the world. The experience was overwhelming for her. She had admitted to the *Today* show's Matt Lauer that right before coming onstage at the Super Bowl, her knees were buckling because she kept thinking that 100 million people were watching. But performing a remix of 'Starships' in the heart of New York was unbelievable. She felt like she was rapping, singing and dancing in the middle of the world. Later she tweeted, "#alltimemoment4life".

Another unforgettable moment would come in the following week, when Nicki happily learned that *Roman Reloaded* had sold 253,000 copies in the first week, debuting at number one. Among her onslaught of achievements, she could now add a *Billboard* Top 200 charts number one album to them.

And she was proud of the album. "It's a better album," Nicki told Lauer, comparing it to her first release, *Pink Friday*. She said the album is constructed better and that "there are more songs". Cleverly, unlike many newer artists, Nicki had involved herself in all aspects of the process of delivering an album, even those processes that fall outside the remit of an artist, but ultimately affect the project. "She wanted to learn about stuff that normal artists don't – small details about shipping, the process of making a CD, the legal side, sample clearances," Joshua Berkman, Cash Money Records A&R, told *Vibe*. "I've never run into that with any other artist. This album is very structured because of that." Armed with this breadth of knowledge, Nicki insisted that she wanted 22 songs on the CD in order to feed her fans more, despite the extra money coming out of her pockets.

"Most albums are not giving [that many] songs. It could have been a double disc, but that would have been more money [for the fans to pay]. No [artist] is giving you 22 songs any more because we lose millions of dollars when we put over 15 songs on an album," Nicki told New York radio personality Angela Yee. "Every time you go over your cap, the label does not pay producer royalties on those songs. So, you gotta pay it out of your own pocket. But, artists don't count that money or live off of it. I will lose $5 million from putting all of those songs on there but I want my fans to feel like they [have enough] to hold off for another year."

This type of sacrifice was the likely catalyst for Nicki's widely reported Twitter meltdown a week after the album release. Nicki had amassed 11 million Twitter followers and on an early Sunday afternoon in April, it all began to unravel. Nicki's fans' devotion to their Head Barb moves beyond fanatical, many of them creating their own fan sites and Twitter accounts with the main goal of promoting their Trinidadian-American idol. For Nicki, it's a win/win – she receives 24/7 love and adulation and free publicity. But, her music is not free. On that fateful day she complained to one of those sites, NickiDaily.com, for posting music from *Roman Reloaded* without permission. Nicki was upset and there were reports that she went all *Mean Girls* on the Barbz involved, blocking NickiDaily.com from her Twitter feed and allegedly trying to turn the other Barbz against the site. After threatening to leave altogether after reading the comments that continued to stream in, Nicki suddenly tweeted: "Like seriously, it's but so much a person can take. Good effing bye... And that's exactly why I'm paying the barbz DUST right now!

182

And deleting my twitter. SMDH – don't cry 4 me Argentina." Along with deleting her Twitter account, Nicki's fan site then shuttered its daily operations with the exception of having the song 'Dear Old Nicki' on repeat on the homepage. During this time, Nicki's former mentor, Fendi, surfaced with his opinion about the Minaj Twittergate; he feels the deletion of her account is simply a reflection of who she has shown herself to be in the past. "Nicki is good at deleting," he told Doggie Diamonds during an interview to promote his latest *Come Up* DVD, which was the springboard for Nicki's career at Young Money. "She deleted me. She deleted Deb. She deleted Puffy. She deleted Twitter with all of her fans. You can't do that! Twitter is the new marketing tool. Eleven million fans and she left everyone hanging? That's Nicki Minaj for you."

While on a promotional tour in London, Nicki explained her side of the situation. "Before the album came out, I saw the website tweeting 'exclusive leaks' from my album! If you made a fan page, I am assuming that you actually care about me and wouldn't do something like that," she told Capital radio DJ James Barr. "So, I just unfollowed them. I did not say anything mean to them. They were rallying other people saying 'She unfollowed us', so I wanted to set the record straight. A lot of times I just don't say anything. But, I did not delete my Twitter because of that. I just needed a moment to myself."

The Twitter debacle came at an interesting time for the artist, with lukewarm reviews from critics and some supposed fans online. Nicki began to feel almost unappreciated and in a shocking move, she hinted that she may leave music altogether. "People ain't giving the kid props for taking it back to the essence. This is my fourth mix-tape," she told UK radio personality Tim Westwood, meaning that *Reloaded* has the same elements that her fans loved about her early mix-tapes. "The kid did it to feed my fans. Now, the kid is thinking she should leave the game." Safaree chimed in: "They're ungrateful," then Nicki clarified: "But, not my babies and my Barbz. All of those other folks." (Nicki returned to Twitter less than two weeks later, with a tweet that said: "★Salutes the Nation of Pinkslam★ ★hugs the Barbz★ ★kisses the Barbz.")

Of course Nicki is not the first rapper to have threatened retirement, and some have even gone through with it, only to return later with a highly orchestrated comeback (for example, Jay-Z). Her sentiments most likely derive from feeling underappreciated: no artist of Nicki's stature achieves an international status without putting in an inordinate amount of work. Moreover, as evidenced by the distinct rap and pop sections of *Roman Reloaded*, she surely listens to both her critics and her fans. She has painstakingly placed music on *Reloaded* that she feels will satisfy their varied tastes and, during her visit to the UK to promote the album, she acknowledged how different types of fans like different parts of the album. After DJ Barr told her that he related to the "second half of the album", Nicki's face lit up with excitement. "I'm going to [ask] that [of] my fans [from now on]: Are you the first half or second half?" And when Westwood asked her to break down the album in terms of her fans, she responded by saying that the "Mix-tape Barbz" love the first half of the album, which includes all of the hardcore hip-hop songs, while the "Poppy Barbz" love the second half, which includes dance songs like 'Pound The Alarm' and 'Right By My Side', her duet with hip-hop star Chris Brown. "As a whole, my amazing grown women out there are liking the songs 'Marilyn Monroe' and 'Fireburns'."

By her own admission then, Nicki's fans are segmented. But she dislikes any claims that she is *only* a pop star. In the first verse from the title track of *Reloaded*, which references the commercial she shot for Pepsi in Argentina, she defends her role as a pop and rap star.

But surely Nicki is aware that the dancier of the songs on the album are pop orientated? Of course she is; her problem lies with the critics who recognise her pop accomplishments (and aspirations) alone, which is essentially to say that she has forgotten her roots and has abandoned the culture that initially put her in the driver's seat to stratospheric fame. "What can I say? What do I have to do, rob a bank? I'm still me. Hip-hop culture is in my heart," she told MTV, in response to the criticism that *Reloaded* leans too mainstream. "I'm always gonna be street. I can't fake that. There are a lot of people walking [around] pretending to be that [street]."

Some see Nicki's mix of pop and hip-hop sensibilities as a side-effect of her penchant for multiple personalities, but one critic takes the theory a step further. "It turns out her split personality shtick isn't so much a product of schizophrenia, but of cowardice," wrote Andrew Nosnitsky for MTV. "Hip-hop artists used to routinely change the pop music landscape, now they change themselves to fit into the existing one."

Nicki is in a peculiar situation as an artist. Having initially gained stardom in the urban world as a mix-tape warrior and an underground rapper, who slayed competitors in street ciphers and on club stages, she made her way to Lil Wayne where the first hit from her first album became a pop hit. Millions of people were introduced to her through 'Your Love', while her original fanbase knew her as the ghetto fab chick from 'Itty Bitty Piggy'. But Nicki says she is a sum of her parts. All of it is her. And she wants dual residency in both the pop and hip-hop hoods. Nicki wants to step out of her doll's house and be able to wave to Katy Perry *and* Rick Ross on the HOV lane.

Overriding any categorisation, Nicki Minaj wants the world to know that she is her own person, her own woman and, most importantly, in this space, her own artist. Kim had initially attained her position as a respected hip-hop star through Biggie's sanctioning; she was an extension of Biggie, his underling. Although Lil Wayne signed Nicki and on occasion she will end a song shouting "I am the female Weezy", at this point in her career she is not his subject. "When she hit the scene, she was just like the pretty girl alongside Wayne," said MTV's director of Hip-Hop News, Rahman Dukes. "Drake was really the next one that everyone was looking out for."

And now, arguably, she is more famous than both of them. And in the hip-hop world, according to MTV's 2011 Annual Hottest List of MCs, the Head Barbie ranked at number four, ahead of Wayne at number five (however, Drake beat both of them, as he made it to number two).

Nicki says that her mission is to set herself apart from Lil Wayne and others who have joined her on triumphant moments in her career so far. "My biggest goal the whole time has been for people to see me as a stand-alone artist," she told *Complex*. "I came out with Young Money, the biggest hip-hop label in the world at that time. And then it was,

'How do I branch away from Lil Wayne?' One of my biggest records was with Drake, 'Moment 4 Life'. Even with the Super Bowl, it was Madonna's moment. I'm just sharing in that moment. It's not Nicki Minaj's moment. Nicki Minaj at the Grammys – that's my moment. I've just been constantly on this quest to stand alone."

Her feelings are not uncommon, especially for females in hip-hop who are talented and know that their skill is not dependent upon the male star they are attached to.

Lauryn Hill is a perfect example. She emerged as the breakout star in the Fugees on their biggest album, 1996's *The Score*, which spawned hits like 'Fu-Gee-La', 'Ready Or Not' and 'Killing Me Softly'. The entire world was enraptured by her beauty, rhyming skills and beautiful voice. *The Score* sold 17 million copies, making her, Wyclef Jean and Pras Michel very rich and very famous. But there was dissent in the ranks. Even though Lauryn was the media darling of the collective, Wyclef was seen as the musical mastermind. And when the time came for Hill to record her solo album, Jean was allegedly against it at first. It was assumed by the world, and Jean, the de facto leader and producer of the group, that once he accepted her as a solo artist, he would take the reigns of Lauryn's project. But Hill had other plans. She turned down his help and set out to make the album on her own.

According to a 2003 *Rolling Stone* story, a source who witnessed Hill's recording sessions said she had underlying motives: "She was aiming for big hits so she could outshine the Fugees and outshine Wyclef." Ahmir "?uestlove" Thompson of the Roots also told *Rolling Stone* that Hill's main objective was to not step, but leap out of Jean's shadow. "Her solo career wasn't based on 'I wanna do an album'. It was based on not being Wyclef's side girl." Hill went out of her way to ensure that her 1998 album, *The Miseducation Of Lauryn Hill* (which sold over 15 million copies worldwide and won five Grammys, including Album of the Year), would largely state that it was written, produced and arranged by Lauryn Hill (she was later sued by several producers who claimed they failed to get fair credit; Lauryn denied the claims, but a spokesman at Columbia Records later confirmed that a settlement had been reached, but the terms – believed to be $5 million – were officially 'undisclosed').

Hill was insistent on becoming her own artist and wanted people to recognise her individual flavour.

Nicki Minaj and Lauryn Hill are disparate artists but their motivations are akin. It is imperative to Nicki that she has creative control over her music and branding. Bryan "Baby" Williams, CEO of Cash Money and an artist in his own right, told *Vibe* that they have always believed in her. "We always had confidence in Barbie. Wayne would like to see her do more branding of herself, and she's doing way more than when she first started. She's everywhere. There's not much you can tell an artist like that."

Artists who have accomplished less have run rampant with inflated egos, but it seems that Nicki's triumphs have not quashed her hunger to be a better artist. "I love collaborating with smart people," she tells Miss Info, a New York media personality. "I am not walking around saying that I know everything. Hell fucking no. I want to build something. I just don't allow anyone around me who drops the ball constantly. All artists should want to learn the business as they go along. If you're in this shit talking about how you just want to be an artist, you're fucking stupid. It makes me cringe."

And Nicki has proven that she is business minded. She and Safaree launched Pink Friday Productions in 2010. Besides producers, they have yet to sign any acts, and there is a definite reason for that. Nicki struggled for years to get to a point where her career could flourish. She knows how anticipation and excitement can quickly turn to disappointment in the music industry. She knows that a "yes" is barely a "maybe" in reality until a person is actually doing what's agreed upon. Even after Madonna called asking to record with her, she did not believe it until she was actually sitting in the studio with her. The same goes for the Super Bowl performance. When she'd told *Good Morning America*'s Robin Roberts that she'd like to work with Madonna, months later, while making another appearance on *GMA* to talk about her MAC Viva Glam campaign, Roberts mentioned how amazing it was that Nicki's wish came true. "OK, I have something to confess," Nicki said to Roberts. "When you asked me that, I already knew I was going to work with her. But, honestly, I don't believe anything until I actually do it!" In the same way that she does not like experiencing disappointments, Nicki does not want to subject someone else to any kind of blighted hope. "I would hate to let someone down," she told Power 105.1. "I don't want someone's dreams in my hands. I know what that feels like."

For that reason, Nicki refuses, at this point at least, to accept a deal from a record company for her to start her own imprint label. Other female rappers have done it: Queen Latifah's Flavor Unit, although not an actual label, has had several successful music acts and secured distribution deals for all of them. In 1999, Lil' Kim started Queen Bee Records (now called IRS Records) and released two artists' albums in 2010 and her mix-tape *Black Friday* (dedicated to dissing Nicki) in 2011. Missy Elliott, the most successful of the female rappers with her own label, The Goldmind, Inc., has released several new artists, with R&B singer Tweet being the most notable. However, no female has reached the level of success that Jay-Z has achieved with his Roc-A-Fella Records imprint, which boasts artists such as Jay-Z and Kanye West.

But Nicki isn't biting... yet. "If I said I wanted to start a label right now, I could get a lot of money because they know Nicki Minaj is gonna promote it and co-sign it," she said to Power 105.1. "But, I won't do it. A lot of dudes, historically, have done it and said they are starting a label and get a $20 million cheque and then peace themselves out."

Nicki may not want her own label, but she certainly runs Nicki Minaj, Inc. every day and is involved in every aspect of its operations. "People assume that I am not the brains behind this operation and they don't give me credit," she told Miss Info. "I couldn't give two fucks about credit. I just want you to leave me the fuck alone. Let me do me. Don't tell me how to pose. I know how to pose. When I am recording I just have to go in [the recording booth] and do it, you know? Even my engineer thinks I am crazy because I'll hear something different on a track and he'll insist, 'No, no, nothing was moved.' [But I tell him], 'Tony, something was moved.' And later, sure enough, 'You were right, there was a two-second delay here.'"

And Nicki's success is enabling the dreams of other female rappers to come to fruition. Before she came along, female MCing was virtually dead in the water; now, there are a few names rising up through the ranks and securing their own record deals. However, in 2012 Nicki told *Vibe* that she doesn't know whether this is due to her influence. "I have no idea. There's really no right or wrong answer for that. I don't know. I'm just doing Nicki Minaj. Anyone that gets in this business, you would have to ask them if I opened the door for them," she told the magazine.

But a couple of months later, while talking to *The Breakfast Club* morning radio show to promote her new album, she was a little more empathetic. "I said a while ago on one of my mix-tape songs 'Still I Rise' that, 'When a door opens for me, then you just got another opportunity to do you.' So, now, in order for my theory to prove right, these girls have to come in the game and get deals because of Nicki Minaj. Because I said it would happen."

One of the girls that has made it happen is Harlem native Azealia Banks. From a young age she pursued a career in musical theatre and starred in off-Broadway productions from the age of 10. Like Nicki, Banks attended LaGuardia High School (drama teacher Harry Shifman mentored both of them). However, Banks dropped out to pursue music. Then going by the name of Miss Bank$, after a failed deal with an independent label in New York she moved to Montreal and began recording tracks under her full name, releasing them onto YouTube. She made the song '212' available as a free download online and filmed a stylish, but D.I.Y.-looking, video. It became a viral sensation.

With an unapologetic potty mouth and an ear for various musical styles, ranging from bare hip-hop breakbeats to nineties Euro-house, Azealia has found a fan in Chanel head designer Karl Lagerfeld (he invited her to perform at his home in Paris for a party celebrating his new fashion line "Karl") and she has impressed Gwyneth Paltrow, who tweeted: "Azealia Banks... Obsessed. Wow." *NME* magazine placed her at the top of its closely watched "Cool List", and Kanye West, when DJing a party in Vegas on New Year's Eve 2011, played '212' and called Banks "the future of music". He is reportedly collaborating with her on her debut album on Interscope/Polydor, entitled *Broke With Expensive Taste*.

Yet Banks told *Vibe* magazine that she does not think Nicki has opened any doors for anyone. "[Rapper] Eve had hot records, movies, a TV show, ad campaigns, etc. Right before she went to jail, Remy Ma was killing it; I don't think Nicki necessarily opened the door for anyone else but herself. She's doing a great job with what she's doing but I don't think any of the female rappers' success is contingent upon anything Nicki Minaj did." Despite her doubts about Nicki paving any roads for females in rap, Banks feels that Nicki has great artistry. "Sonically, *Pink Friday* is great. Nicki has really mastered the art of popular songwriting. I like her mix-tapes a lot [and] she's a brilliant lyricist."

Despite Banks' frank assessment, it is no coincidence that a new wave of oestrogen-fuelled flows are bursting onto the scene now that Nicki has proven herself as not only a profitable rap star, but a pop star as well, with the potential for stadium status. Azealia Banks has garnered the most attention, but other female rappers such as Brianna Perry, Cartier Kitten (associated with Waka Flocka Flame), Kreayshawn, Iggy Azalea, LoLa Monroe (a part of Pittsburg rapper Wiz Khalifa's clique) and Angel Haze are also making waves, with many signing record deals with major labels. So, it seems that Nicki can rest easy: it looks as if her theory is proving true.

Even so, Nicki isn't too worried about the future competition or about the inevitable Minaj clones that music labels will try to produce. "I didn't know who I was as an artist," she told *Complex*. "I knew who I was as a person. My morals and everything, they're still the same. And then I took it upon myself to create this artist, Nicki Minaj. I got help from [my former manager] Deb Antney, Waka Flocka Flame's mother, she helped me. I would meet great people and they would help me. I created my buzz. I wanted to do what a label cannot do. Now, labels are going to think they can re-create this, but they can't."

Nicki simply isn't interested in any of the catfight beefs – real or manufactured – with either the veteran or upstart rap chicks. "The up and coming females… when you guys are coming out and dissing me, and all the negativity," she continued to *Complex*, "they saw me as a threat instead of seeing me as she's going to open the door for us. But it's all love. I am in a great space and I just wish everyone the best."

The song 'Marilyn Monroe', from *Roman Reloaded*, is a personal one for Nicki and it's meaning relates to the space that she once occupied when surrounded by the negative talk. One day, while staring at a picture of the deceased icon, Nicki says she related to the sadness in Monroe's eyes. It's also possible that Nicki relates to Monroe's struggle with balancing the desire for fame and the reality of the loneliness that accompanies such stardom. "It was just like a longing for something," she said to Matt Lauer. "Like a longing for approval. And I feel like a lot of women in power, or successful women, as successful as they are, they have that desire to still be loved. To still be always, you know, great, to still be approved. And it's like no matter how many times you tell them they're great they don't believe it."

But then, in 2009, while she was on the inaugural I Am Music tour with Lil Wayne and her Young Money labelmates, she hit a turning point and Nicki realised that she wanted to achieve that greatness herself. Seeing Wayne onstage every night, and his ability to possess the space and command the crowds, moved her. And she knew she wanted the same thing.

Three years later, Nicki is planning to embark on her own world tour; a journey that will undoubtedly open up even greater possibilities in her career in the same vein as her former tour-mate headliners Wayne and pop princess Britney Spears.

Wayne and Spears are Louisiana natives and were both child stars. Wayne officially signed to Cash Money Records at 15 years old, while Spears is a former Mickey Mouse Club star who became an overnight superstar at 18 with the pop smash '...Baby One More Time'. Thirteen years later, Wayne signed a deal to stay with Cash Money that reportedly pays him in excess of $100 million, while Spears has become one of the biggest female pop stars in history. Jocelyn Vena of MTV wrote that she changed MTV forever with her performance of 'I'm A Slave 4 U' on the 2000 Video Music Awards. "Draping herself in a white python and slithering around a steamy garden setting – surrounded by dancers in zebra and tiger outfits – Spears created one of the most striking visuals in the 27-year history of the show." Spears, and Wayne, are regarded as touchstones in their respective genres. Being that Nicki straddles both the hip-hop and pop worlds, it was more than amazing for Nicki to have her first tour experiences with artists who are both at the top of their game.

Nicki was even more comfortable touring with Wayne the second time because of their professional history. "I thought, OK, on the Wayne tour, this is my audience, everyone that knows Wayne, they know Nicki Minaj," she told SOHH.com. "When I heard those screams, it was one of the best feelings in the world. It changed overnight. I'm pleasantly surprised with the people coming out on this show; they generally are coming out not to critique, but to have fun. The hip-hop community tends to be more critical. On this stage, I felt a little bit more free."

Her tours with Wayne prepared her for going on the road with Spears. Although she was confident in her skills as a performer, she was worried about the differences in demographic. The first night of the Femme Fatale tour, Nicki was concerned that her brand of hip-pop might not connect with Britney's mainstream crowds. "Well, initially, what I thought was I hope this audience will appreciate what I do," she continued. "What I first dealt with was a bit of the unknown: is this something that Britney's crowd will even enjoy? But it all went away the first night. I stood in the transporter, that big prop that we have on the stage, and I could not believe the crowd reaction before they even saw me. It was very emotional for me. I was so shocked."

Not only was Nicki moved by the fans embracing her, it was even more important to her because she had been a longtime fans of Spears. "The fact that she came back out with just so much fire inspires me, and it inspires young women and people all over the world," she told *Out*. "It just inspires you. A lot of my fans feel like they are the underdog and feel like they are the people who aren't ever accepted for themselves, or who are laughed at or poked fun at forever. It just goes to show that once you keep at whatever it is you're doing, people may not like you, people may not love you, but they will have to respect you at the end of the day. And that respect is all that matters."

Part of Nicki's trajectory is to stand alone as an artist and set herself apart from others, which includes staging successful tours on her own. She plans to use what she learned from Wayne and Spears to make her show the spectacle she wants it to be. "Let me just say I'm going to take from Britney and Wayne, because they're both veterans," she told the *Los Angeles Times*. "Being completely honest, I've learned so much from them, in terms of production. Britney's production is so amazing. When I sat out there the first night to watch [her show], I felt like I was a kid at an amusement park. It was so much, the lights, the content and the props."

Beyond having brilliant staging, an artist must know how to get their audience to have a good time. Nicki learned her own Jedi mind tricks from the man who introduced her to the world. "Wayne teaches me how to command a crowd," she continued to the *Los Angeles Times*. "His comfort level and how he makes people feel like he's their best friend when he's onstage. He has that command." Nicki plans for her tour to capture all of the lessons and qualities she received from both Louisiana megastars. "If you can put those two things into a show, you can really do an amazing show – that's my goal. Am I gonna be able to do these humongous venues within the next year? Probably not. But am I gonna put on an amazing show and give everyone something that's gonna be well worth what they paid? Absolutely yes."

Consequently, while she is anxious to get back on tour, she admits that she is looking forward to the smaller, more intimate venues so she can interact with her Barbz. "My fans have been going crazy," she said on the *Today* show. "I'm just excited more than anything, more than the album, I mean, eventually people are going to buy the album, you know. But more than anything for me, it's the fact that this album is now done, out of the way and I can go and see my fans," she explained. "Because I haven't been able to really touch them and feel them one-on-one in a long time because I was doing the tour with Wayne and Britney, [which] you know kind of took me outside of that intimate thing with my fans." However, a Sunday afternoon in June 2012, would not only challenge her all-important relationship with her fans, but also the growth she's experienced over the past four years and even more the notion of whether she still belonged in the hip-hop world.

Hot 97's Summer Jam is not only the premier concert in the New York metropolitan area, kicking off the summer every year, but it's also the stage for the all of the marquee players in hip-hop to perform their hits, bring other celebs on stage and also call out other rappers. The jumbo screen in the MET Life Arena is there for concertgoers in the nosebleed section to see their favorite hip-hoppers, but it's also there for those rappers to flash the pictures (often embarrassing) of the rappers they wish to spark beef with.

Nicki is a veteran of Summer Jam, but this would be her first time headlining the main stage. She may have expected some diss directed at her or one of the Young Money members from another rapper, but never from those who invited her to the party. While on the pre-show stage in the parking lot, Hot 97 Morning Show host Paul Rosenberg took shots at Nicki's double platinum single 'Starships' for being so pop. "I see the real hip-hop heads sprinkled in here; I see them," Rosenberg shouted into the microphone. "I know there's some chicks here waiting to sing 'Starships' later. I'm not talking to y'all right now. Fuck that bullshit. I'm here to talk about real hip-hop shit." The remarks rang through the parking lot and through the entire hip-hop community in seconds. As soon as the words dropped from Rosenberg's lips, everyone was wondering, "Did he just diss Nicki?" His comments made their way to the Young Money Camp, and to Nicki,

Hot 97 was the first station in the world to have a 100% Hip-Hop format and its power in the industry is formidable. Nicki's camp claims they tried to reach out to execs at the station to handle the situation but to no avail. Tyga, a Young Money artist, performed during his 7pm slot on the main stage, but shortly after that, Lil Wayne tweeted: "Young Money ain't doing summer jam." The boss had spoken. There would be no Nicki Minaj performance that night. And although Nicki has been very vocal in the past about Wayne not being able to make her do anything she did not wish to, she went along with the decision. She felt disrespected. She had come too far to allow the reckless comments of a morning show disc jockey to impede her evolution. Back in 2010, she told this author of the inner conflict she was experiencing between the hip-hop and pop sides of her self. Now, in this contentious moment with Hot 97, the issue had clawed itself to the surface once again. "[Rosenberg] has previously derided 'Starships' as 'the most sellout

194

song in hip-hop history,' as if selling out were still an issue," wrote *The New York Times*. "The idea that art and commerce are at odds is a remnant of an old culture war: dogma presented as forward-thinking but really just protecting an outmoded status quo, leading to the unusual and very modern spectacle of a white man deriding a black woman for insufficiently upholding hip-hop values."

Nicki also had a problem with Rosenberg being a white man speaking about her in such in a derogatory manner about her music, which she makes for everyone, regardless of race. She tweeted: "Not blak but on blak radio dissin blak women." Hip-hop legend Dr Dre felt that both parties were at fault "Nicki Minaj was the only one who ruined 55,000 fans' expectations of the night. It has nothing to do with Rosenberg. You go out there and you perform for your fans," he told Fuse.com. And regarding Rosenberg, Dre was less than sympathetic. "We have too many what I call 'semi-super experts' who always try to redefine hip-hop from its infancy. She's an artist whether I like her or I don't like her. My daughter loves her and thinks that she's the world."

The next day, despite his claims that he was going to ruin her career, Nicki called into Funk Master Flex's show to discuss her side of the story and to respond to claims that she deserted her fans. This was an integral moment for Nicki to not only stand up for her fans and let them know their worth, but it was also imperative for her to demand her respect. Although she was still reconciling her two musical halves, she was still a woman and a major artist that had worked hard to grace that stage one day as a headliner. "I have a very personal relationship with my fans, and I'm truly sorry that people's nights were ruined," she told Flex. "You guys have no idea, I've gone through hell and back. I'm not a quitter. I show up and perform. I went with my team's decision, and I made history, and the next time I come out, people won't disrespect me. And for once, I feel like I've really really shown the world, I love and respect myself, and people aren't gonna go there any more."

With each venture, Nicki manages to break new ground. Popular Irish television host Graham Norton declared that she is the "most successful female rapper ever". And he is probably right. Missy Elliott and Lauryn

Hill have sold more records than she has at this early stage of her growing career, but she has already taken the female rap genre and turned it on its head. Sure, she was influenced by her predecessors. But, as most brilliant individuals do, she borrowed greatness and made it sensational. As quick as she is to impress, she is even faster to offend. Her movements are major, but she moves too swiftly to dwell. "Doing the Super Bowl with Madonna doesn't really change Nicki Minaj's personal goals," she told *Complex.* "My goal right now is… to sell five million copies of [*Roman Reloaded*] eventually and tour every country in the world. That's what I've been working toward. So, while the world is talking about, 'Oh, my God, I can't believe Nicki Minaj was at the Super Bowl!' I'm mixing and mastering my music."

Pink Friday: Roman Reloaded is very much a different album from *Pink Friday*. Her debut was more curious. It was Violet wandering around the Wonka Factory touching what she wanted and quickly snapping her head back to see the reaction of the authorities around her. *Pink Friday* was the album she had to make in 2010; she was a woman with abundant options and no reason (or restraint) to refuse any of them. 'Your Love' was the leaked lead-in hit and 'Right Thru Me', its obedient sister, followed behind in a pop procession. Poignant and soulful, 'Moment 4 Life' worked as early morning motivation or a late night reminder; 'Check It Out' with will.i.am. was fun and quirky with a Europop wink. 'Did It On 'Em' was a blatant reminder that underneath the candy-coated façade, the Southside Jamaica, Queens girl was still in residence. The Kanye collaboration, 'Blazin'', added West's signature twist to the set, while the Natasha Bedingfield duet 'Last Chance' added an unexpected pop mix. 'Fly', featuring her gal pal Rihanna, spoke to Nicki's overall desire for the project. She told MTV: "'Fly' is one of my absolute faves. I wanted to work with Rihanna for a long time. I'm very proud of her accomplishments; especially since she was born on an island like me. This song is a female empowerment song. But then again, it's not specific to just women. It speaks about flying, soaring high in the face of every single solitary adversity that comes your way. I speak about how the media has attempted to box me in and how that has made me feel suffocated. After years of being dragged through the mud, I've mustered up the courage to re-define myself. I believe that I represent an entire generation. My fans have become my family; and together we have become a movement. We came to win."

Essentially, therefore, *Pink Friday* showed Nicki as an obvious work in progress, aiming to touch all of the areas she felt her fans and the industry wanted to hear. With *Roman Reloaded* and its one-part hardcore hip-hop and other part hardcore dance pop, she has decided it is unnecessary to define herself. And her lack of self-consciousness is evident. "My first album I was very guarded," she told Ryan Seacrest. "I felt like I was making music to please everyone else, but this album I am just creating music, and there's such a big difference. The music itself you're going to get every side that I've ever shown and then a little bit extra. I've tried to make it very, very balanced, because I don't ever want to be boxed in, and that's always what drives me. So I made a very diverse album."

There is a certain exuberance that runs throughout the project. Al Fox of BBC Music wrote: "The album unfolds an immeasurable amalgam of genres and inspirations, all fused together in a diamond-encrusted bubble of futuristic, day-glo hip-hop. The energy is palpable, the pace rarely lets up, and personality pervades throughout."

The vaudeville show opener 'Roman Holiday' establishes the vigour of the album. The slap-in-the-face funk of 'Come On A Cone' reminds us that the 'Dear Old Nicki' persona is the tour guide at that point on the album. And, as Kanye West and Jay-Z unabashedly swank about their lot in life with the "luxury rap" 'Watch The Throne', the title track is a view into her newly A-list life, of her real-life interactions with talk-show superstar Ellen DeGeneres, fashion goddess Donatella Versace and *Vogue* editor-in-chief Anna Wintour.

The track also finds Nicki presumably addressing the rumours that television mogul Simon Cowell was courting Nicki to be a judge on the American version of the competition reality show *The X Factor.* "I couldn't do your TV show I needed 10 more mill/Not 10 on the back, I need 10 on signing/Give that shit to a wash up bitch, I'm winning," she rhymes. And she lets the world know why she rarely goes shopping herself: "When I'm out, I'm spotted/They gone frame the receipt/If I sign the dotted."

So for those wondering why Nicki is no longer the gutter girl she once was; well, it is because she is no longer that girl. And she is not the first artist in the hip-hop genre to go through huge changes between their first and second albums. The Notorious B.I.G.'s classic debut *Ready To Die* was completely different lyrically and even sonically to his sophomore album, *Life After Death*. On the former, he was still in the mire of hustling while recording it, while on the latter, he had become the King of New York and was on his way to mainstream superstardom.

Nicki is challenging her listeners on her second album, pairing her pop ambitions with her hip-hop origins, as evidenced by the weekend party pop that dominates the second end of *Roman Reloaded*. Jon Caramanica of *The New York Times* writes: "When rapping on the songs of others, she's often the most capable MC around – but on her own material she's often straddling a line between hip-hop and pop that no other rapper is capable of, or would even dare." Rapper Trina agrees: "[Nicki] has challenged herself to not be boxed in just hip-hop or do one kind of music, which is exceptional," she told *Vibe*. "She's already living in that pop-rap space. She's in a space of her own."

And the door is now wide open for Nicki Minaj in other areas of show business. As she proved on *Saturday Night Live* in January 2011 in the skit "Bride of Blackenstein", she has the acting chops to saunter into Hollywood and stake her claim. But unlike Will Smith, a rapper who ventured into acting very early in his career, she says she cannot drop hip-hop and music for any screen: "Will Smith is definitely a friend in [my] head," she said during an interview on The Heat on Sirius FM. "But, it was different with [him] – I don't think he ever saw hip-hop as his be all, end all. He started doing *The Fresh Prince Of Bel-Air* pretty early on in his career. It's a little different for me. I have a movement based just on my music. I have the Barbz and the Roman Empire. It would be different for me to just leave. They won't let me go this soon. I have to put in a lot more work. I will know when it's time. I did the voiceover for *Ice Age* and I want to do movies but just not right now." That part of her career can wait, for now at least. "Acting takes so much of your time," she said to radio personality Angela Yee. "And it's not like you're getting $10 million a picture. So, you really have to think about it. I would rather do it once I settle into my music career," she says.

Will Barbie ever settle down with a Ken and produce a progeny? "I'll definitely be married and I'll definitely have my two children. OK, I might have three, but I do want at least one boy." She also talked to Matt Lauer about kids: "I think a child may be the only thing that could give me true happiness. When I saw Madonna I realised it can be done, because I saw her children were coming to the rehearsals and that really moved me. But no children anytime soon."

But, whatever happens in Nicki's future, she continues to hold Jay-Z's career up as the blueprint. "Jay-Z raps because he wants to not because he has to," she told *Complex*. "I think that's the scary part when, after 10 years in the game, people can't pay their bills and now you're desperate. And that is why, I always say, business first."

The Nicki Minaj that developed through her infamous mix-tapes was a different Nicki Minaj born during the making of *Pink Friday*. And she has been battling with herself and her public over her changing artistry ever since. Nicki may have warring musical souls, and, if so, she refuses to allow either to win. It's not about alter egos, it's about her intentions. "I refuse to define what I do," she told *Vibe*. "You'll feel it. It's more of an experience than a genre. They'll have to create a new genre for this. You can't put it into a genre that's out there right now. You absolutely can't."

Nicki's Pink Friday world tour is poised for success. Her creative director, Laurieann Gibson, told *MTV News* that the show is a "real rap show": "It's Nicki's first outing as a headliner and a lot is riding on its success," she said. Gibson was instrumental in the video and staging success of Missy Elliot, so Nicki is in good hands, but the challenge of creating a credible show for a rapper who has pop success is a difficult one. "The pressure to maintain dominant rappers [on major award shows] and not let them lose street credibility [is tough]," she told *MTV News*. "When I got back to Nicki, I was so happy to be in that soulful music again, in that fight, in the idea that rap is not dead and that somebody like her can be many things in many genres and not be limited."

Whether or not *Roman Reloaded* goes on to sell five million copies or whether she eventually finds the same success as Jay-Z with her own Roman Empire, Nicki Minaj has already etched her mark in history. Speaking to *V* magazine in 2010 she said, "Some will hate it, and some will love it, but all will remember it. And that's what I want: to be remembered."

Whatever becomes of Onika Tanya Maraj, she's serving up a self-curated brand of hip-pop, individuality and sexuality and, in whatever capacity, she will continue to do so for years to come.

Discography

Mixtapes

Playtime Is Over
Dirty Money Entertainment/Young Money
2007

Sucka Free
Dirty Money Entertainment/Young Money
2008

Beam Me Up Scotty
Dirty Money Entertainment/Young Money
2009

Albums

Pink Friday
Young Money/Cash Money Records
2010

Pink Friday: Roman Reloaded
Young Money/Cash Money Records
2012

Compilation albums

We Are Young Money
Young Money/Cash Money Records
2009

Singles

2010
'Massive Attack' (feat. Sean Garrett) #65 R&B

'Your Love' #1 Rap Songs/#4 R&B/#14 Pop/#71 UK

'Check It Out' (feat. will.i.am) #14 Rap/#100 R&B/#24 Pop/#11 UK

'Right Thru Me' #3 Rap/#4 R&B/#26 Pop/#71 UK

'Moment 4 Life' #1 Rap/#1 R&B/#13 Pop/#22 UK

2011
'Roman's Revenge' #23 Rap/#85 R&B

'Did It On 'Em' #4 Rap/#3 R&B/#49 Pop

'Super Bass' #2 Rap/#6 R&B/#3 Pop/#8 UK

'Girls Fall Like Dominoes' #24 UK

'Fly' #9 Rap/#20 R&B/#19 Pop/#16 UK

2012
'Starships' #13 Rap/#89 R&B/#5 Pop/#2 UK

'Right By My Side' (feat. Chris Brown) #24 R&B/#51 Pop/#101 UK

'Beez in the Trap' (feat. 2 Chainz) #24 Rap/#31 R&B/#59 Pop/#131 UK

Compilation singles

2009

'BedRock' (feat. Young Money Roster & Lloyd) #1 Rap/#2 R&B/#2 Pop/#9 UK

2010

'Roger That' (feat. Young Money) #6 Rap/#15 R&B/#56 Pop

Singles as a featured artist

2009

'5 Star' (Remix) (Yo Gotti, also feat. Gucci Mane and Trina)

2010

'Up Out Of My Face' (Mariah Carey) #39 R&B/#100 US

'My Chick Bad' (Ludacris) #2 Rap/#2 R&B/#11 US

'Lil Freak' (Usher) #8 R&B/#40 US/#109 UK

'Get It All' (Sean Garrett) #83

'Woohoo' (Christina Aguilera) #79 Pop/#148 UK

'All I Do Is Win (Remix)' (DJ Khaled, also feat. T-Pain, Rick Ross, Busta Rhymes, Diddy, Fabolous, Jadakiss, Fat Joe, Swizz Beatz) #6 Rap/#8 R&B/#24 Pop

'Hello Good Morning (Remix)' (Diddy–Dirty Money also feat. Rick Ross) #8 Rap/#13 R&B/#27 Pop/#22 UK

'Hold You (Remix)' (Gyptian) #31 R&B/#77 Pop

'Bottoms Up' (Trey Songz) #2 R&B/#6 Pop/#71 UK

'2012 (It Ain't The End)' (Jay Sean) #31 Pop/#9 UK

'Letting Go (Dutty Love)' (Sean Kingston) #51 Pop/#36 UK

'Monster' (Kanye West, also feat. Jay-Z, Bon Iver and Rick Ross) #15 Rap/#30 R&B/#18 Pop/#146 UK

'I Ain't Thru' (Keyshia Cole) #54 R&B

'Raining Men' (Rihanna) #48 R&B/#111 Pop/#142 UK

2011

'The Creep' (The Lonely Island, also feat. John Waters) #82 Pop

'Where Them Girls At' (David Guetta, also feat. Flo Rida) #24 Rap/#14 Pop/#3 UK

'Y.U. Mad' (Birdman, also feat. Lil Wayne) #25 Rap/#46 R&B/#68 Pop

'You The Boss' (Rick Ross) #10 Rap/#5 R&B/#62 Pop

'Fireball' (Willow Smith)

'Feel Inside' (Remix) (Mary J. Blige)

'Make Me Proud' (Drake) #1 Rap/#1 R&B/#9 Pop/#49 UK

'Dance (A$$)' (Big Sean) #2 Rap/#3 R&B/#10 Pop

'Turn Me On' (David Guetta) #92 R&B/#4 Pop/#8 UK

2012

'Give Me All Your Luvin'' (Madonna, also feat. M.I.A.) #10 Pop/#37 UK

'Take It To The Head' (DJ Khaled, also feat. Chris Brown, Rick Ross and Lil Wayne) #17 Rap/#23 R&B/#63 Pop

Other Features/Guest Appearances

2004
'Don't Mess With' Jim Johnston, *WWE Theme Addict: The Music, Vol. 6*

2008
'Gucci Gucci' Enur, *Raggatronic*

2009
'Lollipop Luxury' Jeffree Star, *Beauty Killer*

'Get Low 4 Me' (Remix) Lalo *The Don, Love Life Lyrics*

'Ponytail' Mya, *Beauty & The Streets*

'Grindin Making Money' Birdman, *Priceless*

'Take It Off' Lloyd, *Like Me: The Young Goldie*

'Sex In Crazy Places' Gucci Mane, *The State vs. Radric Davis*

2010
'Coca Coca' Gucci Mane, *Burrprint (2) HD*

'For the Money' Fabolous, *There Is No Competition 2: The Funeral Service*

'Dang A Lang' Trina, *Amazin'*

'In My Head', Jason Derulo, *In My Head*

'She Likes Me' Jadakiss, *The Champ Is Here*

'YM Salute' Lil Wayne, *I'm Not A Human Being*

'Haterade' Gucci Mane *The Appeal: Georgia's Most Wanted*

2011
'Change Change' Verbal, *Visionair*

2012
'I Don't Give A' Madonna, *MDNA*

'Out of My Mind' B.o.B, *Strange Clouds*

'Get Low' Waka Flocka Flame, *Triple F Life: Friends, Fans and Family*

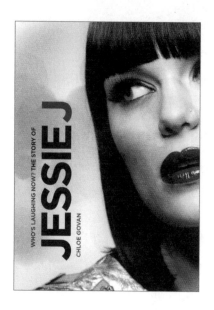

WHO'S LAUGHING NOW
THE JESSIE J STORY
By Chloë Govan

This extraordinary biography tells how Jessica Ellen Cornish from Ilford in north east London overcame being 'not really that good at anything' to reinvent herself as Jessie J and record one of the biggest selling albums of 2011.

Success came in the face of extraordinary setbacks. Childhood bullying, an irregular heartbeat, a serious fall from the stage and a minor stroke at the age of 18 all threatened the health and career of the BRIT school student who first pursued fame through dance and the musical theatre.

Author Chloe Govan has interviewed record producers, school classmates, friends, dance tutors and many others to unearth the real stories behind Jessie J's improbable road to fame.

Chloë Govan has written about travel, lifestyle and music for a variety of publications around the world including Travel Weekly, The Times *and* Real Travel, *where she has a monthly column. She is also the author of* Katy Perry: A Life of Fireworks *and* Rihanna: Rebel Flower, *also published by Omnibus Press.*

ISBN: 978.1.78038.313.2
Order No: OP54505

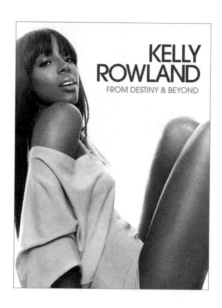

FROM DESTINY & BEYOND
KELLY ROWLAND
By Chloë Govan

From Destiny and Beyond charts Kelly Rowland's rise from painfully shy child to successful backing vocalist and internationally acclaimed solo act. Fleeing a broken home and an alcoholic father, she entered the tough world of show business via what would become one of the best-selling girl groups in the world, Destiny's Child.

A brutal rehearsal regime and a love-hate relationship with the group's manager - bandmate Beyoncé's father Matthew - meant that life was still far from easy. Kelly's eventual emergence from the shadow of Beyoncé to grasp stardom in her own right makes for a truly inspiring story. Biographer Chloë Govan tells it all, from childhood loneliness to success as a solo performer and UK *X-Factor judge*.

Chloë Govan has written about travel, lifestyle and music for a variety of publications around the world including Travel Weekly, The Times *and* Real Travel, *where she has a monthly column. She is also the author of* Katy Perry: A Life of Fireworks *and* Rihanna: Rebel Flower, *also published by Omnibus Press.*

ISBN: 978.1.78038.553.2
Order No: OP54824

CRAZY IN LOVE
THE BEYONCE KNOWLES BIOGRAPHY
By Daryl Easlea

Crazy In Love explores the life and astonishing career trajectory of Beyoncé Knowles, the Texan teenager who rose from performing in her hometown backyards to headlining shows all over the world. Daryl Easlea's biography details her time with Destiny's Child – the troubled group that launched her – and her subsequent spectacular rise to a particularly modern kind of fame.

Beyoncé now spans movies, albums, product endorsements and the obligatory celebrity marriage. Hitched to Jay-Z, she kept changing her hairstyles and was accused of changing her complexion to a lighter shade for a L'Oréal commercial. She even changed her name to Sasha Fierce for one album. Making sense of the chameleonic career that prompted Michelle Obama to declare Beyoncé 'one of my favorite performers on the planet' the author has produced a biography that is both exciting and revealing.

Daryl Easlea was the deputy editor at Record Collector, to which he remains a regular contributor. His work can be found in Mojo *and* bbc.co.uk; *and has appeared in* The Guardian, Uncut, Dazed & Confused *and* The Independent. *He is the author of the critically acclaimed* Everybody Dance: CHIC & The Politics of Disco *and* The Story Of The Supremes.

ISBN: 978.085712.723.5
Order No: OP53988